THE TRANSATLANTIC DESIGN NETWORK

THE TRANSATLANTIC DESIGN NETWORK

Thomas Jefferson, John Soane, and
Agents of Architectural Exchange

DANIELLE S. WILLKENS

University of Virginia Press

CHARLOTTESVILLE AND LONDON

The University of Virginia Press is situated on the traditional lands of the Monacan Nation, and the Commonwealth of Virginia was and is home to many other Indigenous people. We pay our respect to all of them, past and present. We also honor the enslaved African and African American people who built the University of Virginia, and we recognize their descendants. We commit to fostering voices from these communities through our publications and to deepening our collective understanding of their histories and contributions.

First published 2024

9 8 7 6 5 4 3 2 1

Library of Congress Cataloging-in-Publication Data

Names: Willkens, Danielle S., author.
Title: The transatlantic design network : Thomas Jefferson, John Soane, and agents of architectural exchange / Danielle Willkens.
Description: Charlottesville : University of Virginia Press, 2024. | Includes bibliographical references and index.
Identifiers: LCCN 2023052304 (print) | LCCN 2023052305 (ebook) | ISBN 9780813951546 (hardcover) | ISBN 9780813951553 (ebook)
Subjects: LCSH: Communication in architecture—United States—History—18th century. | Communication in architecture—Great Britain—History—18th century. | Architects—Social networks—United States. | Architects—Social networks—Great Britain. | United States—Intellectual life—18th century. | Great Britain—Intellectual life—18th century. | BISAC: ARCHITECTURE / History / General
Classification: LCC NA2584 .W55 2024 (print) | LCC NA2584 (ebook) | DDC 720.92/2—dc23/eng/20240228
LC record available at https://lccn.loc.gov/2023052304
LC ebook record available at https://lccn.loc.gov/2023052305

Cover images: Left, bust of Soane in the Museum Dome of the Soane House (author's photo, ©Sir John Soane's Museum, London); *right,* bust of Jefferson in Monticello's Entrance Hall (Thomas Jefferson Foundation/Monticello)
Cover design: Kelley Galbreath

For my parents, who shared in the travels and trials of this ongoing project; they always looked the other way when I snuck behind gates, and they refused to abandon the adventure to the Désert

CONTENTS

ILLUSTRATIONS

PREFACE

Like many who visit Monticello and Soane's Museum, I distinctly remember my first meetings with these sites. As a transplant to the Commonwealth of Virginia, I did not make the requisite pilgrimage to Monticello during my elementary education, so, instead, I made my first visit as part of another American ritual: the college tour. Enthralled by the fall foliage and the "little mountain," I undertook my undergraduate architectural education at Jefferson's University of Virginia. Following graduation, I served as a "summer guide" at Monticello, shepherding visitors through the house museum. My first, bewildering, visit to Sir John Soane's Museum was nearly a year later with two friends. The following fall, I found myself researching the Codex Coner in the museum's archives, working beneath a signature Soanean starfish ceiling. Here, listening to the occasional sounds of mounted police patrolling the north side of Lincoln's Inn Fields, my imagination easily drifted to a different era when Soane's own students sat reading and drawing.

These initial meetings prompted another series of transatlantic journeys and JefferSoanean investigations. When I returned to the University of Virginia for my master of architecture, I was drawn back to Monticello as a part-time historical interpreter; and the Sir John Soane's Museum Foundation Traveling Fellowship brought me back to London for a summer of intensive research. In both roles, I was fortunate to occupy spaces beyond prescribed hours and tour paths. Slipping behind cautionary ropes and up the stairs to explore rooms closed to the general public, I was able to experience the buildings as homes, not just museums. At Soane's Museum, I found familiarity in the eerie experience of sketching in the crypt during a summer thunderstorm and treasured chats over afternoon tea on the top floor of no. 14. During my years working and researching at Monticello, I discovered that visitors braved myriad conditions; despite torrential downpours, hurricane-force winds, and the unyielding heat and humidity of Virginia summers, it was not uncommon to see nearly three thousand visitors on a busy day. However, on the rare days when few visitors crossed the threshold, it was possible to identify the chimes of individual clocks, the creaks of certain doors, and the paths of the coldest drafts. It has been a privilege to occupy the house museums at different times, but the bustle of spring and summer afternoons are probably closer to the experience of the homes during the lifetimes of Jefferson and Soane. With steady entrance queues at both sites, it is easy to wonder if Jefferson and Soane ever envisioned that in two hundred years their homes would still be filled with curious visitors, eager for a glimpse into their lives and collections.

This book is the result of transatlantic research, buttressed by several grants, fellowships, institutions, and individuals. A Travelling Fellowship from Sir John Soane Museum Foundation, then led by the impeccable Chas Miller, initiated my JefferSoanean obsession. Seed Grants from Auburn University's College of Architecture, Design and Construction as well as the Intermural Grant Program provided invaluable time in various archives and funding for this publication; and colleagues unwearyingly encouraged the project, especially Scott and Charlie, who provided much-needed perspective over tea and toast. I received instrumental feedback from presentations at the Society of Architectural Historians of Great Britain, the Southeast chapter of the SAH, and the Latrobe chapter of the SAH; I will be continually grateful for this international community of scholars who initiated connections to fellow 'lost architect' scholars Julia King and Mark Reinberger.

The American Philosophical Society's Franklin Research Grant and two short-term fellowships from the International Center for Jefferson Studies (ICJS) supported the development of the manuscript. At the Thomas Jefferson Foundation, Jefferson Library, and ICJS, a number of individuals facilitated research, provided access to archives and photographic opportunities, and were always willing to entertain conversations over coffee or a glass of Gabriele's finest: Anna Berkes, Jack Robertson, Endrina Tay, Diane C. Ehrenpreis, Tabitha Corradi, Andrew O'Shaughnessy, Mary Scott-Fleming, Gaye

Wilson, Lisa A. Francavilla, John Ragosta, Whitney Pippin, Gardiner Hallock, Linnea Grim, and Gary Sandling. Over a decade ago, I was welcomed into an amazing family of Monticello interpreters; since then we have enjoyed explorations on both sides of the Atlantic, and they opened their homes to this weary researcher. To Don, Peggy, Shirley, Sharon, Elizabeth, George & Elaine, Wayne, Aurelia, Catherine, Connie, Danna, David, Lou, and many others, you are the "most extraordinary collection of talent, of human knowledge, that has ever been gathered together."

Since I witnessed Tim Knox's dachshunds sparring beneath a meeting table, Sir John Soane's Museum has been a lively, treasured, and atmospheric site for research, where the wealth of the archive is exceeded only by its exceptional stewards, past and present, particularly Helen Dorey, Sue Palmer, Frances Sands, and Stephanie Coane. The University College London's Bartlett School of Architecture was the perfect home to pursue this topic: the Architecture Research Fund sponsored my first trip to Lodi, and I could not have asked for better readers than Professors Adrian Forty and Christine Stevenson. As a fellow Soanean, Jonathan Hill never let me forget the landscape, or smog, and to Barbara Penner, I am eternally grateful for her good humor, patience in reading too many drafts and writing too many recommendations, and the uncanny ability to always ask the best questions. To the Bartletts, you are the most brilliant and beloved cohort of inspiring "transatlantic friends."

THE TRANSATLANTIC DESIGN NETWORK

Introduction

Time wastes too fast: every letter
I trace tells me with what rapidity
life follows my pen. The days and hours
of it are flying over our heads like
clouds of windy day never to return—
more. Every thing presses on. . . .

— Laurence Sterne, *The Life and Opinions of Tristram Shandy*[1]

Although these borrowed lines may read as the prelude to a romantic saga, this is not the story of an affair, or a love triangle. Rather, this is the story of an architectural romance involving two architects from opposite sides of the Atlantic Ocean and their forty-year friendship with a talented and charismatic artist. The architects were Thomas Jefferson (1743–1826) and Sir John Soane (1753–1837); their shared aesthete was Maria Hadfield Cosway (1763–1838). The lines from *Tristram Shandy* are particularly relevant to a discussion about Jefferson, Soane, and their first meetings, respectively, with Cosway. Both encounters were brief, but through the pages of letters that traversed countries and continents, the friends would relive their travels together for decades,

Both Jefferson and Soane were reading *Tristram Shandy* around the time when they first met Cosway. Since the 1760s, Jefferson was familiar with Sterne's work, but he revisited the novel before his transatlantic travels in the 1780s. The lines quoted at the opening of this chapter were especially precious to Jefferson. In September 1782, he and his wife wrote the lines of

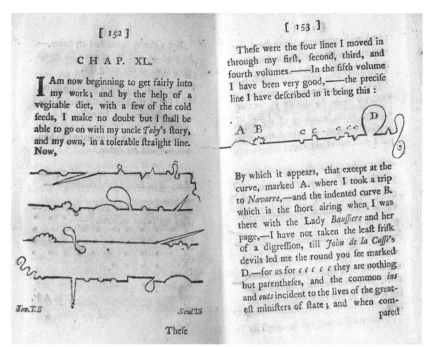

Fig. 1. Soane's copy of Laurence Sterne's *The Life and Opinions of Tristram Shandy* (1769), with a view of the plot lines on 1:152–53. (Sir John Soane's Museum Library)

the passage together, while Martha was on her deathbed. This intimate transcription, written in the last moments of Martha's life, is one of only four known samples of Martha's writing since Jefferson destroyed their private correspondence following her death.[2] Soane's encounters with *Tristram Shandy* were less emotionally charged but occurred at a no less transformative period of his life: Soane received the first six volumes of the novel in 1779 when he was engaged in his Grand Tour. The package came from John Patteson, a Norwich manufacturer and future client, sent in care of the English Coffeehouse at the foot of the Spanish Steps in Rome.[3]

Jefferson and Soane favored works of nonfiction, but they both poured over Sterne's novels multiple times and sought pocket editions for their travels. As a novel filled with ridiculous instances of hyperbole, sexual innuendos, and cultural gaffes, *Tristram Shady* appeared entertaining and simple to many but appealed to those who exercised a deeper reading into Sterne's

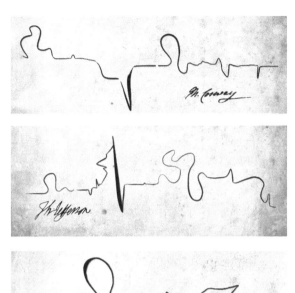

Fig. 2. Timelines for Cosway, Jefferson, and Soane in the style of Sterne's plot line diagrams in *Tristram Shandy*. The upstrokes represent professional successes, the flourishes are significant meetings or events, and the downstrokes represent the death of a significant loved one. (Author's diagrams)

moral tale, filled with a layered and even playful translation of Lockean theory as the title character searched for reason and morality in the world. Like Locke, Tristram thought that his writings could be a conversation with the reader, but this required the reader to examine the novel with purpose, not just as a means of distracting pleasure. Within the novel, there are a series of captivating line diagrams that illustrate the meandering paths of Tristram's narrative, unbridled like a section through a wild and imaginative landscape (fig. 1).[4] As the reader progresses through the course of Tristram's "autobiography," the digressions within his narrative, represented as sinuous curves or abrupt peaks and valleys in the literal plot line, are the most pivotal elements of his journey. Much like Tristram, the initial meetings of Jefferson and Soane with Cosway could be dismissed as insignificant detours along their professional paths; however, these diversions were moments that, like their correspondence with Cosway, stayed with them for the rest of their lives (fig. 2).

KNOWLEDGE AND NETWORKS

There is an interesting lexical gap in the English language. Unlike Romance languages, the English verb "to know" does not make a distinction between the knowledge of a fact or the knowledge of a person. The Italian verbs *sapere* and *conoscere,* as well as the French verbs *savoir* and *connaître,* linguistically recognize the differences between familiarity with an object or concept and familiarity with a person, thereby revealing a vein of epistemology that distinguishes personal interaction as an integral part to the dissemination of knowledge. Architects such as Jefferson and Soane learned their discipline from books, on-site investigations, and, in the case of Soane, formal academic training and apprenticeship. However, for both men, their understanding of art, architecture, and culture was also very much shaped by the interests, observations, and talents of their acquaintances. By reading the letters, diary entries, and account books of Jefferson and Soane, it is possible to trace how conversations in coffeehouses and salons as well as casual journeys undertaken with friends influenced their architectural theories and design goals.

When knowledge is acquired and formed through personal connections, it is often referred to as actor-network theory. In popular culture, it is known as "six degrees of separation," and in scholarly analysis it is typically deployed in twentieth- and twenty-first-century studies as an "anthropology of architecture."[5] For design, these studies set forth people, objects, and flows as critically influential actors that may shape, and are not simply affected by, the form and meaning of architecture.[6] By placing individuals and groups in an active position in the creation of the built environment, this book illuminates how important circles of interpersonal exchange. personal influences, and conversations, not just pattern books and transplanted designers, informed design and America's architectural development in the late eighteenth and early nineteenth centuries.

The Republic of Letters is a significant precedent for the dissection of premodern international communication as a means of theoretical discourse and exchange. As a period of communication and intellectual dissemination, it blossomed with the new availability of paper in the West in the 1500s and then declined with the increased access and affordability of printing in the early 1800s that supplanted letter writing as a primary means of conveying information. The Republic of Letters was composed of transactions through social and institutional networks, and its participants operated within an intellectual community of epistles.[7] Although primarily based in central Europe, some correspondents extended their network to islands in the Atlantic and parts of the Americas via trade routes and colonization.

The Republic of Letters also illustrated the Janus-faced nature of the Enlightenment. In *An Essay Concerning Human Understanding* (1689), John Locke wrote that enlightenment was a product of both an introspective "talk with oneself" and interpersonal discourse.[8] Letter writing was a means of gathering one's thoughts, disseminating those thoughts, and establishing a dialogue that, unlike diary writing, could be directly challenged and influenced by others. Letters could travel through the independent European mail systems that were established in the sixteenth century and, later, through the centralized mail systems of the late eighteenth and early nineteenth centuries. However, these systems could rarely be trusted for delivery or discretion since epistles from prominent figures were often printed in newspapers and leaflets. The invasion of parcels was well known, and many authors found the illicit publication of their letters advantageous for broadening international discourses, or even strategically subversive. Nonetheless, the practice highlighted the fact that letters were not necessarily private.

As maritime travel improved and more noncommercial ships crossed the Atlantic, letters traveled through personal conveyance. This triangulated conversations since the person delivering the note was often provided with a letter of introduction and, consequentially, benefited from access to new organizations, sites, and networks. It is important to underscore that the epistles studied in this book were not always transmitted transatlantically. Sometimes they traveled within the same country or even the same city, but the international composition of authors demonstrated engagement with both sides of the "Western Ocean," the Eurocentric term often used to refer to the Atlantic Ocean.

By applying themes from the Republic of Letters and expanding the definition of correspondence to include exchanged drawings, books, and objects of interest, this book uses Cosway, Jefferson, and Soane as the three core figures to study the nature and composition of the Transatlantic Design

Network: a shared and fluid network of people, sites, texts, and objects that transcended nationalistic concerns. The study of their products and shared network highlights the dynamic, although previously unexplored, cross-cultural exchange of design philosophies between "transatlantic friends" that helped shape the Early Republic era of America.[9] Through the Transatlantic Design Network, this study also reveals a relational reading of architectural development in the young nation that acknowledges the presence of European influences as well as a distinct American identity that was not simply reactionary or derivative but rather collaborative and responsive to the North American environment, character, and national ambitions.

The members of the Transatlantic Design Network were identified by several unique factors: the introduction of newly nationalized "American" individuals and their associated interests, professionally driven travel, and the extension of communication and exchange beyond initial, transitory meetings and social engagements. Cosway, Jefferson, and Soane were selected as the formative figures because of their triangulated correspondence and the characterizations asserted by some of their contemporaries in letters and descriptions, thereby disclosing many of the presumptions and societal conditions that existed in the transatlantic world. The inclusion of cartoons and caricatures in newspapers and flyers blossomed in the 1750s, often portraying characters, such as the Englishman, the American, and the Female. In the case of the selected triumvirate, the caricatures had some merit. Jefferson was labeled "the noble savage," a common stereotype for Americans in Europe, initially propagated by Franklin.[10] In truth, Jefferson was raised in the country and was leery of both big cities and cumbersome governments. As a plantation owner, he also embodied the contradictory nature of many of his revolutionary peers who fought for national freedom while profiting as lifelong slaveholders. Soane's professional and social ambitions inspired the critique among certain Royal Academy colleagues that he was a social climber; this was perpetuated in the satirical poems of the *Observer* and reviews in the *Examiner.* Soane's ambitions were confirmed by his deliberate attempts to obscure his humble heritage, which even included adding an *e* to the end of his surname.[11] His plans to transcend his class took him from the country to the city, and as if by divine intervention, he was "led by natural inclination to study architecture at age fifteen."[12]

Cosway was potentially the most caricatured and, problematically, dismissed of the three. She embodied the image of the attractive artist, and within most scholarship, except that of her steadfast champion Stephen Lloyd, her role as a muse consistently overshadows her numerous artistic commissions and contributions. For example, much has been written about the probability of a romantic relationship between Jefferson and Cosway. The obsession over an imagined affair is understandable given the famously passionate nature of their early letters, but these epistles also illuminate Cosway as a worldly, visually astute, and critical correspondent.[13] Throughout her life, she served as a conduit for her closest correspondents by advancing connections between international figures in the arts, helping circulate publications on architecture and landscape, and providing eyes on the artistic scene of Europe. This book aims to restore Cosway's voice, as well as that of other female colleagues who have, too often, been overlooked by historians and only viewed through the words of their famous male contemporaries.

Jefferson and Soane exchanged letters and material objects with Cosway, such as drawings, books, artifacts, and personal contacts, through which they cultivated a set of shared aesthetic and social concerns. United by a love of picturesque landscapes, they simultaneously valued tradition and technological innovation in architecture, and they were keenly interested in learned institutions. Offering a rereading of Monticello and Soane's Museum through the lens of the network, this book counters the view of Soane and Jefferson as autonomous innovators. Their house museums tested how architecture could be more than an armature for displaying collections: buildings could act as the ultimate artifact, reflective of the architect's careful study of precedents, knowledge of contemporary archaeological and scientific discoveries, and dedication to a design process that lasted more than forty years. By placing formative figures and sites in conversation, it is possible to understand how Cosway, Jefferson, Soane, and others contributed to and benefited from a transatlantic network of exchange that forged distinct architectural links between the Early Republic of America, the Second British Empire, and beyond.

As an interconnected triumvirate, the projects by and longstanding relationships between Cosway, Jefferson, and Soane demonstrate a particularly distinguished sample of the Transatlantic Design Network. The humble backgrounds of each figure distinctly differentiate their travels and experiences from those of aristocratic participants in the Grand Tour who often traveled at a relaxed pace with substantial funds, spent time abroad mostly with their own countrymen, and resisted the full exploration of foreign cultures, much like Smelfungus of Laurence Sterne's satirical account *A Sentimental Journey through France and Italy, by Mr Yorick* (1768). Additionally, the travels of Cosway, Jefferson, and Soane were often sponsored, professionally driven expeditions that, although inclusive of leisurely pursuits, were largely shaped by working interests. As designers, agents, and patrons, they were participants in intellectual circles and highly attuned to aesthetics and new developments in architecture. The ambitions of Cosway, Jefferson, and Soane were also linked to growing movements in the transatlantic community for the broader dissemination of knowledge and the replication of international experiences to larger audiences through localized endeavors. This resulted in museums, more inclusive societies, and educational projects. For example, Cosway founded the Collegio delle Grazie in Lodi, Italy, as a multilingual school that taught the arts, humanities, and science to adolescent girls; Jefferson crafted a house museum at Monticello and founded the Academical Village of the University of Virginia in Charlottesville, Virginia; and Soane developed unprecedented illustrated lectures at the Royal Academy as well as his famous house museum in London, England.

MAPPING THE TRANSATLANTIC DESIGN NETWORK

The correspondence of Jefferson and Soane with Cosway is a unique aspect of their relationship that should not be overlooked. Jefferson was a copious writer with approximately nineteen thousand letters to his credit; however, correspondence with few figures outside of his political and familial spheres matched the frequency and duration of his correspondence with Cosway. Even though they only spent a few weeks together in Paris and a lifetime separated by an ocean, they exchanged nearly a hundred letters between 1786 and 1824. The full extent of Cosway's correspondence with Soane is harder to gauge with fewer conserved letters since, unlike Jefferson, neither figure used copying machines or polygraphs. Forty-five letters from Cosway are preserved in Soane's Museum, revealing shared design interests, and Soane's notebooks relay several travels shared with Cosway, both within London and beyond, to exhibitions and architectural sites such as Stowe. As the distance between the pair increased between 1806 and 1836 due to Cosway's departure for Italy to establish her Collegio, their chain of letters also increased. In the latter years of their letter writing, business dominated much of the conversation since Soane was named the executor of Cosway's English estate. The pair also wrote frequently of personal matters, lamenting their mutual decline in vision and the trials of European correspondence, with Cosway writing, "a weakness in my sight prevents my writing for these two months past and I have no one that can write English for me."[14] For Jefferson and Cosway, it was the "immense Sea" and Jefferson's rheumatism that impacted their correspondence in later years, but the pair maintained conversations about their educational projects and shared transatlantic friends, many of whom had already passed.[15] One of Jefferson's letters to Cosway from 1820 noted that their group of energetic travelers had dwindled, and now, writing from disparate parts of the world, he was like "a solitary trunk in a desolate field, from which all its former companions have disappeared."[16]

Over two thousand letters were consulted in the research for this book, and this sampling of documentary evidence was initially defined by correspondence between Cosway, Jefferson, and Soane. The sample was then expanded to include correspondence between figures who knew at least two members of the triumvirate or were directly engaged in conversations with Cosway, Jefferson, or Soane about the arts, travel, and educational practices (fig. 3). These letters were used to study and map trends within the network, such as the means of cultivating architectural taste as well as the relationship between buildings, people, the design process, and the nature and scope of travel needed to broaden one's visual and experiential catalog. The letters were also beneficial for the identification of additional figures from America and Europe who helped further delineate the nature and composition of the network: Benjamin Franklin (1706–1790), Charles-Louise Clérisseau (1721–1820), John Adams (1735–1826), Madame de Tessé (1741–1813), Charles Willson Peale (1741–1827), Madame de Corny (1747–1829), Maximilian Godefroy (1756–1848), Angelica Schuyler Church (1756–1814), John Trumbull (1756–1843), William Thornton (1759–1828), George Hadfield (1763–

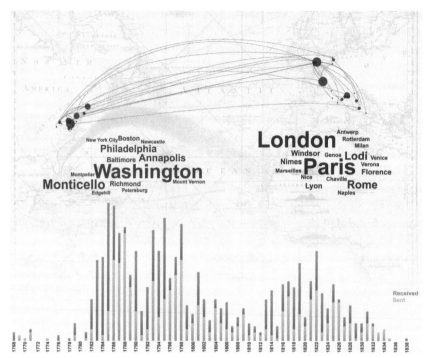

Fig. 3. A visualization of the letters sampled within the study of the Transatlantic Design Network, citing the most prominent sites for sending and receiving epistles. (Author's diagram)

1826), Benjamin Henry Latrobe (1764–1820), and Ellen Wayles Randolph Coolidge (1796–1876).

These figures were not selected because they were the most prolific correspondents of Cosway, Jefferson, or Soane, but because of the ways they interacted: what they sent to each other, where they traveled, to whom they provided letters of introduction, and how their contributions in design, education, curation, or even law may have impacted the forms, collections, and architectural thinking at Jefferson's Monticello and Soane's Museum. Since the complex visualization of the network is not suited to the printed page, an interactive online environment is being developed to explore the flow of letters, as well as the composition of the network, through various strands of association. These include the immediate correspondence, mentorship, patronage, genealogy, and marriage as well as communal membership in other formal networks, such as the London-based Royal Society, the Royal Society of the Arts, the Royal Academy and the U.S.-based American Philosophical Society, the Academy of Fine Arts, and the Columbian Institute.[17]

READING THE TRANSATLANTIC DESIGN NETWORK

This book is arranged in episodes, with three main themes, namely: People, Sites, and Legacies. Within this structure, each of the themes has a set of corresponding chapters, and these may be read chronologically or independently. The theme of People acts as a formative introduction to the key figures within the identified Transatlantic Design Network, illuminating the landscape of their initial meetings as well as the consequences of their association while questioning their awareness of the network's presence and its influence. The theme of Sites places the foundational years and architectural projects of Jefferson and Soane in deeper conversation by focusing on several aspects of their professionally driven travel itineraries and the iterative design processes they exercised at their homes. Finally, the theme of Legacies reflectively explores the museums, libraries, and educational projects of the network members, as well as the ongoing correlations between Monticello and Soane's Museum regarding policy, preservation, and tourism.

Read in concert, the three themes intertwine to present an untold story about ways transatlantic friendships and rivalries shaped architecture and design education. Although Cosway, Jefferson, and Soane are the main foci of the study and, respectively, provide lenses on design interests and occupations in continental Europe, America, and England, this book is a weighted survey that dedicates more attention to the American context. Its intention is to reveal that through the movement of people, letters, and objects in and out of the new nation there was an active transatlantic dialogue filled with the voices of women, overlooked designers, scientists, farmers, and entrepreneurs that collaboratively shaped projects and informed architectural development, physically and conceptually.

PART I

People

During the colonial era and the emergence of the new United States, aspiring North American designers had limited educational and experiential opportunities in comparison to their European counterparts. Typical studies of the early American built environment state that North American occupants could only acquire architectural knowledge by traveling across the "Western Ocean," engaging in the extremely limited field of architectural apprenticeship, or studying architectural pattern books and treatises. This view of architectural development does not recognize the influence of an architectural Republic of Letters. A study of the Transatlantic Design Network aims to bridge this gap by tracing how letters, personal contacts, and material objects such as drawings, books, and artifacts cultivated a distinct set of shared aesthetic, political, and social concerns among an international pool of architects, artists, collectors, and educators.

The theme of People examines the operations of key figures in the Transatlantic Design Network through five chapters. Within this theme, "Meetings" details the extraordinary sites and situations that inaugurated Cosway's lifelong friendships with Soane and Jefferson. "Ambassadors" explores how certain Americans abroad—and previously overlooked women—served as emissaries for design interests, even helping to forward projects in the new nation. "Associates" traces the ways two French architects found *entrée* into the design processes of some of America's most iconic governmental and monumental structures. "Architects" discusses how Cosway's own brother, George Hadfield, became the American government's first internationally commissioned architect. Finally, "Societies" examines the larger scale of interpersonal interaction within the Transatlantic Design Network through the lens of the Columbian Institute, an early American organization with several architects at the helm.

CHAPTER 1

Meetings

I find friendship to be like wine, raw when new, ripened with age.
—Thomas Jefferson to Benjamin Rush, August 17, 1811[1]

The key buildings and areas that formed the backdrops for the initial meetings and burgeoning friendships between John Soane and Maria Hadfield in southern Italy during 1778, and then Thomas Jefferson and Maria Hadfield Cosway in Paris during 1786, also served as an introduction to their shared ardor for aesthetics and architecture. For Jefferson and Soane, the experiences of these sites were singular; neither architect had the opportunity to return to France or Italy, respectively. Consequentially, these events were tied to the memories of meeting a female artist who would become a friend for life. For Soane and Cosway, the memory of their commonly traversed pathways inspired a lifetime of correspondence revolving around the "poetry" of ruins, interest in the preservation of excavations, and, tied to their early situations as poor students in the arts, the intimate trials of financial hardships. The dialogue between Jefferson and Cosway on drawing, agriculture, the relationship between the built and natural environments, and the architecture of sites for entertainment were shaped by an afternoon in the Halle au Blé grain markets of Paris as well as visits to picturesque suburban gardens.[2] These sites served as stimuli for forty years of correspondence, relying on shared memories of cities, landscapes, and follies. These meetings laid the foundations for prolonged friendships amid periods of extended and, finally, permanent separation and immediately assigned an architectural basis to their relationships.

For Jefferson and Soane, their initial meetings with Cosway took place in collective social settings: both architects were surrounded by their creative colleagues when they first encountered Cosway, yet she maintained longer friendships with Jefferson and Soane and corresponded with them more regularly than with any of the other companions in the architects' traveling parties. From the analysis of their overlapping lives from 1778 to 1789, one can understand the many shared connections between the networks of Jefferson and Soane, with Cosway as the critical bridge. Additionally, the distinct places where Cosway met Soane and Jefferson reinforce the importance of a transatlantic design community: the experiential legacy of these sites influenced both the written and the built architectural work of Jefferson and Soane. References to the sites they shared with Cosway appear in their written remembrances, letters to other friends and colleagues, and, most importantly, as physical allusions in the built manifestations of their ambitious house museums.

YOUNG MARIA

While the accomplishments and legacy of Maria Hadfield Cosway have been largely overlooked in the record of history, much attention has been paid to her supposed romances with the famous men such as Jefferson, Jacques-Louis David, Pasquale Paoli, Marquis d'Hancarville, and several others. As a young woman, Maria declined at least two marriage proposals, and her mother warned that she should not encourage the unwanted affections of male suitors and friends.[3] Maria's letters reveal that she took her mother's advice to heart and, if nothing else, simply had several *amitiés amoureuse*— including nationally and internationally significant figures. This captured the primary attention of her biographers and researchers for the last two centuries, except for Lloyd, significantly overshadowing her formative years as well as her artistic and education contributions. Her first nineteen years in Italy included a unique origin story, complete with a mythical family tragedy, a focused study of the arts, and the presence of an almost overwhelming sense of longing for the professional and social opportunities that were denied her because of her gender.

Maria's autobiographical account states that her father, Charles Hadfield, was a Manchester merchant who immigrated to Florence in the 1740s and married her mother, Elizabeth Peacock (Isabella), in Sienna in 1753.[4] Maria's less-than-idyllic remembrances indicate that her mother initially came to Italy as a servant to an English family. As a child, Maria was scarred by the familial fable, later recounted in her autobiographical letter, that a nursemaid smothered her four older siblings. After the nursemaid's dismissal, the Hadfields welcomed four more children: William (b. 1761), George (b. 1763), Charlotte (b. 1766), and Elisabetta (b. 1769). The legend of her close escape from death haunted Maria for the rest of her life, even though it may have been an apocryphal event recounted by a devotedly Catholic mother to encourage lifelong piety, prayer, and repentance.[5]

Located near Brunelleschi's Santo Spirito, south of the Arno, the Hadfields' home was also the family business: one of three inns for foreign travelers. This region of the city served as an English colony abroad, much like the area surrounding the Piazza de Spagna in Rome.[6] The inn's welcoming atmosphere and the congenial demeanor of Charles Hadfield were captured in Thomas Patch's painting *The Punch Party* (1760) as well as an uncharacteristically verbose description within the London printing of *A brief account of the roads of Italy for the use of gentlemen who travel with the post in twenty-three geographical maps* (1775).[7] The author even used Hadfield's inn as a point of comparison in his description of Venetian lodgings: "These houses are not so large as . . . Carlos at Florence. but the[y] are very clean & neat & well Serv'd."[8] The inn was mentioned in every subsequent printing of the travel book, including the Italian edition. This underscored its amenability to families and foreign travelers, even those who were not English, making it one of the best inns in all of Italy.[9]

With such published acclaim and established preference, especially among the English on the Grand Tour, the inn was filled with a steady stream of visitors. Here Maria had the opportunity to meet burgeoning artists and collectors. During the summer of 1775, when she was only fifteen, she met guests who would later form part of Soane's traveling party: Joseph Wright, Henry Tresham, Hugh Primrose Deane, and Edward Edwards. Ozias Humphreys was also with the party, and he would become Maria's drawing companion in the galleries of Florence as well as a close friend for life. Just as the inn was a site for vibrant artistic exchange, a letter from Tresham to Humphreys reveals that politics, too, were a topic of conversation and that the Hadfield patriarch was a zealous supporter of the American Revolution. This may have influenced Cosway's affinity for the Americans whom she encountered later in her life.[10]

During the winter of 1775, Maria outlined her creative pursuits in the city in a letter to Humphreys: "I go every morning at nine [to copy pictures] until one. After lunch I study as usual architecture until half past four. My singing teacher comes at five. At six I go drawing until nine. The evenings of the opera I go to listen to the latest of the prima donna."[11] Her relentless routine for honing her artistic skills was rewarded when she attracted the tutelage of famed painter Johan Zoffany and was honored with induction to the Florentine Accademia del Designo on September 7, 1778.[12] Her practice of painting in the mornings would continue throughout her adult life.

Maria was accomplished in Florentine artistic circles, and word of her talents spread among the English circles traveling through Italy. Yet, living in one of the most popular inns, Maria was the consummate host, never the traveler. She heard the stories of artistic adventures in the ancient cities of Rome, Naples, Pompeii, and Herculaneum. Rome could be reached in a five-day journey, yet the ruins and galleries must have seemed a world away. Later in life, she seized every opportunity to travel in and around London, Paris, Lyon, Lombardy, the Veneto, and Rome. The late 1770s and early 1780s, also the same time she first met Soane and Jefferson, would prove to be transformative for Maria, and she captured the changes in two self-portraits. Talented but deferential, Maria's 1778 *Self-portrait with Turban* depicts a young woman gazing at the viewer; her self-portrait painted nine years later also features what would become her signature turban, though the painting illustrates a well-fashioned lady with arms crossed in defiance. Maria was now a Cosway: an artist of international repute and one of the most famed socialites of Parisian and London salons (fig. 4).

Fig. 4. From a Hadfield to a Cosway: Maria's 1778 self-portrait and an engraving by V. Green after Cosway's 1787 self-portrait. (Public domain and British Museum 1852, 0214.307)

"AMBITIOUS, PROUD, AND RESTLESS"

The first portrait of Soane, made just before he left London for Rome, captures the intense concentration and serious character of a young student, complete with architectural dividers in hand (fig. 5).[13] Despite the polished image presented in the painting, Soane's financial situation in the 1770s was humble. Although he had been working in an architectural office since the age of fifteen, he did not have the independent means necessary to undertake a Grand Tour. Following the precedent of architects such as the Adam brothers, Chambers, and the Dances, travel in Italy was considered requisite for a successful career in London. Lacking the private funds to secure a journey, Soane tirelessly developed his design and drawing talents at the Royal Academy: he won the Silver Medal in 1772, won the Gold in 1776, and was awarded the Traveling Scholarship a year later. Without the annual £60 stipend associated with the scholarship, Soane may never have embarked on

Fig. 5. *Portrait of John Soan* [sic] *as a young man* (1776) by Christopher William Hunneman. (©Sir John Soane's Museum, London, SM P400)

his transformative journey. Capturing his excitement, the notebook entry for his departure date read, "left for Rome on 18 March 1778 at 5am!"[14]

Soane and his traveling companion, fellow student Robert Furze Brettingham, stopped in Paris en route to Rome. They saw Jacques-Germain Soufflot's Sainte-Geneviève under construction and met with architect-engineer Jean-Rodolphe Perronet.[15] The pair arrived in Rome on May 2, and like most English travelers, they probably visited the English Coffee House at the Piazza de Spagna.[16] Here, a few years before Soane's arrival, Sir William Chambers sent sage advice to another young architect, M. Edward Stevens:

You will find great advantage in the decorative art by sketching, or drawing accurately, many of the fragments which lie scattered in all the villas about Rome, and in the environs of Naples. Draw in the Academy the human figure with the same view, correctly if you can, but at least with spirit and taste. Converse much with the artists of all Countrys, particularly with foreigners, that may get rid of national prejudices. Seek for those who have most reputation, young or old, amongst which forget not Piranesi.[17]

Now housed within the archives of Soane's Museum in London, it is unknown how or when this letter came into Soane's possession, but such carefully crafted advice formed a welcome guide for architectural studies in the home of classicism. Soane noted, "My attention is entirely taken up in the seeing and examining the numerous and inestimable remains of Antiquity . . . what impatience I have waited for the scenes I now enjoy."[18] In the fall of 1778, Soane made his first venture south to explore Naples, Caserta, Capua, Pompeii, Vesuvius, Baia, and Paestum. By November 1778, he returned to Rome and met with an ailing Piranesi.[19] Unlike the Adam brothers, Soane and his companions did not have the good fortune of touring southern Italy with Piranesi's French counterpart, Charles-Louis Clérisseau, but Soane eventually collected some of the architect-antiquarian's drawn works for display in the museum.[20]

When Maria met Soane, she was an eighteen-year-old artist whose rapidly blossoming talents had already been recognized in Florence. The energetic character of her figural drawings, along with her vivacious personality and musical talents, prompted the prediction by fellow artists that the young Maria was a rising star in the Italian arts scene and could, perhaps, be the next Angelica Kauffman.[21] Although she had a seemingly prosperous future in the arts, Maria had also expressed an interest in becoming a nun. Throughout her life, she would be torn between the secular world of artistic pursuits and a religious calling.[22] Her indecision was further complicated by family turmoil: the Hadfield patriarch passed away in November 1776, and the business of managing the inn began to take its toll on Maria's mother. Escaping an uncertain future, Maria left Florence with her brother William on December 13, 1778, for her first important trip outside of Florence to explore the landscapes of the Lazio and Campagnia regions.[23]

Maria and Soane were intricately connected to a circle of young British artists and architects in Rome, and their introduction occurred through mutual friends: James Northcote, Tresham, Humphrey, Prince Hoare, and Thomas Banks. These young artists knew Maria through stays at the Hadfields' inn, and Soane through studies at the Royal Academy.[24] Once in Rome, Maria and her brother found accommodation with Banks, an established Anglo resident and a Hadfield inn patron in 1772.[25] Here, sometime between May and December 1778 or early 1779, Maria met "Soan"; the eager architect and son of a bricklayer had not yet added the *e* to the end of his name.[26]

Northcote, a Royal Academician and one of Soane's Italian traveling companions, described Maria's first arrival to the antiquated city of Rome in his *Memoirs:*

She was just eighteen years of age, not unhandsome, endowed with considerable talents, and with a form extremely delicate and a pleasing manner of the utmost simplicity[.] But she was withal, active, ambitious, proud, and restless: she had been the object of adoration of an indulgent father, who unfortunately for her had never checked the growth of her imperfections; she had some small knowledge of painting, the same of music, and about the same of five or six languages but was very imperfect in all of these.[27]

It is unlikely that Soane shared this critical and ungenerous view of Maria, but, unfortunately, little was written during their time together in Italy. The young travelers wandered the Roman Forum, still largely covered with earth, measuring and drawing: the party could have easily been models for Henry Parke's familiar drawing of a student surveying the ruins (1819). Although no architectural drawings exist from Maria's time with Soane, sketching occupied a large portion of the group's time. Three of her brother William's drawings from Rome are preserved in Soane's Museum: *View of the Temples of Vesta & Fortuna Virilias, View of the Forum Romanum,* and *View of the Arch of Septimius Severus & the Temple of Saturn.*[28]

Leaving Rome in April 1779, Maria and Soane ventured south with their group. Despite the popularity of central Rome among architects, Soane preferred Naples: he was unimpressed by the Roman Baroque and favored the funerary monuments along the route from Rome to Naples, such as the Appian Way and the temples and urban ruins of Pompeii.[29] The Roman town had just been discovered in the 1740s, and much of it was still covered in ash, earth, and building rubble. The group climbed the summit of Vesuvius, but it is unlikely that Soane joined since he made the precarious trek in the winter of 1778. Soane then left Maria and the group to travel to Sicily as a commissioned draftsman for five gentlemen, four of whom would become future clients: John Patteson, Thomas Bowdler, Rowland Burdon, John Stuart, and Henry Lewis. By the time Soane returned to Rome, Maria and her brother were gone.

Maria and a very ill William left Rome with the Banks family on May 18, 1779, and returned to Florence. Less than a month later, the Hadfields sold their famous inns, and the family procured passports to travel to London via Paris. William would join the family once they settled into their new accommodations at 9 George Street on Hanover Square in the summer of 1779.[30] The next time Soane saw Maria, by then Mrs. Cosway, was in London on September 14, 1782.[31] After this encounter, Soane did not record an independent meeting with Maria again until 1820, but there are no fewer than sixty entries in his notebooks from 1801 to 1821 listing events and visits with "the Cosways," including excursions to significant architectural sites such as Strawberry Hill and Windsor.

FROM HADFIELD TO COSWAY

The young Maria that Soane met in 1778 was a very different figure than the woman Jefferson met in Paris in 1786. This difference was not simply in name but in experience and accomplishment. Over the course of eight years, Cosway's attitudes and ambitions shifted because of changes in her finances and, consequentially, her social network. Maria's initial arrival in London and change in station were recorded by Northcote, who explained that the family's financial hardships necessitated Maria's marriage: "at that time [he] adored her, though she always despised him."[32] As before, Northcote's tone toward Maria was uncharitable, but he was not alone in seeing her marriage as an unhappy one.[33] Maria Hadfield married Richard Cosway, miniature painter and Royal Academician, on January 18, 1781, at St. George's Hanover Square (1725), a church designed by Wren's apprentice and master carpenter John James. Maria met Richard only a few months prior at the St. James's Park residence of collector and antiquarian Charles Townley, through the introduction of their mutual friend Thomas Banks.[34] Her marriage improved her financial standing and social prospects, and she seemed to view it as a chance for reinvention: "I kept very retired for a twelve month [period] until I became acquainted with the society I should form."[35] Although seemingly hindered by her husband's strict codes for social propriety, she both continued and expanded her artistic pursuits through her associations with the Royal Academy. She began exhibiting the same year she married and consistently presented work for the Academy's annual show until 1789; engravings of her work, executed by Valentine Green and Francesco Bartolozzi, thrust her into publicized success.[36]

Late in the summer of 1784, the couple moved their growing art and antiquity collection from 4 Berkeley Street near Piccadilly to the central block of Schomberg House in Pall Mall.[37] Here the couple entertained more frequently and further cultivated their eclectic collections. Maria Cosway's reputation in the art world, however, was faltering. Her work from the 1785 Royal Academy exhibit was harshly criticized, and between late 1785 and early 1786 she had a bout of "illness," though it is unclear whether this referred to her physical or emotional well-being. While residing with her parents in London during her father's tenure as minister plenipotentiary to the Court of St. James's, the appointed precursor to the position of American ambassador to the United Kingdom, Abigail "Nabby" Adams recorded her impressions of Cosway in nearly identical letters to both her brother and her aunt on January 30, 1786. To Mary Smith Cranch she explained:

I took one [a seat] next to a Mrs. Cosway an Italian artist who is rather a singular character. She paints and her subjects are the most singular that one can imagine- I saw the last year in the exhibition of painting several of her performances. One was a *Dream*—another the deluge. . . . the most extraordinary that imagination could form. She speaks English, Italian, and French vastly well . . . plays and sings, well, but has nevertheless, the foibles, which attend those accomplishments—I mean—I was witness to solicitude from almost every person. . . . I think a woman is never excusable for such a conduct unless she has an inexhaustible fund of wit and good humour to display upon the occasion which this lady had not.[38]

Accounts by fellow Americans John Trumbull (1756–1843) and Jefferson demonstrate that Cosway had reclaimed her "good humour" by the summer of 1786, when she was residing in Paris, perhaps revived by the change in the climate and societal conventions.

THE DOME AND THE DÉSERT

In the late 1780s, Jefferson was in love, and the object of his affection was the city of Paris. On May 7, 1784, Congress appointed Jefferson the new minister plenipotentiary to France, replacing the aging Benjamin Franklin. Two months later, Jefferson sailed from Boston with his eldest daughter, Martha, and his personal secretary, William Short. The eastbound journey to Le Havre was an "unusually short" nineteen days, complete with pleasant weather and the quiet company of only five other passengers.[39] Jefferson's enslaved domestic servant, James Hemings, followed on another ship. Not wishing to dally, the complete party made their way south via carriage and arrived in Paris on August 6.[40]

Jefferson's five years in Paris dramatically changed his lifestyle, architectural knowledge, and social attitudes. The density of the city must have been striking since in the late eighteenth century, Paris was the second largest city in Europe. Although Jefferson spent periods of time in Philadelphia in the 1770s, the largest city of the Atlantic colonies, the population disparity between these top transatlantic centers was significant. The first census of 1790 showed that the combined population of the five largest cities in America was just 123,475. In that same year, France estimated the population of Paris to be 600,000.[41]

The congressional appointment to a foreign post was a well-timed opportunity for Jefferson since the preceding years had not been kind. He was newly widowed, had lost three children, and suffered through a strenuous and harshly criticized term as the governor of Virginia. Although Jefferson was well known in America for his authorship of the Declaration of Independence and his service in the Virginia House of Burgesses, his lack of military training had impeded his judgment as governor during the Revolutionary War. He fled the capital city of Richmond, an indefensible port city, and established a temporary seat of government in his native Charlottesville. Undeterred, British troops led by Lieutenant Colonel Banastre Tarleton followed the group to the foothills of the Blue Ridge Mountains and raided Monticello—his first experiment in architecture—on June 4, 1781. Jefferson sent the delegates and his family away to safety before he narrowly escaped to Montalto, a summit four hundred feet higher in elevation than Monticello, from which he watched the troops destroy his plantation's fields and kill his livestock. Remarkably, Monticello was left unscathed, apart from the wine cellar. A year later, Jefferson's ailing wife died at Monticello after the birth of their sixth child. Only two of those children, Martha and Maria, survived into adulthood and both would, eventually, join Jefferson during his Parisian tenure.

Paris offered Jefferson a fresh start and a broadened perspective. Until the age of forty-one, Jefferson's experience of the greater world was largely limited to his knowledge from books, albeit encyclopedic, and his interactions in America with people who had traversed the physical and intellectual landscape of the transatlantic Republic of Letters firsthand, such as Thomas Paine, the Marquis de Chastellux, and the Marquis de Lafayette. Entrenched in his diplomatic work, Jefferson effectively used his time abroad to also explore the artistic and scientific spheres of Paris that fascinated and inspired him. He watched "aerostatical experiments" in the Tuileries Gardens on September 19, 1784, and enjoyed dining at the Café Mécanique, located near the Palais-Royale, where orders were conveyed to the basement kitchen via metal talking pipes. Food and drink were then delivered through a series of simple machines: dumbwaiters and revolving doors.[42] Jefferson replicated these systems in his American architectural experiments at the President's House and Monticello. While the sights and experiences of the vibrant city were captivating, he was most smitten with the new buildings in the city: "Were I to proceed to tell you how much I enjoy their architecture, sculpture, painting, music, I should want words. It is in these arts they shine."[43]

When Jefferson first met Cosway in Paris during the summer of 1786, he had just returned from two months in London and its environs, partially spent with fellow American diplomatic transplants John Adams and his family. While in residence, the forty-two-year-old Jefferson toured English landscape gardens featured in Thomas Whatley's *Observations on Modern Gardening* (1770), such as Chiswick, Stowe, and Kew, and made notations on scraps of paper. Jefferson also met selected members of the artistic community in London, such as American and founding member of the Royal Academy Benjamin West (1738–1820). If Benjamin Franklin was the best-known American in France, the corresponding title in England certainly belonged to West.[44] A highly successful artist and a favorite painter of the crown, West was paid an extraordinary £34,000 in commissions by King George III between 1769 and 1801.[45] He also served as the president of the Royal Academy from 1792 to 1820, with a brief gap from 1805 to 1806. Unselfish in his successes, West set up a studio in London where he hosted and trained more than twenty American artists, including Mather Brown (1761–1831). The Boston native came to London in 1781 and, three years later, accepted a prestigious invitation to become the second American student at the Royal Academy.[46] Persuaded by Brown's rising stature in the English art world and his American heritage, Jefferson paid £10 and sat for his very first portrait in Brown's studio at 1 Wells Street (fig. 6).[47] While in the studio, Jefferson was introduced to another of West's American protégés and a longtime friend of Brown from Boston who would figure strongly in Jefferson's experience of Paris during the second half of his tenure: John Trumbull.

Although both were Americans and active in the Revolution, Jefferson and Trumbull did not meet until their time abroad. While Jefferson was ensconced in the legal battles of colonial separation, Trumbull was occupied as a colonel with the northern operations of the Continental Army.[48] However, upon meeting at the Adamses' residence in London in the spring of 1786, Trumbull discovered that they shared more than revolutionary roots. Reminiscing in his *Autobiography,* Trumbull wrote that Jefferson "had a taste for the fine arts . . . and kindly invited me to come to Paris, to see and study the fine works there, and to make his house my home, during my stay."[49] Trumbull accepted Jefferson's offer that summer; with the intertwined connections of the Transatlantic Design Network busily in motion, it was through patronage and friendship with Trumbull that Jefferson met Cosway.

After several changes of address in Paris during his first year and a half, Jefferson moved into the unfurnished two-story Hôtel de Langeac at the corner of the Rue de Berri and the Champs-Elysées on October 17, 1785.[50] Trumbull, too, benefited from the new accommodation since its location was ideal for exploring the city; the spacious rooms and gardens also proved to be a productive painting studio for the artist. While in residence, Trumbull took

Fig. 6. *Thomas Jefferson* (1786) by Mather Brown; the portrait hanging in Monticello's Parlor is a copy. (National Portrait Gallery, Smithsonian Institution, NPG.99.66)

the opportunity to study Jefferson for several portraits, including *The Declaration of Independence.*[51] The patriots frequently traversed the city together, and in late August 1786 the pair visited the grain markets of Paris that were housed in the remarkable new structure known as the Halle au Blé (fig. 7). It was amid the cacophony of the urban market and the fascinating new agricultural machinery that Jefferson first met Cosway.

Trumbull met the Cosways earlier in the summer of 1786 and often traveled alongside the couple on their artistic explorations of the city: "I became acquainted and intimate with them, availing myself of all these advantages, I employed myself, with untiring industry, in examining and studying whatever had relation to the arts. I kept a journal of each day's occupation."[52] It is possible to re-create Trumbull's initial excursions with the Cosways from

Fig. 7. Ink wash sketch of the interior of the Halle au Blé by Jean-Baptiste Maréchal, 1786. (Public domain)

these journals. Curiously, however, the diary fails the reader in recounting that famous meeting amid the ambiance of the Halle au Blé, and Trumbull regretfully noted the interruption in his *Autobiography*.[53] Although Trumbull's journals do not narrate the first meeting of Jefferson and Cosway, a fairly detailed reconstruction of their initial architectural experience in Paris can be made by consulting Jefferson's account book and the early letters shared between Jefferson and Cosway.

Much has been written about Jefferson's epic four-thousand-word letter to Cosway from October 12, 1786, known typically as "a dialogue between my head and my heart." Although it is easy to be captivated by its eloquence and romantic overtones, Jefferson's passion for architecture is not to be overlooked. In the letter, Jefferson's head is credited with initiating the excursion to the Halle, since the heart noted, "it might have rotted down before I should have gone to see [it]." The heart conceded that the Halle was the best sight in Paris; however, this was not due to the building's luminous interior or its expressed structural ribbing, but to the company present during the visit.

The Halle au Blé was a massive circular market of brick and stone with a polished ashlar facade and a dome, composed of laminated wood and panes of glass, that flooded the interior of the structure with daylight. Originally designed by Nicolas Le Camus de Mézières, the building was constructed around an open court where six main access roads converged, making the structure the literal core of the agricultural markets in Paris. The ground floor was composed of twenty-five arched openings: six accommodating the access roads and the remaining nineteen barred with iron grilles. The building's dome, however, was its most spectacular feature. After winning an open competition for the design, architects J. G. Legrand and Jacques Molinos executed their ambitious dome using a revived Renaissance system known as the Delorme manner. The dome's segmented assembly system resulted in an expedient construction process, executed between September 10, 1782, and September 20, 1783.[54]

When Trumbull, Jefferson, and the Cosways passed beneath the dome in 1786, the impressive, glazed sections would have illuminated their examinations of the market. Jefferson noted that he immediately imagined the application of the dome's construction methods in America. Once he returned to Virginia, he purchased a copy of Delorme's treatise *Nouvelles invention pour bien batir et à petits fraiz* (1561), which would aid in the design and construction of an octagonal dome for Monticello in 1800.[55] After his own experiment with the fabrication method, he even wrote to the architect of the US Capitol, Benjamin Henry Latrobe, to suggest the use of a Delorme dome for the new House of Representatives. Latrobe was quick to dismiss the idea, writing that "a single leaky joint . . . dropping upon the head or desk of a member will disturb the whole house."[56] Although sharp, Latrobe's structural and functional critique was accurate: when writing to Latrobe in 1805, Jefferson did not know that the dome of his beloved Halle au Blé collapsed in 1802.[57]

It is unknown if it was also Maria Cosway's first visit to the Halle during that late August day. While in Paris, she and Richard resided along the Rue Coqueron near the Halle, so it is possible that she was already quite familiar with the building. After their tour of the market, the group took dinner on the outskirts of Paris in the popular town of St. Cloud before heading to the entertainment venues of Ruggieri's and Krumfoltz. For the next few weeks, Jefferson was a frequent companion of Cosway, with much of their time spent in the company of a larger group consisting of Richard, the Baron d'Hancarville, Trumbull, Short, and others. Jefferson and Cosway were even joined by Jefferson's daughter Martha to see the play *Les Deux Billets.* The only time Jefferson and Cosway may have gone on an independent excursion was September 16 when the pair journeyed to a fantastical garden estate, Le Désert de Retz. This was also their last long visit of 1786.[58]

While exploring the impressive architecture developed from the ruins of an abandoned village, Jefferson and Cosway toured the sprawling landscape of the Racine de Monville's Le Désert de Retz, a site Soane probably toured when he stopped briefly in Paris in the spring of 1778 (fig. 8).[59] The designed landscape included a curious four-story house in the form of a massive ruined Doric column, as well as a wooden chinoiserie, a manmade lake, a pyramidal icehouse that simultaneously served as a Freemason's folly, and an orangery. Aside from a brief note in Jefferson's account book recording payment for entry, very little is known about their impressions of the site.[60] Though now disproved, some scholars speculated that the day ended abruptly when Jefferson took an accidental fall and dislocated his right wrist, as the visit was the last bit of sightseeing that he recorded in his account books before the September 18 entry for the payment of "two Surgeons."[61] The injury, however, did prohibit the diplomat from enjoying the company of the Cosways on additional architectural adventures in the early fall of 1786 and disrupted his copious letter writing: Jefferson wrote fellow American diplomat and John Adams's son-in-law William Stephens Smith that the account of "how the right hand became disabled would be a long story for the left to tell."[62] Three decades after the accident, Jefferson wrote to Cosway from Monticello that "my wrist . . . dislocated in Paris while I had the pleasure of being there with

Fig. 8. A view of the "ruined column" residence at Désert de Retz. (Author's photo)

you, is, by the effect of years, now so stiffened that writing is become a most slow and painful operation."[63]

Nonetheless, ten days prior to his 1786 letter to Smith, Jefferson suffered through the difficulty of writing with his left hand to pen the head and heart letter, the longest letter in his preserved correspondence. In addition to a description of the Halle, Jefferson reminisced about other architectural excursions:

Paint to me the day we went to St. Germains. How beautiful was every object! the Port de Neuilly, the hills along the Seine, the rainbows of the machine of Marly, the terras of St. Germains, the chateaux, the gardens, the [statues] of Marly, the pavillon of Lucienne. Recollect too Madrid, Bagatelle, the King's garden, the Dessert [Le Désert de Retz].[64]

Architectural sites, rather than popular salons or luxurious meals, dominated their itineraries.

Jefferson recalled Le Désert de Retz with awe, especially the exceptional union of architecture and landscape architecture: "How grand the idea excited by the remains of such a column! The spiral staircase too was beautiful. Every moment was filled with something agreeable."[65] Jefferson made no mention of the geometric gardens that were so prevalent in Paris at the time, and his affinity for the picturesque was shared with Cosway. The pair also found the sublime captivating, and Jefferson's subsequent letters urged Cosway to cross the Atlantic to explore America's natural wonders. Although the United States had not yet developed a rich built fabric, Jefferson believed that his nation's natural landscapes were ideal and unparalleled subjects: "the Falling spring, the Cascade of Niagara, the Passage of the Potowmac thro the Blue mountains, the Natural bridge. It is worth a voiage across the Atlantic to see these objects; much more to paint, and make them, and thereby ourselves, known to all ages."[66]

In the same letter, Jefferson's head woefully, and accurately, acknowledged that the Cosways were unlikely to journey to America. The "head and heart letter" does not mention the architectural splendors of Monticello but, instead, the unparalleled condition of this home's natural site. This may be reflective of Jefferson's working plans to dismantle and redesign his home upon his return to Virginia. When Jefferson commenced his transatlantic travels, he left the mountaintop home unfinished, and after two years of travel and architectural explorations abroad, he realized that his residence had substantial shortcomings in terms of its purely symmetrical layout, uniform floor levels that would not allow for spatial connections in section, and lack of opportunities to modulate light, temperature, or views. In later years, after Monticello's substantial remodeling, Jefferson displayed no reluctance in praising his design work, writing his son-in-law in 1812 that the home was the "best dwelling house in the state."[67]

Although Jefferson and Cosway exchanged letters sporadically in the year following their initial meeting, he did not see the artist again until her unaccompanied visit to Paris in 1787. She and Jefferson frequented the newly opened exhibit at the Grand Salon Carré of the Louvre, and Cosway met

Jefferson's other daughter, Mary, then known as Polly, who had just arrived in Paris in July 1787.[68] Coincidentally, upon her return to America with her father in 1789, it appears that Polly preferred the more cosmopolitan name Maria; conceivably, the young girl was as fond of Maria Cosway as her father.[69]

MEANINGFUL EXCHANGE

It is impossible to fully trace the first meetings of Soane and Jefferson with Cosway, since gaps in their correspondence and record books leave questions about everything the friends saw, discussed, and realized during their journeys. However, from their later letters and elements of their house museums, these two gentlemen, along with Cosway, experienced the sites of France and Italy differently from their peers. They extracted new lessons from the built environment that they would use to reinvent the concept of the home as an architectural laboratory and a vessel for disseminating lessons about the greater world to those who did not have the fortune to make continental or transatlantic travels. In later years, as a sentimental and intellectual confidant, Cosway served as the eyes of Jefferson and Soane in continental Europe. In her letters, she painted vivid scenes of familiar sites that the architects would never experience again.

CHAPTER 2

Ambassadors

I desire you would Remember the Ladies.
—Abigail Adams to John Adams, April 23, 1776[1]

The Bicentennial Administration Exhibition held at the Metropolitan Museum of Art in New York City in 1975 focused on Benjamin Franklin (1706–1790) as a crucial conduit between political figures, revolutionary officers, and writers.[2] Conceived as an object-based endeavor with dynamic graphics, the exhibit and catalog for "The World of Franklin and Jefferson" were designed by architects Charles and Ray Eames, who also produced an accompanying twenty-eight-minute film (fig. 9). The bicentennial project marked the final exhibition for the Eames office. It opened in Paris before traveling to Warsaw, London, New York City, Chicago, Los Angeles, and Mexico City. Although the catalog labeled Franklin and Jefferson as the "Architects of Independence," the exhibition featured only a small installation on Jefferson's buildings, bypassing connections with other architects and sites as well as the concept of a transatlantic network of the arts. Of the twenty-nine individuals featured in the exhibition, all were male except for the second First Lady, Abigail Adams (1744–1818).[3] More than four decades after the exhibition, the women of the Transatlantic Design Network have yet to receive their due. Although more attentive to the contributions of women within the transatlantic realm, even Roger G. Kennedy's *Orders from France* relegated his brief discussions of Cosway, Ameriga Vespucci (1805–1866), and others

to their "enormously attractive" appearances and their "number of male friends."[4] Historically, these women have only been seen through the eyes of and through their associations with famous men. Material culture studies have broadened scholarship, yet there is still much to explore within archives and documentary evidence to uncover the stories of female-led architectural patronage, influence, and criticism.[5]

The lengthy entry for "ambassador" in Diderot's 1751 edition of the *Encyclopedia* explains the competing sources for the word: in old Gaul, *ambactus* meant customer, domestic servant, or officer, whereas the Latin root *ambulare* meant traveling.[6] In combining these two roots, the term implies that as a foreign representative, official or unofficial, the "ambassador" exhibits an amenable attitude toward exchange, whether cultural or intellectual. The figures identified here as ambassadors of the Transatlantic Design Network fully embodied Diderot's description. Although not all were architects, they actively participated in the advancement of architectural interests by transmitting ideas, artwork, and books. Selected buildings and sites were frequently referenced in their writings, thereby outlining a collection of prominent precedents, both ancient and contemporary, that were of interest to artists, designers, patrons, statesmen, and socialites within the network. The ambassadors' travels, building commissions, and legacies—such as founding institutions of learning—significantly informed the work and careers of architects in early America. As active agents within the network, they were advocates for architectural interests as well as financiers for important educational and artistic projects. As places to socialize, postulate designs, and make new acquaintances, the homes of ambassadors functioned as the network's 'embassies.'

Within the Transatlantic Design Network, a set of interconnected figures from different national backgrounds were united through travels, and they served as active ambassadors. Some, such as Franklin and Trumbull, were officially appointed American diplomats and treaty negotiators who were also conduits for exchange in international design and artistic circles. Others were female; therefore, they were prevented from serving in official capacities because of their gender. Nonetheless, they served as indispensable points of contact for their compatriots abroad. Additionally, they were benevolent hosts for women from other international circles. As a patron and advocate for the arts who recognized her role as an invaluable architectural emissary—introducing designers to specific sites, figures, and emergent architectural ideas and discoveries—Maria Cosway was the most prominent female ambassador in the network. Yet she was joined by others: Angelica Kauffman (1741–1807), Angelica Schuyler Church (1756–1814), Madame de Tessé (1741–1813), and Madame de Corny (1747–1829).[7]

AMERICANS AND ARTISTS ABROAD

Although it was not yet an autonomous nation, America deployed its first diplomats to Europe in the 1770s. Among these figures was the precocious seventy-three-year-old polymath Franklin. His social persona was far more prominent than those of his American counterparts abroad, such as Adams or John Jay, and his reluctance to conform to European conventions in terms of dress or public etiquette further accentuated Franklin's eccentricity. With hundreds of international correspondents, he was an active participant in the Republic of Letters and, when in London, was a regular visitor to several coffeehouses and the collections of Sir Hans Sloane before the establishment of the British Museum.

Franklin was one of the best-traveled North Americans of his generation, spending nearly twenty-five of his eighty-four years in Europe and crossing the Atlantic six times.[8] Unlike Jefferson or Soane, he was not a designer or an obsessive collector, and he was not substantially involved in aesthetic discourse. But Franklin was a valuable member of the Transatlantic Design Network because he was, in the words of Malcolm Gladwell, a social super-connector.[9] As the self-proclaimed "noble savage," Franklin was the high-profile American in eighteenth-century Europe, and he was one of the most vocal advocates for transatlantic exchange. In addition to garnering support for the American Revolution's cause, he served as an intriguing anomaly within the salons of Paris and the coffeehouses of London: unlike many of his North American contemporaries, who were either born or sought training and refinement abroad, Franklin was an American-born writer, philosopher, printer, scientist, and revolutionary leader.[10] While abroad, he also served as an ambassador for the amicable character and open landscapes of America: he encouraged several notable individuals to traverse the Atlantic, and he provided the letters of introduction necessary to inaugurate careers abroad. For example, after completing his medical studies in Edinburgh and London, British Virgin Island native Dr. William Thornton (1759–1828) sought out Franklin in Paris, immigrated to Franklin's Philadelphia, and became one of the most influential gentleman architects and administrators in the new federal capital of Washington.

As a practiced businessman, critical intellectual, and experienced naturalist, Franklin was part of some of the most significant events in both North America and Europe. He was the author of *Experiments and Observations on Electricity* (1751), a member of the Committee of Five that drafted the American Declaration of Independence, a campaigner for the abolition of slavery, the founder of the University of Pennsylvania, a negotiator and signer of the Treaty of Paris, and a delegate at the American Constitutional Convention. Although momentous, neither Franklin's contributions to these events nor his membership in a variety of established international societies constitutes his most notable contribution to the Transatlantic Design Network.[11] Instead, it was his founding role in two institutions, both based in Philadelphia, that had the most impact on the circulation of design ideas: the American Philosophical Society and the Library Company.

As a founding member of the Philosophical Society in 1743, later known as the American Philosophical Society, Franklin witnessed the organization falter within two years of its establishment. Undeterred, he helped its revival in 1767 by soliciting international members during his time abroad, and he subsequently served as its first president. As a bibliophile in the colonies, where access to printed texts was particularly difficult, Franklin invested in broadening access to education; this prompted his creation of the Library Company of Philadelphia. As a steadily growing, subscription-based institution, the collections of the Library Company were as diverse as its patrons: a century after its establishment, there were 836 members and nearly 44,000 books.[12] The Library Company also facilitated interconnectivity and the circulation of architectural texts: it was the only American institution to exchange books and catalogs with Soane, and in the nineteenth century it was the largest repository for Soane's published works in America.[13]

Soane knew, too, of Franklin's work. He owned Franklin's *Observations on smoky chimneys, their causes and cure; with considerations on fuel and stoves* (1793) and had the text bound with Robert Clavering's *Essay on the construction and building of chimneys* (1793). It is unknown when the volume entered Soane's collections, but Soane described the "many desirable qualities" of the "Penseilvanian Stove . . . from the celebrity of Dr. Franklin" in a Royal Academy lecture, noting that the invention lessened the smoke drawn into a room and efficiently produced warmth.[14] Franklin and Soane, like many members of the network, often viewed architecture as applied science. In June 1752, Franklin anxiously awaited the completion of Christ Church in Philadelphia, as its bell tower would be the tallest structure in the city and would thus allow the scientist to use the steeple to demonstrate his hypothesis that lightning was electricity. His impatience with the construction process, however, led to his now-legendary experiment of lofting a kite with an attached metal key to the skies during a storm while his son, William, stood witness to the literal spark of Enlightenment curiosity.[15] Franklin's close friend Benjamin West painted a phantasmagoric vision of the moment in *Benjamin Franklin*

Drawing Electricity from the Sky (1816). Although not painted from life, the two men spent many years in proximity when Franklin was living in rented accommodations on London's Craven Street. West's second son (b. 1772) was named after Franklin, and the Philadelphia scientist-diplomat was also the boy's godfather. With such close connections to West, it is likely that Franklin frequented West's artistic circles in London and was familiar with the founding Academicians of the Royal Academy, including another key member of the Transatlantic Design Network: Swiss artist Angelica Kauffman.

Kauffman came to London in 1766 under the sponsorship of Lady Wentworth. She served as a portrait artist but was also busily employed as a decorative painter in the Adam brothers' residential work. These interior paintings illustrated Kauffman's spatial sensibilities, as many were directly responsive to their architectural context: figures in different panels were connected through their positions and the direction of their gazes.[16] Three years after her arrival in London, her status within the world of professional artists was solidified when she was installed as one of the forty founding Academicians of the Royal Academy; she and Mary Moser (1744–1819) were the only two females, and their election had been at the urging of King George III.[17] As women, "decorum" prohibited their inclusion in life drawing courses, so within Zoffany's painting *The Academicians of the Royal Academy* (1771) the depictions of both Kauffman and Moser are relegated to lifeless and incomplete portraits in the background of an active studio populated by their fellow male Academicians.[18] Perhaps as a conspicuous critique, one of Kauffman's four "Elements of Art" thematic canvases commissioned by the Royal Academy in 1778 for the Council Chamber of Somerset House emphasized that drawing sculptural casts was the only way females could study human anatomy at the Royal Academy. The allegorical series (*Invention, Composition, Colour,* and *Design*) exclusively features females, but the figure of *Design* shows a student intently studying the Belvedere torso on a pedestal, with the evidence of her labors strewn at her feet.[19]

Although Kauffman was a pioneering member of the Royal Academy who had nearly eighty submissions in nineteen annual exhibitions between 1769 and 1797, she was not able to edify a place for female artists within the academy.[20] Besides the two female founding members, no women were elected until 1923, when Annie Swynnerton (1844–1933) became an Academician.[21]

This apparent gender hierarchy, informally codified during the academy's foundation, may help explain why Maria Cosway was never a candidate for Academician despite her professional successes and close relationships with key Academicians, including her husband and Kauffman, who, nearly twenty years her senior, was a consummate mentor.

As an ambassador, Kauffman served as a conduit for transmitting letters of introduction, favors, and even gifts within artistic, design, and political circles. In 1775, for example, Tresham sent Kauffman a copy of Vignola's *Regola delli cinque ordini d'architettura* to convey to another English friend in Rome.[22] When she moved to Italy permanently in the early 1780s, she continued to receive travelers from the Grand Tour, capturing their images in her studio near the Spanish Steps and the Caffé Anglois, a popular gathering place for the English that Soane frequented during his travels. Kauffman's work and affable personality were so well known that members of the network named their children after her: "Angelica" was the middle name of Cosway's only child, and Charles Willson Peale (1741–1827), an American painter and museum entrepreneur, named his daughter after the vibrant artist he met while studying under West in London from 1767 to 1770. Aptly, Angelica Kauffman Peale (1775–1853) became a pioneering female painter in America.

Trumbull can also be considered an ambassador within the Transatlantic Design Network. As both an appointed diplomat and a painter who traveled between America's East Coast, England, and continental Europe, he was responsible for facilitating introductions between political figures, artists, and writers. In his autobiography, he wrote that he had painted sixty-eight works "before I had received any instruction other than was obtained in books."[23] Like Jefferson, his education was substantially ameliorated by his travels abroad. He went to London in 1780 with letters of introduction from Franklin to West; however, tensions in London resulting from the Revolutionary War prompted his arrest. Under accusations of espionage, he was imprisoned for seven months before he was deported.[24] Undeterred, he returned to London and, in the spring of 1786, met Jefferson, who invited the artist to pursue his work in Paris. Through his travels and continued correspondence, he was thoroughly engaged in transatlantic dialogues; it was because of Trumbull's knowledge of the architectural struggles in America's capital city and his fervent advocacy for a trained architect that Cosway's brother, George Hadfield, received a commission to travel across the ocean and pursue a career in Washington, albeit a curious and tumultuous one.

Modern historians often criticize Trumbull's key works, such as *Declaration of Independence in Congress, at the Independence Hall, Philadelphia, July 4th, 1776,* because they portray notable moments in America's foundation as historical fiction. In *Declaration,* Trumbull depicts a room filled with delegates of the Second Continental Congress, yet he was conscious that it was a crafted re-creation since the fifty-six signers never occupied the same space, let alone a space as polished as the one rendered, complete with British regalia. Heavy drapes, such as those depicted in the painting, would not be present in the heat of a Philadelphia summer, and cracks would have marred the plaster walls due to the expansion and contraction of the wooden armatures in the high humidity. Yet the building—and even its occupants—present a calm state amid the sweltering physical conditions and ominous political implications. From the late 1780s until the early 1790s, when his artistic work was interrupted by his diplomatic service as one of the negotiators of the Jay Treaty, Trumbull traveled through London, Paris, and America capturing images of the signers of the Declaration of Independence so he could present accurate portraiture in his painting. This self-initiated journey by one of America's earliest and most famous painters is even more remarkable since he had significant vision impairment: he was nearly blind in the left eye from damage sustained by a fall down stairs as a young child.[25] Trumbull's dedication to the arts fueled his travels, and the formation of his extensive interpersonal network illustrates that although he painted an imagined scene of patriots gathered in Philadelphia, he was masterful in his own life at bringing people together.

THE WOMEN OF THE COTERIE

As the diplomat's residence, Jefferson's Hôtel de Langeac in Paris was an informal embassy for international exchange and debate: critical discussions about the Declaration of the Rights of Man and of the Citizen occurred over dinner while figures from both America and Europe formed lasting relationships. Here, the familiar party of Jefferson, Trumbull, and Cosway welcomed another foreign compatriot: Angelica Schuyler Church. Both Jefferson and Trumbull knew of Angelica as the daughter of General Schuyler, and both were happy to become acquainted with another American living in Paris.[26] She came to the city with her husband, John Barker Church (1748–1818), a British émigré who served as commissary general in the Revolution under the alias of John Carter; the pair met in New York and eloped before moving to London.[27] Business eventually motivated the couple to relocate to Paris, where Angelica was reunited with other revolutionary figures who were close associates of her family, including Lafayette.

In Paris, the group of friends and artistic ambassadors expanded to include Madame de Corny and Madame de Tessé. They dined and traveled together in and around Paris and introduced one other to new acquaintances. Jefferson corresponded with Madame de Corny about the mechanical arts, the design of country houses, and his daughters, for whom she served as a surrogate parent when Jefferson was called away from Paris for diplomatic duties. As Lafayette's aunt, Madame de Tessé instantly welcomed Americans into her social circles, often entertaining at Château de Chaville (1766), her home designed by Étienne-Louis Boullée.[28] Here Jefferson found a home that was compact in plan but expansive in section through its use of double- and triple-height vaulted spaces. The compact stairways were like the two-quarter winders Jefferson would employ in the redesign of Monticello: they used space efficiently, and the absence of a newel post left a rectangular void that, although vertigo-inducing for the downward traveler, allowed light to cascade through the vertical passage. A skylight illuminated Chaville's vestibule, nested within a trapezoidal recess like those Jefferson would install in his bedchamber and dining room at Monticello. However, unlike Boullée's use of skylights, positioned horizontally on the roofline, Jefferson angled his skylights to be parallel with the slope of the roof. This allowed for better drainage and permitted afternoon light to wash the walls of these double-height rooms. Jefferson did, however, borrow a bit of visual trickery from Boullée: instead of using a festooned parapet to conceal the skylight from the exterior, Jefferson put a railing along his roofline to distract the eye from the twelve skylights that punctured the roofscape of the home. Overall, Jefferson found Madame de Tessé's home so compelling that he made a playful suggestion to her: if the exuberant *superintendant de Bâtiments du Roi* moved the Maison Carrée to Paris, her Chaville could be relocated to Nîmes as a fair trade, providing de Tessé a more favorable climate and closer proximity to her beloved "remains of antiquity."[29]

In Paris, this group of ambassadors—both French and American, male and female—established a circle of correspondence in which they shared news from their countries, discussed the arts as well as gossip, and served as agents for each other in various capacities. Jefferson's letters with Madame de Corny provide an invaluable lens onto his impressions of England's gardens and scientific instruments; curiously, these observations were not recorded in other letters, diary entries, or the abbreviated notes of his memorandum books. With Madame de Tessé, Jefferson exchanged plants: although the American *florae* planted at Chaville have been lost, some of the seeds from France are still preserved at Monticello's seed bank.[30] For Jefferson, these two French correspondents proved particularly endearing because they shared a zeal for architecture, and their letters contain some of his most impassioned passages on buildings and landscapes.

The ambassadors were together in Paris for only a short time, but they maintained dedicated correspondence and visited each other when possible. In the summer of 1788, when the Churches returned to London, Jefferson wrote: "if you will install me your physician, I will prescribe to you a journey a month to Paris."[31] Beyond their shared friendship with Cosway, Jefferson and Church were drawn together because their daughters attended the same convent school in Paris, the Abbaye Royale de Panthémont. Church was also the sister-in-law of Federalist Alexander Hamilton, an instrumental figure in the Revolution but Jefferson's ideological adversary during their service in the nation's first cabinet. Jefferson eventually installed a bust of Hamilton by Giuseppe Ceracchi in Monticello's Entrance Hall, but he also placed a larger-than-life Ceracchi bust of himself in the hall, installed upon a gifted marble pedestal from Madame de Tessé, so that the pair could be "opposed in death as in life."[32]

Trumbull's friendship with the Churches was beneficial to his artistic pursuits abroad, not least because John Church acted as his "banker," a financial patron who charged minimal interest on the loans he granted Trumbull from the summer of 1786 to 1797.[33] When in England, Trumbull often spent time

Fig. 10. An 1882 engraving and ca. 1907 postcard of Down Place showing Church-era features such as the crenellation, the semi-circular portico of the north facade, and the long, gothic gallery (far left). (Public domain and British Museum MAPS 136.a.1.[17])S

with the Churches at their London residence on Sackville Street and made at least one journey to their Berkshire estate near Windsor, Down Place (figs. 10 and 11).[34] This Neo-Gothic country house along the River Thames was constructed around 1750, and the crenellation as well as the meandering plan resembled a smaller, simpler version of its western London neighbor, Strawberry Hill. Down Place underwent several additions and alterations during

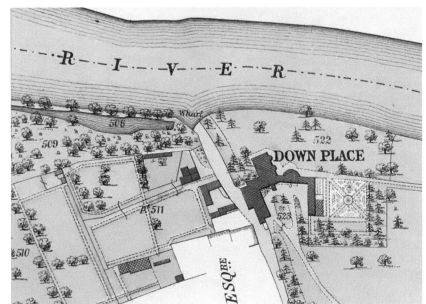

Fig. 11. Plan and detail of the Down Place estate from an 1882 sale. Although outbuildings and interior elements were altered, the footprint of the main building was similar when the Churches were in residence. (British Museum MAPS 136.a.1.[17])

the late nineteenth century, predominately service quarters and conservatories, and again throughout the twentieth century, even functioning as the Bray Film Studios from 1949 to 1985.

When it was the Churches' residence, a long, winding path brought visitors from the main road to the home's southern entrance, bounded by the oldest part of the home to the west and a long picture gallery to the east. On the north, a semicircular portico supported by Doric columns looked toward the Thames. The area was a popular riverside retreat from the city and had once been a part of a Roman road to Londinium. Popular residences such as Water Oakley and Toad Hall were nearby, and from the banks of the Down Place estate visitors could see Windsor Castle, Eton College, and Monkey Island with its two Palladian pavilions by Robert Morris, commissioned by the 3rd Duke of Marlborough and decorated with fishing-themed *singerie* by Andien de Clermont.[35]

Gouverneur Morris visited Down Place repeatedly and noted that it was

Fig. 12. An engraving of Cosway's proposed monogram for Angelica Church. (Williamson, *Richard Cosway, R.A., and His Wife and Pupils* [1897])

just twenty-five miles "along good road" from Hyde Park Corner, making it convenient to visit the residences of both Church and Cosway, often conveying letters from other American friends.[36] According to Morris's diary, the group regularly found themselves discussing the arts. In May 1790, Cosway, who had recently given birth, had plans to paint the ceiling of a garden folly at Down Place featuring the letter *A* surrounded by the graces, but illness later that summer prevented the work. Morris and Church found shared interests in architecture, and Morris accompanied Church in 1796 when she visited Joseph Bonomi, an Italian architect well known in England for his work on country houses, perhaps envisioning some additions or alterations to Down Place (fig. 12). Church abandoned the project when she returned to New York, but she and Morris resumed their visits in the United States after a chance encounter in December 1798.

As a frequent gathering place for several women in the Transatlantic Design Network, Down Place served as an embassy of retreat and a place from which the women made visits to other country houses in the area, describing their excursions in letters to Trumbull and Jefferson. Of the Parisian coterie, Madame de Corny visited multiple times. During one stay, she wrote to Jefferson that although she had missed the companionship of Cosway, she was able to visit London where "everything is in motion." When exploring the countryside, she dismissed Jefferson's fascination with the picturesque and found that the *"garden l'angloise"* of Kew, Hampton Court, and Claremont could not imitate those of France.[37]

Down Place and its associated company were so precious to Cosway that she frequently wrote to Jefferson and Trumbull expressing her anxiety that Church, whom she called her "sister," would one day leave England to return to America permanently.[38] Church made a brief journey across the Atlantic in 1789 to attend the inauguration of President Washington in New York City; in 1797, as Cosway feared, Church moved to an upstate New York estate situated along the upper Genesee River. In 1806, the Churches commissioned Latrobe to design a home on the expansive site in the federal style, complete with an Ionic portico with attenuated wooden columns. The decision to hire Latrobe, an architect who was not actively practicing in New York but rather working as the Surveyor of Public Buildings in Washington, further illustrates the Churches' dedicated sponsorship of professional designers.[39] Unlike Down Place, however, Church never hosted any of her transatlantic friends at Belvidere. In 1802, when Madame de Corny inquired if Jefferson and Church frequently saw each other in America, Jefferson wrote, "we are 350 miles apart; a distance which in this country is not easily surmounted."[40] As two Americans who met abroad, Jefferson and Church never convened in their home nation; like Cosway and the other ambassadors of the network, she only knew about Jefferson's cherished Monticello from his letters.

For Jefferson, the group of female ambassadors that he associated with in Paris represented some of his closest architectural confidants. That Jefferson did not actively insert himself into the circles of professional architects working for the monarchy and associated aristocrats indicates that he did not directly mix the political agenda of his diplomatic appointment with his personal architectural interests. Jefferson consciously distanced himself from the realm of state-sponsored architecture, and this may also reflect support of the quickly approaching French Revolution. To satiate his curiosity about the ancient and contemporary architecture of France, he instead aligned himself with a cohort of well-connected women who were visually astute and conversant in the language of architecture through their own travels, studies, and patronage. While abroad, and even when separated by an ocean, the coterie sustained their dialogues about built composition, other transatlantic friends, and the wish to reunite for tea and "libations" at Jefferson's Monticello.[41]

CHAPTER 3

Associates

How is a taste in this beautiful art to be formed in our countrymen, unless we avail ourselves of every occasion when public buildings are to be erected, of presenting to them models for their study and imitation?
—Thomas Jefferson to James Madison, September 20, 1785[1]

While Jefferson and Soane, the two architects at the core of this transatlantic exploration, were busily occupied in their respective nations from the 1790s, Cosway served as their eyes on continental Europe. She kept her two correspondents apprised of her travels, intellectual encounters, and artistic discoveries in France and Italy. Yet, Jefferson and Soane shared other associates who functioned as architectural collaborators and conduits for news on continental endeavors: Charles-Louis Clérisseau (1721–1820) and Maximilian Godefroy (1765–1848). The connections with both Clérisseau and Godefroy further underscore the fact that although Jefferson and Soane never met or corresponded, similarities between their architecture and approaches to epistemology are not simply coincidental: they were known as critical points of contact for designers in the Atlantic realm. Through the transmission of letters and an array of interpersonal connections, it is evident that they were part of a creative transatlantic network that was far more dynamic than studies of late eighteenth- and early nineteenth-century American or British architecture usually recognize.

Clérisseau was a well-known figure in the realms of neoclassical design and archaeological exploration in the late eighteenth and early nineteenth centuries who proved instrumental to the education of numerous architects. To Soane, Clérisseau was known primarily for his painted visions of sublime classical grandeur. Although it is unclear if Soane and Clérisseau ever met, Soane's admiration for this artist, architect, and expert on Roman ruins is well documented: Soane eventually became the second most prolific contemporary collector of Clérisseau's work, albeit with a substantially smaller collection than Catherine the Great's extensive assemblage of more than a thousand works that had been commissioned through her agent, Baron Friedreich Melchior von Grimm.[2] As a member of the D'Holbach's Coterie, von Grimm belonged to the same French Enlightenment group where Jefferson found André Morellet, an economist and writer who translated Jefferson's only published book, *Notes on the State of Virginia* (1785), into French.[3] Jefferson met Clérisseau at another salon in late 1784 or early 1785 and later collaborated with the antiquarian to create one of the most significant pieces of civic architecture within the nascent United States: the Virginia State Capitol. Although Clérisseau influenced one of the first authentic examples of neoclassical architecture in America, his contributions were made remotely, essentially by working as an antiquarian architectural consultant. Even though Clérisseau never made the physical journey across the Atlantic Ocean, his work traveled fluidly in the forms of plans, models, and printed texts.

A native of Paris, Clérisseau immigrated to Italy as the recipient of the 1746 Prix de Rome and spent 1749 to 1754 as a student in the French Academy. In addition to his physical surveys of ancient ruins, Clérisseau was known for his imaginative *vedute* and his fascination with *capricci*. With more than fifty-five years of survey experience in Italy and France, Clérisseau was the expert on Roman era ruins. In his early career, he was primarily a painter of architecture; however, he eventually transitioned from simply drawing architectural scenes to painting illusionistic architectural *trompe l'oeil,* such as the Ruin Room executed within the monastery of Trinità dei Monti (c. 1766).[4] Eventually, Clérisseau practiced as an architect, working on commissioned projects in England, Russia, and America. Nonetheless, few of his works were executed as envisioned: he saw several projects through the design phase, but most schemes were either abandoned or passed along to another architect for modification and construction.

Clérisseau's contributions to architectural history were largely tied to his role as a coveted guide for foreign architects, introducing them to the sites and details of classical architecture. While in Rome, he tutored burgeoning architects such as William Chambers (1723–1796) and Robert Adam (1728–1792). In 1771, the same year Soane entered the Royal Academy as an architectural student, Clérisseau moved to London to enter what would become a doomed architectural partnership with Adam.[5] The following year, both Clérisseau and Soane exhibited their work at the Royal Academy for the first time as painter and architect, respectively.[6] Financial troubles compelled Clérisseau's return to Paris in 1775; here his interests in Roman ruins were revived when he began a survey of the extant monuments in France. The project resulted in his landmark publication *Antiquités de la France, Prèmiere partie: Monumens de Nismes* (1778). The richly illustrated tome was one of the earliest in Soane's vast library, purchased in 1780 and itemized in the 1782 catalog. Although some scholars assert that Jefferson knew of Clérisseau's publication prior to his diplomatic journey to France, and that this may explain why Jefferson sought out Clérisseau while abroad, it is more likely that the pair met in the salons of Paris, possibly that of Madame de Corny, and discovered a shared admiration of ancient architecture.[7] As evidenced by Clérisseau's invoice from June 2, 1786, Jefferson was able to purchase his copy of *Antiquités* directly from the author.[8]

As an essential reference text on classicism, the volume was a welcome addition to Jefferson's collections. At the time of his departure from America, Jefferson was engaged in discussions with the directors of public buildings in Virginia, William Buchanan and James Hay, regarding the construction of a new state capitol building in Richmond. As a virtual *tabula rasa* along the picturesque falls of the James River, the Commonwealth could construct a new built identity divorced from its English roots. Jefferson's commission as a civic architect was, however, interrupted by his congressional appointment on May 7, 1784, as a minister plenipotentiary to France; he set sail for Europe just two months later. Despite the directors' assumptions that Jefferson's obligations abroad would preclude his desire to continue work, Jefferson did not abandon the project. Instead, he leveraged his time abroad to make beneficial connections: through friendship and their shared aesthetics, Jefferson engaged Clérisseau's expertise.

The directors' impatience almost thwarted the collaboration. In Jefferson's absence, they began construction on a haphazard capitol building in spring 1785, and Jefferson realized that a written reply urging the pair to stop work would not be as effective as an in-person appeal.[9] Upon Jefferson's beseeching, close friend and fellow gentleman architect James Madison (1751–1836) interceded in the construction currently under the supervision of local builder Samuel Dobie. He presented Jefferson's new scheme, crafted alongside Clérisseau, that was based on the "Maison quarrée of Nismes," a classical structure that was "very simple, but it is noble beyond expression, and would have done honour to our country, as presenting to travellers a morsel of taste in our infancy, promising much for our maturer age."[10] By creating a capitol building based upon a first-century temple, Jefferson saw the opportunity to achieve architectural excellence in early America through the calculated manipulation of an established precedent. He would repeat this pattern throughout his architectural career.

Madison's appeal was successful, and Jefferson received a letter from the directors in October 1785 apologizing that they did not "sollicit your aid in the business at an earlier day."[11] In France, Jefferson and Clérisseau continued to work on the design. Although Jefferson's letters to the directors adamantly championed the superiority of his design, he had not yet visited the Maison Carrée. When Jefferson was finally "nourished with the remains of Roman grandeur" and visited the capitol's precedent in the spring of 1787, he recorded his impressions in what has become one of the most evocative epistles elucidating his architectural interests:

Here I am, Madam, gazing whole hours at the Maison quarrée, like a lover at his mistress. . . . This, you will say, was a rule, to fall in love with a female beauty: but with a house! It is out of all precedent. No, Madam, it is not without a precedent, in my own history. While in Paris, I was violently smitten with the Hotel de Salm, and used to go to the Thuileries almost daily, to look at it. The loueuse des chaises, inattentive to my passion, never had the complaisance to place a chair there, so that sitting on the parapet, and twisting my neck round to see the object of my admiration, I generally left it with a torti-colli [twisted neck].[12]

Interestingly, his letter was not addressed to a diplomatic colleague or fellow gentleman architect but rather to Jefferson's Parisian friend and correspondent Madame de Tessé. During Jefferson's visit, the site was surrounded by dense residential blocks, but an early nineteenth-century "preservation" project razed the area: when Soane's prized apprentice John Sanders visited the Maison Carrée in 1817, he encountered a "perfectly insulated" site, and although the temple had been "repaired in several places, the original parts may easily be distinguished."[13] Although Soane planned a journey during his Grand Tour, he never managed to explore the Roman ruins of Nîmes in person. But, like Jefferson, he found the Maison Carrée an extraordinary "object of admiration," and he referenced the classical structure in four of his Royal Academy lectures, even presenting a perspective of the pseudoperipteral temple during lecture 3 (fig. 13).[14] The image removed the temple from its urban context and placed it on a plateau, with hills in the background as if it were a Francophile's Paestum.

Jefferson's initial knowledge of the Maison Carrée was limited to written descriptions and engravings in *Antiquités*. Clérisseau's understanding of the site, thus, largely shaped Jefferson's perceptions, and this may explain why Jefferson called Clérisseau an architect in his lengthy January 1786 letter to the directors.[15] Clérisseau's *Antiquités* contained nine engravings of the temple, and his surveys of the structure informed his design for the shell of the Virginia Capitol; in collaboration with Clérisseau, Jefferson conceived the interior as "it was impossible for a foreign artist to know what number and sizes of apartments would suit the different corps of our government, nor how they should be connected with one another." Jefferson's letter underscored the fact that their design would occupy only two-fifths of the footprint of the capitol building currently underway, that their scheme would use half the number of bricks and columns, and that the beauty of their proposal was "ensured by experience and by the suffrage of the whole world." With practical consideration for conserving materials and funds, Jefferson advised the directors that rebuilding the foundations already in place would not be that difficult since the mortar was still fresh. This advice highlights Jefferson's

Fig. 13. Drawing from Soane's office for a Royal Academy lecture, featuring "La Maison Carrée Nîmes." (©Sir John Soane's Museum, London, SM 19/10/3; photo by Ardon Bar-Hama)

practical knowledge of building technology and foreshadows the substantial renovation work that he would undertake at Monticello in the 1790s.

Jefferson's January 1786 letter was accompanied by a ground plan as well as front and side elevations. He explained that Clérisseau had not yet finished the sections and that a plaster model was underway. The 1:60 model, executed by Jean-Pierre Fouquet (1752–1829), was sent from Le Havre in December 1786 and arrived at the Richmond worksite on February 28, 1787, where it is still on display in the redesigned Jefferson Room of the Virginia Capitol.[16] Soane, too, would commission Fouquet models: in 1834, he purchased twenty works in plaster by the master modelmaker's son, François.

In the early 1800s, Soane yearned to collect Clérisseau's *vedute* for his house museum. Through estate sales and other collectors, Soane eventually amassed twenty-one watercolors and drawings by Clérisseau.[17] The antiquarian's tutelage of Adam may help explain Soane's particular fervor: between the 1818 Robert Adam sale at Christie's and an 1833 auction, Soane purchased an archive of more than nine thousand of Adam's drawings. Even without evidence of a personal connection, Soane expressed his great esteem for Clérisseau in Royal Academy lecture 5: "the beauties and almost magical effects in the architectural drawings of a Clérisseau, a Gandy or a Turner."[18] The three artists were linked by their ability to capture architectural space and atmosphere in a way that resonated powerfully with Soane, "painting with light."

At Soane's Museum, the majority of Clérisseau's gouaches were placed on the folding panels of the Picture Gallery's north wall, devoid of windows since it faced a utilitarian service road, Whetstone Park. The framed images of Canaletto's Venice and Clérisseau's *vedute* of Rome act as fictive extensions of space, providing viewers with vistas of foreign sites. Although Clérisseau produced architectural drawings for the Virginia State Capitol, he did not execute any of his signature renderings for the project. Nonetheless, it is not difficult to imagine a stylized *vedute* of the Virginia Capitol, illustrating the building on the knoll above the rocky falls of the James River, hanging on the walls of Soane's Picture Gallery and imaginatively transporting visitors to a landscape across the Atlantic Ocean.

THE CIVIL ARCHITECT

As Clérisseau's career stagnated in 1805, another French architect with connections to Jefferson and Soane was starting to build his professional reputation abroad: Maximilian Godefroy. Although his life began and ended in Paris, his career as an engineer, educator, and architect covered three different nations. Yet, like many of the figures explored within the assessment of the Transatlantic Design Network, Godefroy's legacy has been overlooked in most American and European surveys of early nineteenth-century architecture. In France, his work is seen as an anticlimactic version of Ledoux; in America, his designs are eccentric in comparison to those of his more prolific peers, such as Latrobe or Mills; and in England, his career never really blossomed.[19] Nonetheless, a brief foray into Godefroy's career demonstrates two key facets of operations within the Transatlantic Design Network. First, some architects were quite mobile and multinational in their practice: Godefroy worked, in various capacities, in France and then had a productive fifteen-year tenure as an architect-engineer in America before returning to France via England. Second, Jefferson and Soane were recognized points of contact for foreign architects. Within the civic, social, and professional circles that facilitated commissions in their respective nations, letters of introduction to Jefferson and Soane were highly desirable for designers looking to establish careers abroad.

Forays into the complex and often dizzying nature of Godefroy's transatlantic career are further complicated by the fact that documentary records frequently provide contradictory accounts of his life and movements.[20] Godefroy varied the spelling of his name; however, unlike "Soan," who simply adopted an additional letter for his surname in 1784, Godefroy's letters illustrate continuous fluctuations: he was Jean Maur Godefroy during his youth in France and then adopted the name "Maximilien" before shifting the spelling to "Maximilian" in America, where he later fluctuated between two variations on his surname, "Godefroy" and "Godfroi," and insisted upon using an old-régime aristocratic title of Count St. Mard.[21] Changes to his moniker may reflect Godefroy's active desire to reinvent his career and its trajectory. Despite a fascinating history that includes stints as an engineer, geographer, educator, artist, and architect, few scholars examined Godefroy's work, aside from Robert L. Alexander and Mark Reinberger.[22] The dispersal of scant documentary evidence in three countries has deterred further investigation, but there are previously unmapped connections between Godefroy, Jefferson, and Soane as well as unpublished letters that shed new light on the transatlantic architect.[23]

Godefroy's career as an architect did not truly begin until he relocated to the United States in 1805 at the age of forty. The first half of his life in France was uneventful in terms of his contributions to the built environment: it consisted of eighteen months of service in the army, and he was possibly part of the Davidian circles of Paris around the years of the French Revolution.[24] In 1803, Napoleon's secret police seized him for demonstrating opposition to the régime. Although never charged, he was held for nineteen months and released only when his sister negotiated his deportation to America. Godefroy's first forty years were fraught with turmoil, but upon his departure to America on March 12, 1805, he managed to position himself as a well-connected figure, with letters of introduction to several merchants in New York City and Philadelphia as well as two key letters from Dutch financier Theophile Cazenove: one to then secretary of state Madison and the other to then president Jefferson. [25]

Godefroy arrived at the port of New York after a month and a half of transatlantic travel. By the summer of 1805, he had settled in Philadelphia. There he met Latrobe, who was actively occupied in the creative circles and building programs of several sites. He was the presidentially appointed Surveyor of Public Buildings of the United States, an architect of the Bank of Pennsylvania, a hydraulic engineer for Philadelphia's pumping stations, a published author on landscape design, a commissioned architect for several private buildings in Philadelphia, a member of the American Philosophical Society, and, by the fall of 1805, a charter member of the Philadelphia Academy of Fine Arts. As an immigrant architect-cum-engineer, Latrobe served as an ideal liaison for the transplanted Godefroy. In France, Godefroy pursued private property management and civil engineering projects, but in the United States he actively sought more ambitious design and construction projects. Godefroy's admiration of Latrobe's practice eventually led to collaborations and even a close friendship, until an unfortunate professional fallout over the Baltimore Exchange project in 1816.[26]

Perhaps under Latrobe's guidance, Godefroy left Philadelphia, where commissions were competitively conferred on established designers, and moved to the growing city of Baltimore in December 1805. The transition from the dense urban atmosphere of Paris, where over half a million resided, to Baltimore, with its mere twenty-six thousand inhabitants, must have been striking. Instead of stone cathedrals and densely populated boulevards of mansion blocks, he found Baltimore as a city in transition. Like many developing urban centers in America, the city was generally composed of temporary wooden structures and only a few modest brick buildings. Although not aesthetically compelling, Baltimore was attractive to Godefroy as an active construction site, straining to meet the needs of a population that was practically doubling every decade.[27]

Godefroy's initial employment in Baltimore was as a teacher at St. Mary's College, a preparatory boys' school managed by the Sulpician Order. From late 1805 until his resignation in the fall of 1817, Godefroy taught a range of subjects, including principles of architecture, engineering, and fortification. This teaching appointment connected him to some of America's leading figures—he served as tutor to Madison's stepson—and led to his first architectural commission in the United States. Constructed between 1806 and

1808, St. Mary's Chapel is considered one of the earliest examples of Gothic Revival in America.[28] In an expression of utility, Godefroy used simple materials: bricks and sandstone quarried from Acquia Creek, a tributary of the Potomac River. Although composed of locally sourced materials, there is little rational order to the rest of the building. It is a perplexing mix of forms and styles that lacks the clear structural expression of Gothicism and demonstrates Godefroy's amateur approaches to physical construction and composition. The compressed Latin cross plan contains a vaulted nave flanked by symmetrical rows of columns and ribbed aisles. These tightly bundled and attenuated compound columns are capped with acanthus leaf capitals that resemble the papyrus columns of Egyptian architecture, but in a strange juxtaposition, these columns support pointed arches. The facade of the building, braced with flying buttresses that are parallel to the nave, looks like an elaborate stage set: the flattened screen has little relation to the arrangement of the rest of the building, especially considering the use of blind windows. Although a patchwork of architectural references, the building is striking for its uninhibited experimentation, and the Sulpicians appeared to be satisfied, as they commissioned Godefroy to design the church of St. Thomas (1812) for the newly founded order in Bardstown, Kentucky.[29]

While he was engaged in the design of St. Mary's Chapel, it is probable that Godefroy also executed the adjacent home that was to be used as a chapter house. Since the brick cornice profile matches the chapel's aperture jambs and there is an unbalanced pattern of quoins on the home, it may have been composed of the chapel's remnant brick stock. The home's interior is full of unique details and unconventional spatial manipulations, such as a top-lit cantilevered staircase, curving hallways, and a complex arrangement of rooms. There were also two alcoves on the second floor, one used for a bed and the other for a domestic chapel. Wooden-slatted apertures in the walls of the alcoves allowed "borrowed light" to permeate these small spaces, reflecting Godefroy's reading of Durand. Such inventive interiors would have been foreign to many American builders, who consulted pattern books that typically lacked interior elevations, but the home's interior reflected contemporary trends familiar in French domestic architecture—and familiar to Godefroy.

While working on projects at St. Mary's, Godefroy was simultaneously unreserved in his self-promotion, developing a publication extolling his knowledge of civil engineering in hopes of obtaining future commissions. The unillustrated treatise, *Military Reflections* (1807), asserted his authority in fortification design as an "Ex-Officer of the Etat Major" who sought asylum within the "tranquil borders" of the United States but found substantial deficits in the American defenses along the mid-Atlantic. [30] Eliza Crawford Anderson (1780–1839), a Baltimore native and accomplished writer who was both the first female editor of a magazine in America and the founder of *The Observer,* translated Godefroy's French text into English for publication.[31] Godefroy and the single mother found the working partnership fruitful, and the pair married in 1808. Now connected to an established Baltimore family, Godefroy began posting advertisements in Baltimore's *Federal Gazette* for drawing lessons, hosted at his father-in-law's residence: "[open] to young ladies Tuesdays, Thursdays and Saturdays from 11–1; to gentleman every evening except Sunday 5–7."[32]

As Godefroy's employment blossomed in Baltimore, so did his sophistication as a designer. The eccentric architect generally worked between several styles, as evidenced by the Commercial and Farmer's Bank (1812, demolished 1955), with a coffered exedra similar to Ledoux's Hôtel Guimard (ca. 1770), and the First Unitarian Church (1817) that transformed the two main elements of the Pantheon—a circular cella and an extruded portico—into a singular, compressed square in plan.[33] His most celebrated design, Godefroy's Battle Monument (1815–1825), has appeared on the official seal of the city of Baltimore since 1827.[34] Each element of the early American *architecture parlante* composition, commissioned both to celebrate Baltimore's role in the American victory over British forces in the War of 1812 and to commemorate those lost in the bombardment of Fort McHenry, contains allegorical references and patriotic symbols (fig. 14).[35] Standing thirty-nine feet tall, the rusticated pylon's eighteen courses represent the number of states in the Union, and the four griffins on the pylon's plinth bear features of the American bald eagle. A bundled column of thirty-nine rods, representing the thirty-nine Baltimore citizens who perished, forms the second tier of the monument and supports a statue of "Lady Baltimore." Purportedly modeled after Eliza, the figure holds a laurel crown and a rudder while gazing toward the bay where the battle occurred. Additionally, the frieze directly below the banded column contains an ancient Greek symbol of mourning: tear jars known as

Fig. 14. Godefroy's Battle Monument in Baltimore, with details of the American *architecture parlante*. (Author's photos)

lacrymatories. Illustrating knowledge of Stuart and Revett's *Antiquities of Athens* (1762), this motif had been employed a few years earlier by Robert Mills at Richmond's Monumental Church (1812), a tomb built to house and commemorate the seventy-two victims of the Richmond Theater fire.

Throughout his trials and architectural successes in Baltimore, Godefroy maintained connections to Jefferson. In his first letter to Jefferson in 1806, he appealed to the president's Francophile sensibilities, penning a lengthy explanation in French that one of his letters of introduction from Stephen Etienne Cathalan (1757–1819) had been destroyed by fire.[36] Although Godefroy's career is full of contrived histories, it is likely that he had obtained this letter. Cathalan served as Jefferson's agricultural agent in France from 1786 and was later appointed United States vice-consul at Marseille.[37] The pair remained in correspondence about agricultural operations for thirty years, and Cathalan sent Jefferson figs, seeds, and wine until 1816. Ashamed to present the Cathalan letter in its ruined state, Godefroy explained that he was recently exiled from France after experiencing "great injustices from suffering as a Prisonnier d'état." He hoped that the president would entertain the "inconvenience" of his independent inquiry to "be used in the service of the United States in the proper manner." At the end of his four-page letter, Godefroy asked the president for a job. At this point in Jefferson's hard-fought second term as president, the prospects of the country were rapidly expanding with the recent Louisiana Purchase, yet the nation's naval resources were suffering from the effects of the first Barbary War, and Jefferson was on the eve of enacting the ill-fated embargo of 1807. With more pressing matters at hand, Jefferson did not have any direct commissions to offer Godefroy.[38] Nearly a decade after his initial inquiry, however, Godefroy found himself employed at Jefferson's Virginia State Capitol to devise a solution for subsidence and erosion.

While employed in Richmond, Godefroy took an excursion through central Virginia with his wife, stepdaughter, and two sons in the fall of 1816. On their way to Natural Bridge, they encountered Jefferson at Wood's Tavern.[39] He was en route to Poplar Forest and encouraged the family to visit Monticello during their travels; since he would not be in residence to give the architect a tour, Jefferson penned a letter of introduction for Godefroy to present to his granddaughter, Ellen, who oversaw the household in the absence of both her grandfather and mother. Monitoring the wine stock, winding Jefferson's clocks, and tending to visitors were just a few of the assigned duties for this young woman, just shy of her twentieth birthday. Ellen recorded the Godefroys' visit to Monticello in a letter to her mother, noting that they stayed only an hour.[40] As evidenced by its brevity, Godefroy's visit to Monticello was architecturally driven, rather than the social or supplicatory nature of visits the Jefferson family was accustomed to receiving. If Godefroy recorded any impressions on the architecture or collections at the elevated plantation, they have been lost. Following their short visit to Monticello, the family continued to Natural Bridge and, here Godefroy wrote to Jefferson about the unparalleled "beauties de la nature" and offered to purchase the property. Much to the chagrin of Jefferson's family amid mounting financial concerns, the naturalist declined.[41] Had Jefferson accepted, he would have discovered Godefroy's overstated exuberance and inadequate funds: the family had been struggling since Dr. Crawford's death in 1813 and were approaching bankruptcy.

Godefroy's later career in America was hindered by a national economic depression, and this lack of work prompted the family's return to Europe. Their transatlantic journey was wrought with trouble from the outset: before the ship left the Chesapeake Bay, his stepdaughter died of yellow fever. Upon reaching England, the ship ran aground, and Godefroy's professional possessions that survived the accident were detained at Liverpool's Custom House. Three letters detailing this harried ordeal are held at Soane's Museum, but their presence within the archive escaped researchers because they were misfiled, either during Soane's lifetime or during the reorganization of the museum by its first curator, George Bailey.[42] The Godefroy-related documents consist of one letter of introduction from James Biggs to Soane, dated February 25, 1821, another note from Biggs to Soane on August 8, 1821, and an enclosed letter from Godefroy to Soane requesting aid in the return of his possessions, outlined in an accompanying inventory (figs. 15 and 16).[43] Biggs's first letter to Soane confirmed a prearranged visit to the museum that would afford Godefroy the opportunity to explain his predicament to Soane in person.

Although there is no evidence to confirm Godefroy's visit, the preserved correspondence illustrates several key points, including that most visits to Soane's Museum during this period were made by appointment and through interpersonal connections with the architect. Additionally, Godefroy's predicament was a topic of conversation between Soane and Biggs, in person and through letters, for nearly six months. Godefroy's inventory provides fascinating insight on the packing list of an architect who was looking to reestablish himself. Finally, through their shared interests in the arts, especially architectural practice and the exhibitions of the Royal Academy, Soane and Godefroy were part of a transcontinental and transatlantic network that forged architectural alliances and circumvented aristocratic and political circles. Although Godefroy did not know Soane directly, Soane expressed sympathy for the architect and was willing to intervene with authorities on his behalf.

Godefroy's inventory outlined the contents of ten cases and trunks that were initially detained in Liverpool on November 8, 1819, as "the objects nec-

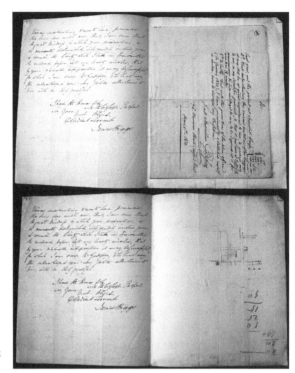

Fig. 15. A spread of Biggs's letter to Soane, August 8, 1821, showing Godefroy's enclosed inventory (folded) and a series of small annotations in Soane's hand as well as a thumbnail sketch of a staircase. (©Sir John Soane's Museum, London, XVI.H.2-3; author's photo)

essary to his Profession without being intended for sale, without duplicates; but exclusively intended to be used as Instruments of his Business." He detailed the exact contents of each piece of luggage and the corresponding conditions of the objects contained within; for almost every drawing and book, he noted substantial damage from saltwater. He also listed missing items, such as "2300 Study Engravings of the various schools, there may be about 1400 at most remaining"; of the salvaged documents, he categorized many as "almost rotten." In hopes of imploring Soane's assistance, Godefroy's letter ended with an impassioned plea, outlined in five points. First, Godefroy highlighted that most of his possessions were not damaged by the trauma of the shipwreck but instead by the "frequent & hasty packings & unpackings it had to undergo" during his visits to the Customs House in 1819 and 1820 when he

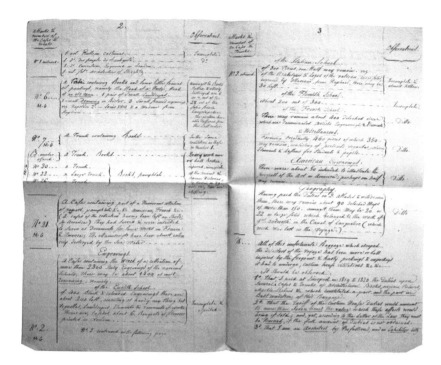

Fig. 16. A portion of Godefroy's inventory. (©Sir John Soane's Museum, London, XVI.H.2-3; author's photo)

paid the duties levied for the undamaged contents. Second, the new tariffs imposed would "amount to more than Seven times the value" of the complete contents if they were sold in pristine condition. Third, hoping to rouse the attentions of Soane as a professor of architecture, he underscored that he had exhibited at the Royal Academy's two most recent shows. His fourth point, appealing to Soane as a sentimental collector, stated that despite "the ruinous condition of this baggage it may still be of great importance to me, & perhaps only to me, in my scientific pursuits." If the tariffs were not paid, the Custom House advised Godefroy that the contents would be burned. Finally, Godefroy assured Soane that his professional interests in England were not transient since he had received permission to establish himself in London from the Alien Office in January 1820.

The architect's appeals were unsuccessful. After eight years in London, Godefroy returned in 1827 to France, where he spent his final years working on civic commissions in what he called the "Siberia" of the French provinces. Godefroy's time in London was not, however, without consequence. Although he was never nominated or elected for membership, he exhibited nine works at the Royal Academy between 1820 and 1825.[44] With the exception of two pieces, all of these works introduced foreign audiences to several aspects of America: renderings of his own architectural experiments in Baltimore, a bold depiction of the bombardment of Fort McHenry by the British during the War of 1812, vernacular architecture in the form of a slave cabin, and a landscape of Jefferson's beloved Natural Bridge that included dimensions and a quotation from Jefferson's *Notes*.

For Clérisseau and Godefroy, their associations with the Transatlantic Design Network facilitated the dissemination of their written and drawn works as well as the successful completion of built projects on American soil. Such accomplishments were not easily made in even their native countries since they were not consistently aligned with the monarchy or aristocracy. Using Jefferson and Soane as points of entry, Clérisseau and Godefroy were able to use the network to reinvent their professional careers. For America, Clérisseau's reinterpreted Roman classicism shaped federal buildings and state capitols across the nation, and Godefroy's *architecture parlante,* using Greek and Egyptian motifs, helped established a language for the memorials and monuments of the new nation.

CHAPTER 4

Architects

He is much respected in Washington, and, since the death of Latrobe, our
first architect, I consider him as foremost in the correct principles of
that art.

—Thomas Jefferson to Maria Hadfield Cosway, October 24, 1822[1]

Collaborative, international networks of patriots, orators, farmers, lawyers,
and botanists fueled the foundation of the United States and shaped its architectural development. Maria Hadfield Cosway's brother, architect George
Hadfield (1763–1826), was a beneficiary of the Transatlantic Design Network
through his connections to several key figures, including West, Trumbull,
and Jefferson. When Hadfield's architectural prospects in Europe were uncertain, his career was transformed through a flood of letters and introductions that led to a federal commission in the new capital city of Washington.
Following a brief, tumultuous tenure as superintending architect of the
United States Capitol, Hadfield practiced in the Washington area for more
than thirty years, completing a few other federal commissions and several
homes for notable families in Washington and Virginia. He even held a US
patent for the streamlined production of bricks and tiles.[2]

Hadfield's prominence, however, had faded by the time of his death, and
his work was little more than a footnote within the plethora of scholarship on
architectural contemporaries such as Soane and Latrobe until Julia King's
George Hadfield: Architect of the Federal City (2014) established a record of
Hadfield's works in England, Ireland, and America. When viewed through a

transatlantic lens, Hadfield's role as the first internationally commissioned federal architect in America, along with his career in the nation from 1795 to 1826, illuminates the power and scope of the network: he was specifically drafted as an architect for the new nation because of Trumbull's artistic pursuits in London, his career was sustained by federal commissions during Jefferson's presidency, and he worked closely with other members of the network, such as Latrobe, Thornton, and Washington. His extant built works are some of the most iconic structures in the Washington metropolitan area, and his work should be reappropriated within American architectural history, not least because he was largely responsible for introducing professional standards into the practice of architecture.

GEORGE HADFIELD: LOST ARCHITECT

Hadfield grew up alongside Maria and their three other siblings in the Florentine inn, and he immigrated to London with his mother and sisters in June 1779. Once situated in London, he began his initial forays into the artistic world with entries to the Royal Academy's annual exhibit. After his eighteenth birthday, he was accepted as a student of architecture. Both Maria and George exhibited works from 1781 to 1784, and when their brother William joined the exhibition with architectural watercolors in 1783 and 1784, the Hadfields earned unique status as the only family to have three siblings exhibit concurrently in the eighteenth century.[3] George Hadfield's success within the competitions of the Royal Academy's architecture school was also expeditious: in the year of his entrance to the school, he was awarded the Silver Medal, and he won the Gold Medal after only a year of studies for his designs for a National Prison. In 1790, he followed in the academic footsteps of Soane when he was awarded the prestigious Traveling Scholarship that sponsored his return to Italy. Although a new mother, Cosway left her husband and infant daughter in London to join her brother on portions of his Italian journey, traveling with him to Venice before Hadfield went on, alone, to Rome.[4] Cosway did not actively maintain her correspondence during her travels, falling silent for more than four and a half years with friends such as Jefferson, so the details of the siblings' tour are unclear. Of

Hadfield's few preserved documents from this period, two letters to the Royal Academy stated that he could be reached at the Piazza di Spagna, possibly referring to the same English coffeehouse that Soane used for his correspondence when he was in Rome.[5]

Like Soane, Hadfield was a serious student of architecture during his nearly five years in Italy. As evidenced by his later design work in the United States, especially Arlington House, Hadfield was enraptured with the bold proportions of the Greek Doric temples of Paestum. When he returned to London in 1795, Hadfield submitted his last entries to the Royal Academy exhibit: a "design for a national mausoleum" and two measured drawings of temples from Rome.[6] Although it is unknown if he took these drawings with him to America, his firsthand architectural fieldwork in the spectacular classrooms of the ancients would have been entirely unprecedented within the architectural circles of the Early Republic.

After completing a rigorous education at the Royal Academy, working under the tutelage of James Wyatt from 1784 to 1790, and five years of extensive travels in Italy, Hadfield's theoretical foundations as an architect were impeccable.[7] However, he had yet to complete an independently built project. Upon his return from Italy, he was faced with the promise of little work in London beyond his connections to Lady Chesterfield, and associates at the Royal Academy offered few immediate commissions beyond chimneypiece work.[8] There was also little room for advancement within the formal structure of the academy since the majority of the forty prescribed positions of Academician were occupied by artists, not architects. As a result, Hadfield sought other professional networks, such as the Architect's Club.

Founded on October 20, 1791, by Samuel Pepys Cockerell, Dance, Holland, and Wyatt, this subscription-based social organization met for dinner on the first Thursday of every month. Membership was open only to those with the highest educational credentials, and this signified a shift in attitude for selected members of the architectural profession: apprenticeship alone was no longer satisfactory training for those hoping to practice architecture in the world's largest city. Membership was exclusive to Royal Academy medalists, associates, and Academicians, or those who were elected members of academies in Rome, Parma, Bologna, Florence, or Paris.[9] As a recipient of the Royal Academy's Gold Medal, Hadfield was eligible, and he was nominated by Holland and Wyatt shortly after his return from Italy.[10] His election on January 2, 1795, however, received one critically detrimental black ball that Farington attributed to either Soane or Brettingham.[11] It is unlikely that Soane cast the black ball, since he found the club quarrelsome and predicted it would be short lived.[12] Although this was disappointing, Hadfield's career prospects did not rest solely on the Architect's Club since, at the time of the election, he was already engaged in negotiations with the commissioners of the District of Columbia for a superintending architect position in America's new capital. Coincidentally, on the very day Hadfield's election to the Architect's Club failed, the commissioners drafted letters to President Washington in Philadelphia and Trumbull in London expressing their interest in officially offering Hadfield the position of architect of the Capitol.[13]

THE FIRST INTERNATIONAL ARCHITECT OF THE FEDERAL CITY

Selected scholarship on Hadfield suggests that his architectural commissions in America were directly attributable to his association with Jefferson and Jefferson's fondness for Cosway, but correspondence disproves this theory. Hadfield met Jefferson briefly in Paris late in the summer of 1789, when he was traveling through the city with Trumbull and was tasked with delivering a letter from his sister to the statesman.[14] The two planned to meet again, but Jefferson's dinner invitations did not reach Hadfield at his hotel due to a French porter's mishandling.[15] Although other instances within the operations of the Transatlantic Design Network prove that transitory introductions could lead to more in-depth collaborations or correspondences, this was not the case with Jefferson and Hadfield: the pair did not interact again until Hadfield's arrival in America. Instead of a familial connection, Hadfield's initial employment as an architect in the federal government can be explained by his friendships with two Americans at the Royal Academy, Trumbull and the foreign-born president known as the "American Raphael."

While neither Trumbull nor West practiced architecture yet, they were professional artists closely tied to a larger community of designers through their work with the Royal Academy and their travels in continental Europe. Through these connective veins, Trumbull and West had the ability to serve as mentors and patrons for aspiring designers on both sides of the Atlantic. Therefore, when Trumbull received news from his brother that the commissioners of the newly founded capital city were looking for a new "principal architect" to assist Thornton with the construction of the Capitol Building, he did not suggest a fellow statesman or even an established European architect for the position. Instead, he offered the commissioners a series of nine letters that extolled the architectural merits of a close friend from the Royal Academy: Hadfield.

In the fall of 1794, Trumbull wrote his brother with an enclosed letter to the commissioners that recommended Hadfield for the position of superintending architect of the Capitol:

Mr. Hatfield . . . just returned from this Tour. Before he went abroad he was considered as possessing Talents and Knowledge in Architecture superior to any of the young men his contemporaries; he has not mis-used his time in Italy and is now considered by Mr. West the President of the Academy as well as by others, to possess the Theory of Civil Architecture more perfectly than any young man in England. The War damps Architecture as well as all the other arts in this country and as Mr. Hatfield is neither rich nor connected with powerful friends, his prospects here, notwithstanding his superiority of knowledge, are for the present not flattering.[16]

Trumbull knew that even if America could attract a foreign architect for the position, it would not likely be a seasoned designer. As an agent for Hadfield, Trumbull made it clear to the commissioners that Hadfield was aware of the precarious nature of work in Washington: he was not expecting high pay or a secure position.[17] Despite such an open offer to receive a well-trained architect, the commissioners expressed reluctance in their letters to Trumbull, due in part to the bitter battles over the design for the Capitol between Thornton, the gentleman architect who won the competition for the building and served on the Board of Commissioners, and émigré architect Etienne Sulpice Hallet (1775–1825), the appointed superintendent of works.[18] According to the commissioners, Hallet was "capricious and obstinate," which forced his dismissal from the position in 1794.[19] Records from the commissioners note that the superintending architect was continuously hindering work on the building by refusing to be subservient to Thornton's plan. The superintendent was primarily in charge of the workmen and not the design; therefore, constant deviations from the plans as originally proposed were seen as costly and even subversive.

In his initial letters to the commissioners, Trumbull repeatedly stated that Hadfield was "not yet engaged in any work which he cannot quit," thus underscoring a sense of urgency to the commissioners in the matter of obtaining a trained architect for the position. Although Hadfield's architectural prospects were not promising, he was undertaking work in England at a variety of country estates. The pressing need to appoint a new superintending architect would be repeated in letters from the commissioners to President Washington that asked for funds to initiate Hadfield's tenure. Washington, having heard several objections to the work at the Capitol by both the commissioners and his architecturally inclined secretary of state, Jefferson, must have been tired of receiving news of the troubles in the new federal city and, like many other elected officials, may have wondered if moving the government from Philadelphia to Washington would even be worth the strain on the newly developing government infrastructure and its limited finances. Nonetheless, funds were appropriated, and by January 1795 the commissioners were able to make an offer to Hadfield. He accepted by letter on March 8.

In 1795, at the age of thirty-two, Hadfield crossed the Atlantic for the first, and only, time. His passage was paid by the commissioners in addition to the promise of a salary of 300 guineas a year and a housing allowance.[20] The commissioners also issued their hefty expectations of Hadfield in writing: "Our undertakings are of such moment that we require the aid of superior talents. Genius demands a high price every-where, and we should be unwilling to underrate its worth in America." When Hadfield arrived in Washington, he came with a letter of introduction to the commissioners from Trumbull, whom he had known for a decade, avowing that Hadfield was "modest, unassuming, and correct in his taste and judgment, and should any difficulties occur in the executive part of the plan he will state them with candor."[21] Trumbull knew of the intense deliberations surrounding the precision and refinement of Thornton's plan, but he felt that Hadfield possessed the skills necessary to execute the project effectively, with regard to both structure and style, while maintaining professional decorum.

As an example of international architectural headhunting in the late eighteenth century, Hadfield's commission as the first professionally trained architect to work on a federal project is of note. Today, it is not uncommon for national governments to engage famous, foreign architects to design new federal structures, both as a symbol of prestige and to show government dedication to development. Hadfield had educational credentials but lacked the built record needed to make him a notable architect. This form of speculative architectural appointment would become a theme for the new republic due to the absence of established professional practices. When Hadfield arrived in Washington in the fall of 1795, he discovered that the city's design circles were filled with foreign entrepreneurs. The Revolutionary War funneled opportunists into the new nation: without codified architectural schools, training schemes, or establish professional organizations, the United States was a welcoming atmosphere for designers who lacked the funds, formal education, or social connections to undertake architectural endeavors within the established conventions of practice found in European cities such as London.[22]

In fact, five of the most influential designers for the new city were born abroad: Pierre Charles L'Enfant (1754–1825), James Hoban (1758–1831), Thornton, Latrobe, and Hallet. L'Enfant, a Frenchman who was skilled in large-scale planning endeavors, came to the American colonies in 1777 to serve as an engineer in the Continental Army. As an officer and a friend of Washington, he was perfectly placed to assume the position of lead urban designer in the new federal capital. A French surveyor and a member of the *Architectes Experts-jures du Roi 1re Colonne,* Hallet came to the United States in 1787 and would eventually work alongside both L'Enfant and the foreign architects engaged in the design of the Capitol. Hoban arrived in 1785 after serving an apprenticeship in Ireland under Thomas Ivory; although more of a builder and draftsman than a formally trained architect, he enjoyed early architectural successes in Charleston, South Carolina, before moving to Washington in 1792, when he won the architectural competition for the design of the President's House. The competition for the Capitol Building brought Dr. Thornton, a British Virgin Island native, to Washington. He migrated to Philadelphia in 1786 after the completion of his medical studies in Edinburgh and travels through continental Europe. Thornton would later use these travels, as well as his "two weeks in the Library of Philadelphia," as the justification for his architectural expertise when Latrobe, who arrived in 1796, publicly questioned the doctor's abilities.[23] Surrounded by Washington's key designers, Hadfield was not unique as an immigrant, but he was the first of these foreign-born designers to have his services specifically solicited.

As foreshadowed by Hallet's relationship with Thornton, Hadfield found the original proposal for the Capitol deficient and, in some instances, unbuildable (fig. 17). Hadfield's letters to the commissioners chronicle his initial impressions of the project and relay a steady stream of concerns about the feasibility and cost of the building. His first letter, composed less than two weeks into his tenure as superintending architect, spoke of "unwarrantable defects in the plan"; he would spend the following months making estimates for reinforcing the foundations, addressing aesthetic issues with the elevations, requesting better building materials, and completing work related to the north wing.[24] Frustrated with his salary, the level of craft from the workmen, and a lack of professional support, he appealed to President Washington. The design and management of the Capitol project was floundering, and countless letters pointed to Thornton as the obstinate party, yet Washington offered Hadfield no consolation. Instead, he deferred the resolution of the disagreements back to the commissioners, of which Thornton was an appointed member.

In hopes of garnering some good will with the national executive, Hadfield aligned himself with fellow immigrant Hoban, who was also enraged by the architectural micromanagement levied by the commissioners. In the fall of 1795, the pair went to Philadelphia to present their case to President Washington in person.[25] Washington, who was a surveyor by training and had constructed elements of his own home at Mount Vernon, did little to remedy the architectural stalemate. In a letter to the commissioners, drafted shortly after their visit, Washington wrote that even as chief executive he could not comment on the architectural matters at hand because he did not "have sufficient knowledge of the subject, to judge with precision."[26] It is unclear whether Washington was referring to his knowledge of neoclassical design and the organization of structural components on such a large scale, or if he was specifically referencing unfamiliarity with the details of the Capitol's design. Despite Jefferson's architectural interests in federal projects, he was

Fig. 17. Hallet's front elevation drawing of the US Capitol, ca. 1793–95. (Library of Congress, Prints and Photographs Division, Washington, DC, LC-USZC4-1255)

silent during these Capitol disputes. He had resigned his post as secretary of state and retired to his mountaintop to initiate Monticello's substantial remodeling project, so governmental work, design-related or otherwise, was not at the forefront of his attentions.

Without the backing of the executive, Hadfield gave the commissioners notice of his intended resignation on June 24, 1796. A few days later, the commissioners issued their own harsh ultimatum, stating that instead of finishing his last three months on the site, Hadfield should be immediately relieved of his duties. In lieu of three months' salary, they would pay for his return passage to England.[27] Following the commissioners' letter, Hadfield withdrew his resignation and asked for his immediate termination to be reconsidered. He would stay on the project for nearly two more years and would be well respected by both the workers and his colleagues. Despite the Capitol battles, the commissioners engaged Hadfield in the design of the public offices that were to flank the President's House: the Treasury and War Departments. After working on designs in 1796 and 1797, Hadfield refused to submit his finalized plans to the commissioners without the assurance that he would be appointed superintending architect of the works. This refusal to relinquish control of construction supervision was the last straw for the commissioners.[28] On May 18, 1798, Hadfield was formally dismissed. Latrobe and others defended Hadfield's untimely dismissal in letters and public notes for the next twenty years, but their claims of unjust treatment fell on deaf ears in the federal city: "when Hadfield went down, [Hoban] took charge, with no better fortune than his predecessors. Thornton was still impracticable, and the Commissioners offensive."[29] In 1799, realizing his reputation was on the line, Hadfield even appealed to the Commissioners for an investigation into his actions and abilities at both the Capitol and the Public Offices, but neither party pursued the matter further.

JEFFERSON AND HADFIELD

On March 4, 1801, Jefferson was inaugurated as the third president of the United States. Recognizing the potential of an architectural ally in the executive office, Hadfield wrote Jefferson on March 27. He stated that he had accepted the DC Commissioners' invitation in 1795 to "visit this country, for the purpose of superintending the building of the Capitol" and that his dismissal had been of "great injury."[30] With hopes that federal architectural projects would be managed differently under the new administration, Hadfield pledged Jefferson that he would "endeavour to make myself useful, and thereby obtain a subsistence in a country which I have chosen to spend the remainder of my life."[31] As Hadfield hoped, architectural commissions in Washington were different under Jefferson's supervision: in 1802, he eliminated the district commissioner positions that had caused such grief to immigrant designers such as Hadfield, Hoban, and Hallet. Additionally, Hadfield received several federal commissions, including the Marine Barracks and Commandants House at the Navy Yard south of the Capitol (1802), the City Jail (1802), and the Arsenal at Greenleaf's Point (1803). Designs for the jail revealed common interests between professional architect Hadfield and gentleman architect Jefferson: both men had previously explored projects that posited social reform through new architectural configurations.[32] While in London in 1786, Jefferson investigated Newgate Prison and later submitted designs for a jail in Richmond. Hadfield's interest in the typology began at an earlier age with a design for a jail that earned him the Royal Academy's Gold Medal.

Confident that his professional prospects were more secure, Hadfield became an American citizen in August 1802 and was elected a city councilman in the following fall. Busy with his new life and commissions in America, it seems that Hadfield neglected his connections abroad. Cosway wrote to Jefferson in 1805 and 1819 inquiring about her brother. Later, in 1821 and 1822, she enclosed letters to Hadfield within her correspondence to Jefferson since it appeared that the statesman had the best chance of intercepting the immigrant architect. In a letter, Jefferson informed Hadfield that Cosway was leaving London for Lodi and, since he received free postal and diplomatic pouch privileges as a former president, Hadfield was welcome to correspond with Cosway through him: "should you have no better means of conveying a letter to her than under the cover of mine, I shall forward it with pleasure."[33] Hadfield made use of this offer at least five times.

Jefferson's letters to Cosway commented on Hadfield's work in America: "I believe he is doing well, but would he push himself more, he would do better."[34] According to Jefferson's assessment, Hadfield's practice in Washington was not slow due to a lack of work but rather to a lack of motivation. Hadfield's letters to Jefferson and his sister, however, protested: "there is here a stagnation in the building line, owing to the scarcity of money, that is very ingureous both to Architects and mechanics."[35] The Panic of 1819 impacted Hadfield's practice in the federal center and surrounding regions. The constricted lending market and the reestablishment of the Bank of the United States amid an unregulated system of independent banks and unclear legislative management crippled the practice of fellow immigrant Godefroy and forced his return to Europe.[36]

Although Hadfield's career in America benefited from his personal connection to Jefferson, especially from 1801 to 1809, the relationship between these two gentlemen does not seem to have been particularly close. The pair may have engaged in conversations in the boarding houses of Washington, but there is not a capacious record of letters between the two: Hadfield's affiliation with the Transatlantic Design Network helped his career but did not define his most immediate friendships. According to available records,

Hadfield never visited Jefferson at Monticello, and Jefferson's letters do not indicate that he consulted Hadfield on the design of the University of Virginia.[37] This last point may shed the most insight on the nature of their relationship, and potentially on Jefferson's opinion of Hadfield's taste with reference to his affinity for Greek architecture. From 1814 until his death in 1826, Jefferson was in correspondence with both Latrobe and the ever-argumentative Thornton regarding the overall scheme and design of individual pavilions for his "academical village." Jefferson's university was to be a model of refined Roman architectural proportions and decorations, not the robust Greek orders that Hadfield favored.

Hadfield's federal commissions continued beyond Jefferson's presidency with the City Hall (1820–1826). Here, he used several architectural quotations that alluded to the work of Englishmen such as Smirke and Soane through the five-bay design of the Greek revival building that had planar manipulations within the surfaces of stucco-coated brick. Of Hadfield's domestic commissions, the best preserved is Arlington House (1802–1818). Perched at the crest of Arlington National Cemetery, the Greek revival home receives an estimated four million people annually, but it is only tenuously connected to Hadfield because of the site's more prominent historic associations with Washington, Robert E. Lee, and the cemetery itself. Arlington House has been called the first residence in America with a Greek temple front, ultimately initiating the domestic application of Greek revival architecture. Although Hadfield never constructed a house museum for himself, as Jefferson and Soane did, he may have been given such an architectural program under the direction of George Washington Park Custis (1781–1857). In addition to a functional plantation and a residence for the family, he wanted to cultivate a museum and shrine to Washington at the property, a reincarnation of Mount Vernon. When Mary, the only surviving child of Custis and Lee Fitzhugh, married Robert E. Lee in 1831, the history of Arlington House dramatically shifted into one focused on a divided nation rather than an architectural landmark.[38]

Located on the highest point in Georgetown, the Oak Hill Cemetery is home to Hadfield's last architectural project, the Van Ness Mausoleum, and this commemorative temple commission illustrates his established connections with the District of Columbia's elite.[39] General John Van Ness (1770–

1846) was a US representative from New York who enjoyed a successful political and military career in the new federal city. In 1803, Van Ness was appointed by Jefferson as the major of militia for the District of Columbia, and he served as the mayor of Washington from 1830 to 1834. Van Ness's ties to the city went beyond his professional ambitions, as his wife was the sole heir of David Burnes. The federal capital was built on swamp land once owned by Burnes, so the Burnes–Van Ness families were dominant figures in the city. Their acts of philanthropy included the donation of a site that would become home to the Washington Theater, a project completed to Hadfield's design, and the establishment of an orphan asylum in the city. In their personal lives, however, the Burnes–Van Ness family was less fortunate. The couple lost their only child, Ann Elbertina Van Ness Middleton (b. 1803), in 1823 and shortly thereafter commissioned Hadfield to design a family mausoleum. Often cited as a model of the Temple of Vesta in Rome, the mausoleum's stylistic resemblance is closer to the Temple of Vesta in Tivoli due to its simple circular peristyle, the lack of pilasters on the cella, and the domed roof.[40] The design of the brick and sandstone mausoleum is reflective of Hadfield's European roots in terms of both his travels in Italy as a young student, where he had the opportunity to visit the ancient ruin, and his time as a student with James Wyatt. Hadfield's design bears similarities to Wyatt's drawing for a mausoleum in Brocklesby Park, Lincolnshire; the design was well known within the Royal Academy, and Turner even gifted Soane an engraving of the image.[41]

FROM PROSPERITY TO OBSCURITY

Hadfield passed away in his home on February 6, 1826. Breaking conventions employed by others in the Transatlantic Design Network, Hadfield did not write an autobiography, leave copious journals, or publish a treatise. His sole architectural apprentice, William P. Elliot, became the executor of his estate and served as a vocal advocate for his work. Hadfield's documents, except for those held by others in the network or in federal collections, were lost. The few drawings that he retained during his career were left to the Columbian Institute, but these, unfortunately, were lost after 1900. Founded in 1816 as the Metropolitan Society, the institute sought to establish intellectual and scientific independence from Europe. Although it may seem odd that Hadfield, an immigrant, would be drawn to such an organization, his involvement with the institute illustrates his supreme desire for independence and sole control over his work and legacy. Robert Little delivered Hadfield's eulogy to the institute, referencing his unparalleled international training but simultaneously underscoring the lasting effects of his dismissal from the Capitol project: "for many years he struggled with contracted circumstances, and poverty; but his reputation was never sullied by object severity, or injustices."[42]

For Hadfield, the Capitol commission marked both high and low points in his career. It was an opportunity to literally help build a new nation and work within a community of designers that, unlike in London, was unencumbered by aristocracy or architectural dynasties. Nonetheless, he discovered that America lacked appropriately trained practitioners and professional architectural standards, particularly in reference to his insistence that a design drawing represented intellectual property. Although Hadfield was a beneficiary of the Transatlantic Design Network, he was not an active participant. He did not generate new transatlantic conversations, nor did he help perpetuate the network by inaugurating new connections. Additionally, he did not adhere to many of the network's common practices, such as lifelong participation in extramural organizations.

Although it was positive that this international architect became an American nationalist who was vested in the amelioration of the new country, Hadfield did not engage in international exchange. Nor did he work as an agent for his peers abroad, attracting other foreign architects to the capital city in hopes of establishing a rich community of academically trained designers. This would have been particularly advantageous to Hadfield's insistences on design ownership and cohesive construction processes: if a designer's project was accepted by a client, that architect should be responsible for the project's construction. If the designer could not successfully execute the plan as proposed due to issues with the structure or arrangement, elements of the plan should be amended, and this was the only instance when the designer should be removed from the position of superintending architect. Although commonplace within Europe, this set of professional standards was alien in the developing sphere of American architectural practice, a field composed of engineers turned architects, draftsmen, and gentleman designers who were neither formally trained in architecture nor experienced through apprenticeships. In America's Early Republic, architectural projects commissioned by federal and local governments were characterized by collaborative practice. Despite his trials, Hadfield's objections to certain practices within federally sponsored architectural projects in the late 1790s laid the groundwork for the professionalization of architecture within the nation's capital and paved the way for full-time American-born practitioners, including Charles Bulfinch and Robert Mills.

A brief obituary appeared in the *National Intelligencer* a week after Hadfield's death, highlighting his travels in Italy and that he was "selected" by West and Trumbull, on behalf of General Washington, to serve as "Architect to superintend the building of the Capitol."[43] The obituary paid the highest

Fig. 18. Hadfield's headstone in Congressional Cemetery, Washington, DC (Author's photo)

patriotic praise to this naturalized citizen, noting "his love of liberty and independence was unconquerable, to which he sacrificed all his prospects of wealth and fame." Hadfield severed many of his transatlantic ties, but he certainly did not become an antisocial figure: Little's obituary stated that although Hadfield left no relatives, he had "many friends." The reluctance to participate in international exchanges may simply be explained by a shy disposition, noted in Cosway's penultimate letter to Jefferson.[44] In Washington's Congressional Cemetery, where he was buried alongside some of the nation's patriots and key governmental figures of the Early Republic, Hadfield's tombstone proved that he was laconic in death, as in life. The simple Portland Stone marker contains Hadfield's name, year of death, and a single word: architect (fig. 18).

CHAPTER 5

Societies

Through the representatives of the people, coming from various sections of our country, of different climates and soils, whose minds are illuminated by the rays of science; and through the scientific citizens and foreigners who visit this metropolis.

—Edward Cutbush, January 11, 1817[1]

Washington's first learned society was founded by 105 members on June 28, 1816.[2] Initially named the Metropolitan Association for the Advancement of the Sciences, the organization quickly changed its title to the Columbian Institute for the Promotion of Arts and Sciences. It was incorporated by constitutional ordinance on April 20, 1818. The new name of "Columbian" aligned the institute with a sense of American independence and ingenuity, referencing both the nation's capital city and the person then credited with the discovery of the New World, Christopher Columbus. Although the Columbian Institute ultimately failed, losing its governmental charter after only twenty years, its existence proves that international exchange was essential to the development of artistic, architectural, and scientific communities in America. The Columbian Institute faltered because it tried to foster a nationalistic attitude of intellectual independence, contrary to other institutions of the era that encouraged international collaboration and welcomed foreign members, such as the American Philosophical Society, the Royal Society, and the Royal Academy.

FOUNDING AMERICA'S EARLY ORGANIZATIONS

By the late eighteenth century, London was a city of societies. From liveries to aristocratically sponsored organizations, practically every interest and facet of intellectual exploration was covered within the charter of a formal institution. In addition to all the sponsored organizations, London was bustling with informal exchanges that occurred at the tables and thresholds of the city's more than three thousand coffeehouses.[3] While amid trade-driven travel or educational endeavors such as reading law at the Inns of Court, many merchants, politicians, planters, and lawyers from the young American nation experienced the vibrant atmosphere of formal and informal exchange in London.

Enthused by the spirit of academic, artistic, and scientific curiosity that they experienced abroad, well-traveled American colonists such as Franklin pioneered intellectual organizations in the New World. With fellow polymath John Bartram (1699–1777), Franklin founded the American Philosophical Society in 1743 in Philadelphia. Largely inspired by the work of the Royal Society, the American Philosophical Society was formed to encourage, enlighten, and share the intellectual undertakings of the colonies with organizations abroad. Despite its ambitious charter, the American Philosophical Society suffered from lackluster organization; without elected officers, the organization faltered and almost disappeared from the record of early American history. It was revived in 1768, however, when it merged with another small organization, the American Society. By the 1780s, the society's numbers were growing—with the support of 172 individual pledges, it instituted its meeting and exhibition spaces in Philadelphia's Philosophical Hall.[4]

From its foundations, the American Philosophical Society was conceived as a North American institution that would provide a platform for international exchange. It represented an attempt to formalize the interactions already taking place between individuals in the Atlantic world. These exchanges were initially facilitated by the international composition of the American colonies, especially in the planned city and trading center of Philadelphia. The subsequent transatlantic political and military actions of the American Revolution were quite beneficial to these intellectual societies. For example, an influx of European figures came to the aid of the colonial cause, and this brought new and diverse members—including Lafayette and Tadeusz Kościuszko (1746–1817)—to the society. After the war, many of these figures left the new nation to spread the revolutionary spirit in their home countries but maintained their transatlantic communications.

Through interpersonal networks of correspondence, the American Philosophical Society attempted to maintain transatlantic exchange at an academic level through the turn of the nineteenth century. However, with the foundation of several independent museums, public universities, and other organizations, America was moving toward the development of an educational and intellectual culture independent of European precedents.[5] The War of 1812 further polarized relations between America and Europe due to trade embargos. It is not surprising, then, that as Washington, DC, was literally rebuilding from the ashes of the British invasion of 1814, key American figures sought to establish new intellectual and interdisciplinary organizations that were entirely divorced from their European counterparts. Out of this interest to cultivate independent American intellectual enterprises, the Columbian Institute was established.

The institute's home in Washington, liberated from past governmental centers such as Philadelphia or New York City, also signified the desire to establish a new scholarly center in the nation that would be aligned with the federal capital. Congressional support of the Institute was intended to provide intellectual stimulus to the city, a capital comprising a mere ten thousand occupants in 1816. As a scientific and literary society that included members of Congress, doctors, lawyers, military leaders, and engineers, the Columbian Institute planned its meetings to coincide with congressional sessions so that the institute could deliver weekly reports to the nation's elected officials. These reports would fall within one of five classes of study outlined in the institute's charter: mathematical sciences, physical sciences, moral and political sciences, general literature, and the fine arts.[6]

As indicated in its charter, the institute's membership language differed from that of the American Philosophical Society. The institute's "resident members" were those who lived in the District of Columbia, while its "corresponding members" lived outside the city and were specifically solicited from "different sections of the United States." In contrast, American Philosophical Society applied the term "resident" to any member within North

America.[7] Nonetheless, with its focus on the federal capital, the membership of the Columbian Institute comprised the most influential figures of America's Early Republic and the Antebellum period. Every American president from 1816 to 1838 belonged, though all were honorary (and thus inactive). The exception was John Quincy Adams, who served as the institute's president from 1822 until its termination. In comparison to other organizations of the era, the institute also had the largest subscription of architects, all of whom were practicing in Washington by 1818: Bulfinch, Elliot, Hadfield, Hoban, Latrobe, Mills, and Thornton.

The institute's charter and the records of its first years present an organization poised for success in the nation's capital, especially with respect to architectural interests, as it was at the center of new building initiatives, had government support, and included the nation's leading architects. As a profession that melded the arts and sciences, architecture was an ideal medium for the organization's efforts and advocacy. Under different circumstances, the institute could have been the first professional architectural organization in America, far preceding the establishment of the American Institute of Architects in New York City in 1857. However, despite a very clear mission and an impressive cohort, it was plagued by inactive members and a lack of dedicated funds.

Of the Columbian Institute's approximately 150 resident members, 122 corresponding members, and a few honorary members, only a fraction were ever in good standing with paid memberships. The apathy of the membership prompted an amendment to the organization's constitution, altering the definition of a quorum from 7 members to 5 members in 1820.[8] Even then, the organization often failed to reach the required quorum at their meetings. Although never explicitly prohibited in the charter, the institute did not have a single female member. The American Philosophical Society, on the other hand, inducted its first female member in 1789; generally, there was very little overlap between the two organizations. Jefferson became an active member of the American Philosophical Society in 1780 and eventually served as its president from March 1797 until January 1815. Yet, even as the consummate "joiner" for America's early discourses on architecture, education, and intellectual exchange, he never actively participated in the institute, replying to his honorary membership with only an encouraging note that the institute could be fortuitous to the "future destinies of our beloved country."[9]

The institute was operated by only a handful of men who were elected annually to take charge of the organization's original communications, archive, library, and collection of specimens.[10] In addition to an indifferent membership, the Columbian Institute suffered from the presumption among members and other societies that, as a federally chartered organization, it had financial backing from Congress. The institute often found itself without funds or meeting space. Members gathered in various Washington hotels and taverns until the summer of 1824, when the institute was given a small room in the Capitol, but the space was revoked just a few months later.[11] The lack of a physical institution was a problem that the American Philosophical Society never encountered: it had successfully cultivated financial sponsorship for its "neat, sufficient building" in Statehouse Square and had established a sustainable economic plan by renting space in the building to tenants such as the University of Pennsylvania, the College of Physicians, artist Thomas Sully, and the Philadelphia Stock Exchange.[12]

Rather than aligning itself with the working model of the American Philosophical Society, the Columbian Institute sought independence through the guidance of its core members and established only a few international partnerships, such as the seed exchange with the French Geographic Society. Proving that it was not wholly insular, the institute published its proceedings in Washington's available newspapers, the *National Intelligencer* and the *National Register,* between 1818 and 1828. Although the Columbian Institute did not have an open membership policy, the publication of its activities expressed an interest in the dissemination of its nationalistic agendas, such as establishing an independent meridian in Washington.

To advance the mission of the organization that was increasingly drawn toward scientific pursuits, the institute began collecting technological objects and natural specimens for a museum. Hadfield donated a solar microscope and reluctantly partnered with Thornton to curate a "cabinet of the minerals of the United States, and other parts of the world." Oddly, this pair of active architect-members was not consulted on the institute's only building proposal, a design for a museum and greenhouse.[13] As a way to contrib-

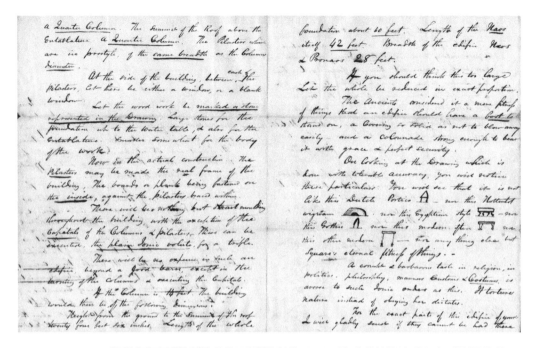

Fig. 19. Letter from Henry Meigs to Joseph Meigs detailing a proposal for the Columbian Institute, June 7, 1820. (Smithsonian Institute Archives RU007051)

ute to the "civilizing of Washington," the institute petitioned for funds in support of the foundation of a national botanic garden, comparable to those found in the capital cities of Europe, such as Kensington, Regents Park, or the Tuileries.[14]

A lease of five acres on the west side of Capitol Hill was given to the institute in 1820, and additional land was added in May 1824. Instead of using the expertise of its architectural membership to craft an aesthetically pleasing and functional greenhouse at the foot of the Capitol, lawyer and Congressman Henry Meigs set forth the only known design proposal: a curiously illustrated letter, with thumbnails sketches of a "Dutch Portio," as well as a "wigwam," "Egyptian style," "Gothick," and "modern" form, and an accompanying naive perspective in watercolor for a simplified Ionic temple, made of wood but rendered to look like stone (figs. 19 and 20). His proposal was un-

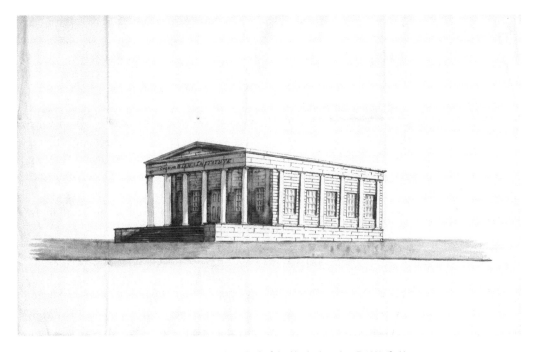

Fig. 20. Watercolor perspective by Henry Meigs of a proposed home for the Columbian Institute, June 7, 1820. (Smithsonian Institute Archives RU007051)

answered, and the institute never erected a single structure. It did, however, manage to place a few walkways through its swampy gardens and enclose the site with a fence in 1826. Even then, small victories in Washington's building program were to be celebrated.

By the middle of the 1820s, the Columbian Institute's activities had slowed substantially. Founder and first president Edward Cutbush even resigned his membership on December 9, 1826, and left the capital city to pursue other educational interests.[15] After the Columbian Institute's charter expired in 1838, the surviving members and scant activities of the organization were absorbed in 1840 into a new, federally sponsored organization called the National Institute for the Promotion of Sciences. Six years later, it became part of the Smithsonian Institution. Despite the string of failures and disappointments that characterized its short life, the organization had a few significant and lasting impacts for intellectual culture in Washington. As the first items within the National Institute's holdings, the Columbian Institute's legacy of a small museum of specimens of geology, botany, ethnology, archaeology, and fossils represents the beginnings of the Smithsonian Institution's vast collections. The Columbian Institute's early interest in establishing a federally sponsored garden at the base of Capitol Hill also led to the establishment of the National Botanic Gardens and the construction of its first conservatory after the Civil War. The institute's ambition, however, to produce a "national reservoir for improvements in the arts and science" on Capitol Hill was not actualized until the latter half of the nineteenth century with the federal development of a grand landscape plan that included museums and monuments, now known as the National Mall.[16]

At its foundation, the Columbian Institute was primed to act as a professional architectural organization with a few key designers at its helm. Unlike their peers in the sciences, the architects of the institute did not use the organization as a platform for international exchange within their field. Locally, they did not address issues found in architectural practice in the nation's capital, investing instead in their own individual projects. Overall, the short lifespan of the Columbian Institute proved that proactive international exchange was essential to an organization's longevity in the Atlantic world and that architectural discourse in early America largely operated within informal circles of exchange.

PART II

Sites

The assessment of post-Revolutionary architectural and aesthetic relations between the newly formed American states and England is often characterized by a one-sided view of development: early American architecture was born by reacting against or copying English architecture (usually badly). Although American designers and architects sought to create independent architectural character, projects such as Drayton Hall (1738) illustrate that it was clearly influenced by Anglo-Palladianism. The aesthetic identity of these structures has been characterized by architectural historians such as Dell Upton as a "collection of visual quotations" that were representative of derivative and muddled design efforts rather than original architectural invention.[1] These commonly held views of American architectural development in the Early Republic do not acknowledge the presence of a larger and highly influential transatlantic network of relationships that activated the exchange of design ideas and books while shaping architectural careers.

The theme of Sites places the designs of Jefferson and Soane in conversation and reintroduces their architecture within a transatlantic context. Privileging design process, technology, and building performance, the following chapters analyze the four-decade development of their house museums through travel and moments of exchange within the network. "Foundations" introduces parallels within both their formative years and the selected location of their house museums. "Landscapes" demonstrates that the house museums of Jefferson and Soane have similar architectural characteristics in terms of their arrangement, program, and relationship to their surroundings. "Libraries" reveals that Jefferson and Soane were reading similar texts and responding to scientific discoveries as well as the availability of new materials. By studying the schematic and design drawings, often represented as loose, annotated sketches, as well as extant architectural fabric of the homes, "Cabinets" places Monticello and Soane's Museum in parallel to see how both men tested different structural systems and forms, continually refined spaces for private study, thereby underscoring their shared dedication to both lifelong learning and an active record of correspondence. "Laboratories" demonstrates that, as they aged, they became more experimental with their use of glass, manipulations in section, and the boundaries between the inside and outside. Finally, "Pasticci" illustrates that although Jefferson and Soane were aware of international dialogues and discoveries, their work paid close attention to national histories and the cultivation of personal narratives through architectural form.

CHAPTER 6

Foundations

When all the goods from a lifetime of buying were stuffed into it
[Monticello], the house must have resembled the most crowded parts of
John Soane's famous museum-house in London.
—Garry Wills, "The Aesthete"[1]

At first glance, Jefferson's plantation home in Charlottesville, Virginia, near
the Blue Ridge Mountains and Soane's townhouse in the bustling metropolis
of London, England, have little in common. One man sought to establish a
place of picturesque self-sufficiency within the frontier of colonial Virginia,
close to his family's homestead, while the other chose to divorce himself
from his rural roots to live in one of the world's largest urban centers.[2] For
Jefferson, the ultimate ambition was to live in an enlightened, agrarian uto-
pia, albeit flawed in its reliance on enslaved labor. For Soane, he created a
place of concentration and quiet amid one of the busiest cities in the world.
Despite the obvious differences in the physical locations of Monticello and
Soane's Museum, there are important conceptual similarities between the
sites, especially concerning the origins and intentions for placemaking used
by the respective architects. Read in parallel, the formative years of Jefferson
and Soane established their lifelong interests in education and aesthetic exploration and suggested that their greatest experiments in architecture and
ideology would be their own homes.

"PRECIOUS CLUTTER"

In 1993, historian Gary Wills reviewed an exhibit at Monticello and the corresponding catalog, *The Worlds of Thomas Jefferson at Monticello,* that restored many of Jefferson's collections, albeit temporarily, to the house museum.[3] When Jefferson's family was forced to sell Monticello following the death of the patriarch on July 4, 1826, many of his possessions found new homes in museums, with family friends, and in the hands of individuals who were already collecting Jeffersoniana. The exhibition was, thus, the first time in more than 165 years that Monticello resembled its creator's vision in terms of the diversity and number of objects that filled the home to stimulate the minds of curious visitors; yet the collections represented only a quarter of what would have filled Monticello during Jefferson's retirement years. After viewing the exhibition, Wills commented that it attempted to "restore Monticello to some of its original air of precious clutter," and, consequently, the mountaintop home was akin to Soane's Museum.[4] It is significant that Wills, a classicist by training and a historian with interests in American politics and religion, envisioned a correlation between Monticello and Soane's Museum. In his review, he made no additional commentary on the connection and consequentially his assessment was based purely on appearance or, perhaps, sheer volume. Despite the quantity of scholarship produced on Jefferson and Soane, it is interesting that during the three decades since Wills's review no researchers have explored his intuitive association between two of the Western world's most famous house museums.

For Jefferson and Soane, compulsive collecting and purposeful curation resulted in homes that illuminated their personalities, insecurities, ambitions, and desired legacies. As customized architectural laboratories crafted within a shell of domesticity, Monticello and Soane's Museum embody the concept of an "essay in architecture."[5] Jefferson and Soane opened their built experiments not only to family and friends but also to colleagues and students. For Soane, his hired servants managed the household; however, for Jefferson, the founder's experimental plantation was only possible due to the forced labor of the enslaved community. Beyond both human labor and the "precious clutter," Monticello and Soane's Museum should be read as residences that contained places of retreat and arenas for exploration (and exploitation). Despite their frozen states, the house museums are far more than reliquaries or cabinets of curiosity. As representative figures within the Transatlantic Design Network who were also prominent within their respective nations, Jefferson and Soane crafted house museums that were reflective of a dynamic atmosphere of exchange.

Today, the house museums of Jefferson and Soane exist largely in stasis: walls are not continually "put up and pulled down," and the collections do not move unless under the watchful eye of curators clad in protective gloves.[6] The design process at Monticello and Soane's Museum was a never-ending exercise for the architects, shaped by new discussions, discoveries, and acquisitions (figs. 21 and 22). Since the architects lived on-site, many of the decisions for Monticello and Soane's Museum were made without drawn record;

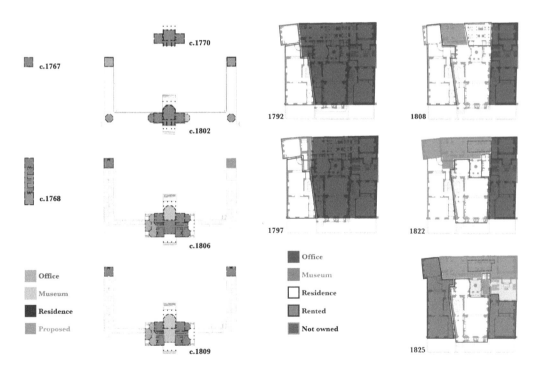

Fig. 21. Design progress at Monticello. (Author's diagrams)

Fig. 22. Design progress at Sir John Soane's Museum, overlaid on the plan of the house museum's configuration from 1837 (Author's diagrams)

however, their letters and the observations of visitors, written and drawn, illuminate the more than forty years of design and construction at each home.[7] In order achieve a new reading of Monticello and Soane's Museum, it is essential to look beyond the modern conditions of the house museums that represent the last years of the architects' lives. By examining the genesis of the house museums as well as the experiences that launched the architects' interests in crafting them, it is possible to understand how Jefferson and Soane participated in design dialogues and why the choices of specific sites for their architectural experiments were so critical to the character of their house museums.

"FIXING THE DESTINIES"

Although Jefferson and Soane were born on opposite sides of the Atlantic Ocean, their lives shared remarkable parallels that may help explain some of the basic similarities in their approaches to designing, collecting, and disseminating educational principles to the masses. Jefferson was born at Shadwell, a farm located at the base of the mountain now known as Monticello, on April 13, 1743. The farm was named for the east London parish that Jefferson's mother, née Jane Randolph (1721–1776), once called home. After immigrating to Virginia, she married Peter Jefferson (1708–1757), and of the couple's eight children who lived to adulthood, Jefferson was the eldest son. Soane, the youngest of Martha (née Marcy, d. 1800) and John Soan's five children who survived infancy, was born a little over ten years after Jefferson, on September 10, 1753, in Goring-on-Thames, England. To quickly quell the coincidental notion that Jefferson and Soane were distant cousins, it is important to note that Soane added the *e* to the end of his name in 1784, and he was not a descendent of Jefferson's great-great-grandfather, Henry Soane (1626–1660/1), who immigrated to the Virginia colony in 1651 and served as the Speaker of the Virginia House of Burgesses during the last year of his life.[8]

As children, both Jefferson and Soane had the privilege of private education, and both of their fathers were accomplished in professions tangentially related to architecture: surveyor and bricklayer, respectively. Even though Jefferson's father settled in a remote part of Virginia that was home to only a few other families in the 1730s, his wooden home had ample furniture, three mirrors, several maps, and a variety of surveying and mechanical instruments.[9] Jefferson was also familiar with the rich and inventive carpentry at his family's residence at Tuckahoe.[10] At Reading, Soane grew up in a similar atmosphere where drawings were present in map, diagram, or plan form, and measured details were critical. Their eyes were trained to perceive space in a quantitative manner, and these skills would be further developed through their own initiatives in reading and observation. Jefferson never abandoned the legacy of his father's occupation and surveyed properties throughout his life, applying mathematical precision to his building book and calculating measurements to the sixth decimal place in some instances. The family's heritage in masonry informed Soane's construction knowledge and may have helped him to develop his signature manipulation of brick surfaces in unconventional, proto-modern ways.

At the age of fourteen, both men lost their fathers, but these misfortunes led to transformative educational experiences. Jefferson was put under the tutelage of a classical scholar, James Maury, and then went to study at the College of William & Mary, where he was introduced to one of America's largest colonial centers, its architecture, and his mentor William Small, who, in Jefferson's words, "fixed the destinies of my life."[11] Soane followed a similar path, leaving his home for school in Reading and then apprenticeships in Chertsey and London that led to his work with the Dances' architectural dynasty and his entry to the Royal Academy to study architecture. In these formative years, shaped by personal loss and scholastic opportunity, both Jefferson and Soane first displayed the bookish and introspective tendencies that would inform the cultivation of libraries and private working spaces at their homes.

SELECTING A SITE

For Jefferson and Soane, the sites and configurations of their house museums were reflective of both their personalities and ambitions. Jefferson supposedly selected the site for his residence as a young boy when he told friend Dabny Carr (1743–1773) that he would one day build his home on the little mountain west of the family's farm.[12] As a boy, it is doubtful that Jefferson recognized the problems such a site would pose: the mountaintop lacked a natural spring, so water was always precious; skilled craftsmen had to be solicited; and the transportation of certain materials, such as fragile glass, was treacherous along the steep, winding, and narrow mountainside roads. Despite Jefferson's varied travels in the young nation, and even abroad, he maintained the conviction that Monticello would be his ideal residence. While traveling around Lake Champlain, Jefferson wrote to his daughter Martha, extolling his native state's rich landscape: "On the whole I find nothing any where else in point of climate which Virginia need envy to any part of the world. . . . [W]e have reason to value highly the accident of birth in such a one as that of Virginia."[13] The surrounding region was not densely populated, but Albemarle had been established the year after Jefferson's birth, and the gridded town of Charlottesville became the county seat in 1762, five years before Jefferson started to level his mountaintop in preparation for construction. Jefferson was not in an entirely remote location, and in letters the Jefferson family often referred to the 'neighborhood' surrounding Monticello. Although Virginia was not home to any of the nation's largest urban centers (Philadelphia, New York, Boston, Charleston, or Baltimore), the first official American census in 1790 demonstrated that Virginia was the most populous of the thirteen states and four districts that composed the nation.[14]

Standing a little over three hundred feet taller than the elevation of central Charlottesville, Jefferson's mountaintop afforded him a view of the developing town to the northeast as well as the expansive landscape that stretched across mountains, valleys, and rivers. When advising two young Americans about their travels in Europe, Jefferson wrote that upon arriving at a new town one should first buy a map and guidebook, walk the perimeter of the town, and then climb a steeple to "view the town and its environs."[15] Jefferson's steps for establishing Monticello mirrored this process: as the son of a mapmaker, he knew his surroundings well and chose a site that allowed him to continually observe the world below.

At the mountaintop, Jefferson encountered a difficult task as a designer: a blank slate. As evidenced by the early design sketches for the home, Jefferson contemplated a variety of initial configurations and orientations for his home, most of which favored a Palladian *parti* that featured a centralized home and flanking, symmetrical dependencies. Progress, however, at the site was frequently thwarted by his career as a statesman. During Jefferson's tenure as secretary of state (1790–1793) he wrote to Angelica Schuyler Church that he wanted "to be liberated from the hated occupation of politics, and to remain in the bosom of my family, my farm and my books. . . . I have my house to build."[16] The plantation was an active construction site from the late 1760s until 1809, but Jefferson was in residence for less than half of those years. On March 4, 1809, James Madison was sworn in as the fourth president of the United States, and Jefferson happily traded his residence at the President's House in Washington for retired life at Monticello. At this point, much of the home was complete, but Jefferson continued to refine his home and the plantation's landscape as a laboratory for architecture and agriculture until his final years.

During his only visit to London in 1786, Jefferson passed through Lincoln's Inn Fields, but this was six years before Soane purchased his first townhouse. Like Jefferson, Soane's selection of a townhouse on the north side of Lincoln's Inn Fields was the result of careful study. The site put Soane in proximity to many of the larger building initiatives in London as well as the social circles where patrons operated. As later stated in one of his Royal Academy lectures, the establishment of a home and architectural practice in London reflected Soane's drive to infiltrate the building program of a rapidly growing city where the "wealthy and enlightened of every class are congregated."[17] The site also possessed generous southern light and a pristine view of the largest garden in central London, complete with a designed landscape of pathways and a central basin.[18]

Soane's site resulted in a different set of challenges than those of Jefferson's open plot of land. Soane's first purchase at Lincoln's Inn Fields, no. 12, consisted of an established structure: a mid-seventeenth-century townhouse with a meandering party wall that followed medieval plot lines.[19] The site was further complicated by the numerous strict building codes that governed Lincoln's Inn Fields and were enforced by a board of trustees that had been established by an act of Parliament.[20] Through the continual manipulations of his amalgamated townhouses, Soane tested the limits of the architectural review board and eventually went to court over alleged infractions.[21] Therefore, he focused his working attentions for the site behind the facade: his creative impetus was internalized, and he spent more than forty years shaping and reshaping the interior and its connections to the ground and sky.

Although seemingly disparate, the site selections of Jefferson and Soane share crucial qualities. Both gentlemen chose sites that were the most conducive to their personalities. Jefferson, the ever-introspective naturalist, sought a place for agricultural development and expansive connections with nature, abandoning both the chaos and conveniences of the urban sphere. Soane, the ambitious self-promoter, chose to be in the center of professional, social, and bureaucratic groups. As it developed, Jefferson's Monticello stretched further and further into the landscape while Soane's became more internalized; the experience of Monticello as a site could be likened to using a telescope since it was best understood from a distance, whereas Soane's Museum was a kaleidoscope, an interlocking and dynamic site best comprehended from within.

CULTURES OF DOMESTICITY

Jefferson and Soane married their wives at similar ages, twenty-nine and thirty-one, respectively. Soane had three decades with his Eliza, but Jefferson lost his wife after only "ten years of unchequred happiness."[22] As neither man remarried, they might be seen as wedded to their house museums for the latter portions of their lives. However, the early incarnations of the house museums, especially in terms of locations and arrangement, reflected the families that occupied the homes.

The death of Eliza's uncle, George Wyatt, on February 23, 1790, left her with a considerable inheritance that afforded the family the opportunity to purchase and reconfigure the first townhouse at Lincoln's Inn Fields.[23] The residence initially housed Soane's young family, but when Soane's two sons, John and George, reached adolescence he purchased a twenty-eight-acre property west of London in Ealing: Pitzhanger Manor. Here, as illustrated in Soane's seventh Royal Academy lecture, he could develop a villa to get away from both the city and unexpected visitors. When Soane purchased Pitzhanger in 1801, he immediately began demolishing and renovating the home as a working architectural studio dedicated to the education of his sons.[24] This strong, almost obsessive interest in creating an architectural legacy was, in part, due to Soane's early experiences in practice. At fifteen years old, Soane was apprenticed to the office of George Dance, and one of his first projects was to assistant George Dance the Younger with the construction of an extension to Pitzhanger. As a young man, Soane saw the advantages of establishing an architectural lineage firsthand: before even reaching the age of thirty, Dance the Younger had inherited his father's prominent position as London's clerk to city works.[25]

After three years of construction that drastically altered the family areas and external arrangement of the home, Soane's Pitzhanger was finished in 1804.[26] Contemporary scholars called Pitzhanger a "self-portrait" of Soane, as architect and collector, and the home's configuration, decoration, and use of ruins were certainly spatial precursors to the designs that would be executed at the combined townhouses of Lincoln's Inn Fields.[27] Despite myriad casts, artifacts, and books made available to John and George, neither son expressed interest in pursuing architecture as a career. Frustrated, Soane sold the property in 1810 and returned his attention to central London. As a retreat that never fully realized its purpose to inspire his sons' architectural ambitions, Pitzhanger can be viewed as an abandoned experiment that strongly informed the development of Soane's London house museum.

Whereas Soane's urban retreat was a precursor to his main house museum, Jefferson's secondary residence benefited from lessons learned in terms of design, construction, and functional operation at Monticello. Poplar Forest was a five-thousand-acre plantation located approximately ninety miles south of Charlottesville. Here Jefferson crafted a home that distilled many of the themes and spatial devices originally tested at Monticello, such as polygonal rooms and skylights. Designed between 1806 and 1809, the octagonal home featured a piano nobile, flanked by earthworks, dependencies, and freestanding octagonal privies. Compared to the interrupted design processes at Monticello, construction at Poplar Forest was streamlined, and Jefferson even took a two-month break from the presidency to oversee the laying of the foundations at his second home. Unlike Monticello, Poplar Forest functioned as a profitable plantation, and the residence truly served as a retreat for the retired statesman.

One of the critical assumptions to dispel is that Jefferson's residence at

Monticello was a remote and tranquil home. From a geographical standpoint, Jefferson's choice of a site on the developed edge of western Virginia illustrated his interest in creating a home that would evoke Pliny's concept of *otium,* or leisure. But in practice, as evidenced by Jefferson's letters as well as those of his family and other visitors, Monticello rarely, if ever, functioned as a quiet retreat. Although located in a rural site, Monticello probably had more visitors than Soane's Museum during the architect's lifetime. Soane opened his home to clients, friends, and students but only at selected times: even Maria Cosway wrote to Soane to ask "permission to see your house," and during the 1833 Parliamentary debates about the establishment of Soane's Museum as a national institution, one of the minsters objected that it was rarely open, and the museum limited its visitors to a select demographic.[28]

Several architectural survey texts perpetuated the misperception that Monticello was a tranquil American villa, similar to many of the large, eighteenth-century estates in Virginia and the Carolinas that embodied coherence and grandeur through their romanticized interpretation of "plantation Palladianism."[29] Early Jeffersonian biographer Henry Adams (1838–1918) even wrote that at Monticello Jefferson built himself "a château above contact with man."[30] In fact, Monticello was a hectic site: aside from Jefferson's siblings, his daughters and their children, friends, and transatlantic acquaintances, Monticello was a named destination for those hoping to meet the founding father, as well as strangers passing through Charlottesville to the hot springs in western Virginia. The traffic on the mountaintop increased following Jefferson's retirement in 1809, and in 1816 Jefferson's granddaughter Ellen wrote, "we have had many several large parties from the springs, and a coach of four is by no means an uncommon sight at the door."[31] The number of visitors increased again when the University of Virginia opened in 1825. Moreover, as an active plantation with industrial operations along Mulberry Row, there would have been a variety of noises and smells to disrupt Jefferson's *otium;* it also would have been difficult to overlook the commotion from the nearly two hundred people that composed the enslaved community on the plantation.

Built as a retreat from the chaos of his home and its visitors, it was Poplar Forest that provided respite for Jefferson through his retirement years. Despite the sometimes-harried conditions on the mountaintop, Monticello always remained the center of his architectural focus and his primary house museum. Conversely, Poplar Forest's furnishings were sparse, and it was a seasonal residence. Unlike Pitzhanger Manor where Soane tested the placement of collections in a site with only privileged access before removing them to a more accessible, urban setting, Jefferson did not deposit his precious collections at Poplar Forest: these were reserved for "public" display at Monticello.

UNDERSTANDING EARLY AMERICA

Soane's Royal Academy lectures, delivered between 1810 and 1835, predominately focused on English architecture; he also referenced classical works, polite architecture, and examples of the vernacular in continental Europe, India, China, and Mexico. His lectures were, however, entirely devoid of discussion on American architects or architecture.[32] Soane owned texts that referenced the buildings of North America and had interpersonal connections to figures across the ocean. Therefore, the absence of discussion about the architecture of the United States does not reflect a lack of knowledge but rather a conscious decision. Soane perhaps imagined that his students would never travel to America, and he did not foresee a reason to make the journey.

Soane did not possess Jefferson's only published work, *Notes on the State of Virginia* (1785), but within the text he would have found a less than complimentary assessment that reinforced the European assumption that America was filled with substandard architecture: "The genius of architecture seems to have shed its maledictions of this land. Buildings are often erected, by individuals, for considerable expense. To give these symmetry and taste would not increase their cost. It would only change the arrangement of the materials, the form and combination of the members."[33] Furthermore, young America did not conform to the material standards that would have been familiar to Soane in London. The Great Fire of 1666 and resulting building policies largely eradicated wooden structures. Jefferson criticized the American built landscape, filled with impermanent structures, and emphasized that it was a nation to be mined for its resources rather than style.[34] Jefferson had firsthand experience with the problem of wooden architecture in America, considering that on February 1, 1770, an inferno engulfed his Shadwell homestead and his treasured library. Jefferson wrote that the blaze caused the loss of "every paper I had in the world."[35] It is possible that he lost some of the earliest of his architectural drawings for Monticello, but more importantly, the Shadwell fire prompted the codification of Jefferson's architectural palette. Situated in the humid climate of the western edge of the Piedmont Plateau, Monticello had soils particularly conducive to making a fire-resistant material: brick.[36]

As illustrated, drastic changes during their formational years, the conditions of their family life, and experiments with other residences largely informed the architectural foundations of Jefferson's Monticello and Soane's Museum. In the late 1700s and early 1800s, the transatlantic world was not as harshly divided as one might think from contemporary texts that referred to the civilized world and the New World; even maps, such as those by popular cartographer Aaron Arrowsmith, depicted the Atlantic Ocean as a geographical feature that bisected the globe, yet the personal and professional connections between the sides of the "Western Ocean" were both ample and active.

CHAPTER 7

Landscapes

The gardening in that country is the article in which it surpasses all the earth. . . . This indeed went far beyond my ideas.
—Thomas Jefferson to John Page, May 4, 1786[1]

In 1786, Thomas Jefferson spent fifty-six days in England, and this was the only period that Jefferson and Soane were in the same country. As a congressionally appointed agent, Jefferson traveled to London on a diplomatic mission to aide John Adams in treaty negotiations with Portugal and to meet with the Tripoline ambassador; however, between the elongated weeks in arbitration, Jefferson found time to shop and undertake some personal excursions within the city and its environs. On Jefferson's list of forty-eight figures whom he hoped to call upon in England, Soane's name was not present: the young architect was still building his practice and had not yet begun his built experiments at Lincoln's Inn Fields. According to the documentary evidence available, the pair never crossed paths in a London coffeehouse, but the two certainly would have found shared interests in their appreciation of Roman architectural precedents and the importance of civic architecture for shaping growing societies.

Jefferson's English garden tour was the most extensive study of the built environment that he undertook during his lifetime, and it was the longest time that Jefferson and Adams spent together, outside of a political context. The extent of the tour, however, has been continually misstated. By closely examining the timeline of Jefferson's garden tour, a series of journeys focused on exploring landscape architecture projects, it is possible to better understand Jefferson's autodidactic architectural education and how his travels shaped his practical and aesthetic theories. Soane, too, played the architectural tourist during his twenty-three-day stay in Paris in 1819, a city that Jefferson knew well from his time as minister to France.

By examining the American Francophile in London and the Englishman in Paris, it is possible to read the personal travels of Jefferson and Soane in parallel: they both had limited time to explore sites and left only sporadic notebooks documenting their inspection of agricultural and engineering practices while drawing references to works of history and fiction. Both gentlemen were encumbered by ambitious careers, so personal travel was a distinct privilege. Therefore, the sites selected for their respective journeys illustrate that although Jefferson and Soane never met, as members of the Transatlantic Design Network they were operating within an extended community that guided the references they used as well as the sites they visited, drawing inspiration for the landscape architecture elements of their respective house museums.

RE-PLOTTING JEFFERSON'S JOURNEY

Many historians portrayed the garden tour of Jefferson and Adams as a luxurious, two-week excursion where the pair used a copy of Whately's *Observations on Modern Gardening* as the primary guide for their travels.[2] This version of the Jefferson-Adams garden tour is, however, a confused and somewhat fictionalized account that not only misrepresents the chronology of the journey but also its motivations.[3] The misrepresentation of the tour is due to the fragmentation of primary sources and may also be traced to the account presented in Marie Kimball's *Jefferson: The Scene of Europe* (1950).[4] Although Kimball's work consulted Jefferson's writings, her abridged reconstruction of the travels intimates that Jefferson and Adams traveled together for an extended, uninterrupted period of time.[5] Jefferson's built work clearly demonstrates his Francophile architectural interests, yet it also demonstrates that he preferred the picturesque and sublime elements of English landscape gardens over the formal geometry of French landscape design, thereby creating a unique mix of references at his mountaintop plantation. Jefferson's interests in the picturesque were apparent in his descriptions and sketches for Monticello's landscape from 1771, yet the application of these design principles evolved significantly following his experiential research in England, transforming the landscape architecture at Monticello from a scheme characterized by disparate elements to an executed arrangement that was more cohesive and inventive.

By weaving the complex chronology outlined in various primary sources, it is possible to reconstruct a more accurate picture of Jefferson's only first-hand encounters with English landscape gardens and dispel several myths: his tour was not a two-week jaunt in April but rather a series of five separate excursions that took place over the course of eleven days between March 31 and April 20 (fig. 23). Since Jefferson was uncertain about the length of time

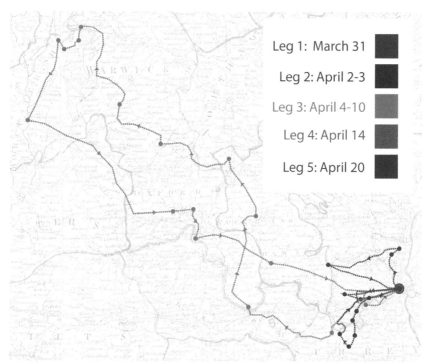

Leg 1: March 31
Leg 2: April 2-3
Leg 3: April 4-10
Leg 4: April 14
Leg 5: April 20

Fig. 23. Jefferson's garden tour in England and Wales, drawn over *The most accurate surveys containing all the cities, boroughs, market towns & villages* by John Rocque, 1790 (Author's diagram)

he would be dispatched in England on diplomatic duties, unraveling the sequence of his garden tour into the five distinct trips presents a clear prioritization of his interests. Writing to Page upon his return to Paris, Jefferson referred to England as "that nation hates us," but he also asserted praise for English gardens, divorcing his political beliefs from his aesthetic appreciation. During his time in England, Jefferson managed to see key architectural and landscape works by some of the most notable designers: Adam, "Capability" Brown, Burlington, Chambers, Gibbs, Holland, Kent, Shenstone, Vanbrugh, and Wren. Jefferson's studies of English landscape gardens, through readings and on-site observations, far surpassed any of his American peers, such as Latrobe or Thornton, and with this in mind, Jefferson was America's first landscape architect. He put his studies into practice at Monticello, Poplar Forest, the University of Virginia, and several other private residences, melding architectural design with nature, both wild and cultivated. He relied on his encyclopedic knowledge of plants, understood grafting, maintained controlled experiments in Monticello's greenhouse, correlated weather and plant behavior, tried to employ local materials whenever possible in his landscape designs, and understood that built landscapes needed to be efficient, productive, and beautiful. Not to be overlooked, this was a collaborative landscape practice, albeit forced, considering the maintenance of Jefferson's designs and execution of cultivation practices were powered by an enslaved community.

THE GARDEN TOUR

The ever efficient Jefferson made the most of his brief stay in England by visiting a number of theater productions and sampling food from some of the most famous venues, but he found much of his time was "lost in ceremony."[6] From his rented accommodation at 10 Golden Square, he made several formal and informal diplomatic visits in the city, including one to the court of King George III, where the former patriot recorded an "ungracious" reception.[7] An undated note in Jefferson's hand details some of the people and sites of interest, ranging from Counts of Bavaria and Russia to other Americans living in the city, such as artists under West's tutelage. Jefferson also proposed a visit to Scottish baronet Sir James Riddell at Stratford Place, the site that the Cosways later transformed into a house museum.[8] Recalling that Jefferson did not meet the Cosways until the summer of 1786. the group was not yet acquainted during Jefferson's time in London.[9] This gap in their encounter, separated by only a few months, may account for an extraordinary lost opportunity: through a connection with the Cosways in London, it is likely that Jefferson would have been introduced to a close friend of Maria's whom she knew for nearly a decade: architect John Soane.

As Jefferson wandered through parts of the city, particularly Westminster, he made efforts to see specific buildings and garden squares but observed that the architecture was of the "most wretched styile."[10] The shopping, however, was more gratifying. While in London Jefferson bought maps, books, clothing, and scientific instruments, noting that the "mechanical arts in London are carried to a wonderful perfection."[11] Jefferson's visit to London in March and April was also, fortuitously, timed with spring blossoms, and this conceivably made his English gardens tours even more enticing, enlivening his sensibilities as both architect and gardener.

During the first of the five trips in the garden tour, Jefferson independently explored South Lodge, Enfield Chase, and Moor Park on March 31. He left no notes about South Lodge, and his descriptions of Enfield Chase and Moor Park were less than complimentary, noting several "improvements" for both sites that could ameliorate both the architecture and landscape.[12] After returning to London for a day, Jefferson made his second garden excursion on April 2 with William Stephens Smith (1755–1816), Adam's secretary and future son-in-law, and Smith's servant, Petit. The group traveled to Chiswick, Pope's garden at Twickenham, Hampton Court, Esher Place, Cobham, and Paynshill and then spent the evening in Weybridge before returning to London. Oddly, the group did not visit Walpole's Strawberry Hill, a site frequented by Soane and the Cosways. Instead of illustrating an aversion to Walpole's Whig politics or even a dislike of the Gothic Revival, Jefferson's omission of Strawberry Hill may have simply been due to a lack of time and his pressing interest in Twickenham's other prominent site, Pope's Grotto, since it featured a picturesque garden, geological collections, and substantial subterranean earthworks in the form of a fabricated grotto.[13] Soane, too, admired the work of Pope and often discussed the "poetry of architecture" as well as the use of unexpected elements within the landscape; much of Soane's Museum is a physical reflection of Pope's Epistle to Lord Burlington.

Throughout Jefferson's notes from his garden tours, he preferred picturesque landscapes but also favored practicality over designed frivolity. For example, he noted that the octagonal dome of "Cheswick" had "an ill effect, both within and without; the garden shews still too much art; an obelisk of very ill effect. Another in the middle of a pond useless."[14] Despite his critique, Jefferson would eventually employ a number of these features at Monticello: the home was capped with an octagonal dome in 1800, he placed a small fishpond on the West Lawn, and he designed his own obelisk tombstone to be placed in the family graveyard. Despite critical notes, this leg of the journey was certainly influential to Jefferson's design sensibilities, and the rapidity of the first two portions of the garden tour illustrates his voracious appetite for architecture and landscape design: in three days he covered eleven sites.

Adams joined Jefferson for the third portion of the tour. From Adams's diplomatic residence in London's Grosvenor Square, the pair started an excursion that spanned April 4 through 10, making it the longest and most geographically ambitious portion of Jefferson's landscape tour. Although Adams wrote three diary entries about their tour, he did little to detail the specifics of their visits, displaying aesthetic ambivalence by noting that Stowe, Hagely, and Blenheim were "supurb," Woburn, Caversham, and Leasowes were "beautiful," and Wotton was "both great an[d] elegant tho neglected."[15] Finding the "artificial incitements" of follies unnecessary, Adams's diary entries did not focus on the architecture or landscape details of certain sites. Instead, he turned his attention to history, describing the sites related to Shakespeare at Stratford and expressing his general displeasure with the financial extravagance of landscape gardens, writing that he hoped it would be long before "Ridings, Parks, Pleasure Grounds, Gardens and ornamented Farms grow so much in fashion in America."[16] Adams noted that the "larger scale" of the American landscape needed no artificial improvements, such as the cascades of Hagely or extended river of Blenheim. Although Adams and Jefferson were lifelong correspondents, Adams never visited Monticello, so it is unknown if he would have approved of Jefferson's mountaintop experiment or perhaps viewed it as an ornamented farm.[17]

By contrast, Jefferson's notes on this portion of the garden tour, although brief, were clearly written by an astute critic of design: he measured distances between elements and commented on the distinct features of the landscape, ranging from the pitch of slopes to the composition of specific sight lines. Although he often recorded the architects of primary buildings at the various sites, his notes were written from the perspective of a budding landscape architect, recording observations on the experiential qualities of the gardens such as the materials used in the walking paths, the clarity of the water, and the contrasts between the ornamented gardens and bordering farmland. In his laconic notes, he recorded only a few complimentary thoughts, such as calling Esher Place "a most lovely mixture of concave and convex."[18] On the whole, his notes were critical, calling the architecture of Paynshill "incorrect" and stating that there was "no one striking position" in Blenheim. He did, however, make lengthy notes about Stowe. He was disapproving of the on-axis approach to the site and Corinthian arch, yet he found the various temples as well as most views within the site pleasing. It does not appear that Jefferson and Adams toured the interior of the home, a site where Soane would later design a Gothic Library (c.1806).

For the fourth leg of the garden tour, Jefferson made a solitary day trip from London on April 14 for a tour of Kew.[19] Here he made no notes about Chamber's eclectic architectural composition. Instead, he focused on the construction of an Archimedes' screw for lifting water and copiously annotated a rough sketch. At this point in his travels, it seems as if Jefferson was trying to make the most of his dwindling time in London: the day before his visit to Kew he toured the Tower of London, and in the following days he made trips to see the Raphael cartoons at "Buckingham house" and Ashton Lever's Museum.[20]

The fifth and final component of Jefferson's garden tour was a day trip with John, Abigail, and their daughter Nabby on April 20 to two Robert Adam projects: Osterley and Syon House.[21] In his diary, Adams described Osterley as well as the flora and fauna at both sites in detail, but Jefferson left no record of his impressions, noting only payments to servants at both sites. Unlike Soane, who was enthralled by the work of the Adam brothers and collected their drawings, Jefferson may have been unimpressed by their lack of integrated landscape plans. For Soane, the Adams' architecture was masterful at crafting complex and surprising interior arrangements, especially within the confines of existing urban fabric; as a resident of a rapidly growing country with a predominantly rural population, Jefferson was more intrigued with designs that used the land rather than those than manipulated compressed interiors.

BIRTHDAY TOURS

Despite the diplomatic duty that instigated Jefferson's trip to England during the weeks around his forty-third birthday, his garden tour provided much needed moments of respite. The same could be said for Soane's twenty-three-day trip spent touring sites in and around Paris in 1819 for his sixty-sixth birthday. He had enjoyed recent professional successes with the completion of the Dulwich Picture Gallery and an appointment as one of the attached architects to the Office of Works; however, he was also a recent widower, and this tragedy partially coincided with the commencement of ocular troubles that would plague the rest of his life.

Soane's 1819 trip to Paris was not his first time in the city: he passed through at the beginning of his Royal Academy–sponsored Grand Tour in the spring of 1778, then again for nearly a month in the late summer of 1815. The 1819 excursion was his last trip to the continent. This recreational trip was spent in the company of his housekeeper, Sally Conduit, and her husband as well as one of his students, Henry Parke (1790–1835).[22] Drawing was Parke's primary occupation during the Parisian excursion, and several of the sites they visited were later crafted into large illustrations for Soane's Royal Academy lectures.[23] During his visit, Soane stayed at 18 Rue Vivienne, just a few blocks north of the Palais Royal and the eastern edge of the Tuileries Garden. Had their time in the city overlapped, Jefferson would have been a close neighbor, considering his primary residence was on the corner of the Rue de Berri and the Champs-Elysées.

Soane's three weeks in the city were filled with architectural excursions and shopping. His abbreviated notes, recorded in a pocketbook, closely mirror Jefferson's memorandum and account books from his time in Paris: both men spent multiple afternoons "book hunting"; they toured several sites within Paris but also ventured to St. Denis, Versailles, and Malmaison. On

September 10, Soane's sixty-sixth birthday, he visited the Canal de l'Ourcq and sketched with Parke. Then, they traveled to the Halle au Blé, the site where Jefferson first met Cosway. This was not the only time the paths of Jefferson and Soane crossed as architectural tourists. They both investigated famous domed structures in Paris and made multiple visits to St. Cloud. However, many of the sites and surroundings of Paris that Jefferson knew differed drastically from the ones that Soane visited three decades later. The French Revolution and reign of Napoleon had changed the landscape. Soane was disappointed to find that Josephine's beloved Malmaison was unfurnished, and the floors were rotting. At St. Cloud, where Jefferson and the Cosways frequently dined before the king commandeered the residence, Soane found that the "interior is full of cracks and settlements, so much as to offend the English eye."[24] Nonetheless, the shifting conditions of sites that both Jefferson and Soane visited may have appealed to their respective aesthetic sensibilities: Jefferson, interested in the development of new architectural projects in his nation, observed the construction processes at buildings such as the Hôtel de Salm and the Panthéon while Soane wandered through sublime ruins, catching glimpses of fragmented Mignard ceilings, gilding, and mirrors.

RETREATS AT HOME

Jefferson's 1786 English garden tour and Soane's 1819 trip to Paris were two rare occasions when the respective designers were able to indulge in concentrated periods of architectural and landscape tourism. Perhaps driven by the realization that they were unable to freely travel due to professional obligations or motivated by the awareness that many of their countrymen did not have the opportunity to travel, both Jefferson and Soane brought the world to visitors of their house museums. Objects, paintings, and architectural elements enlivened the buildings, transporting visitors to foreign sites and times through eclectic constructions. Although the house museums were intended to provoke the intellectual and aesthetic curiosities of visitors, they were also didactic manifestations of the respective architect's interests and travels.

As much as Jefferson's Monticello and Soane's Museum were intended to bring international experiences to their visitors, the homes were also designed to provide their owners with places for reflection. Retreats out-of-doors were crafted at both sites; however, Jefferson and Soane approached the design of their exterior "rooms" in opposite ways. At Monticello, where Jefferson's land stretched across five thousand acres, he created a Garden Pavilion on the kitchen terrace. This symmetrical construction was a naturalist's temple, a room within a dramatic landscape that had arched, triple sash windows on each of the four walls.[25] His plans for garden pavilions predated his European trip and had been part his earliest designs for the grounds of Monticello. In December 1771, he wrote a lengthy design proposal in his memorandum book: there would be "a small Gothic temple of antique appearance" to serve as a mausoleum for his beloved sister, Jane, and a number of follies to populate the mountaintop, ranging from a grotto to a bathhouse rendered in the style of "Chinese, Graecian, or in the taste of the Lantern of Demonsthenes at Athens."[26] His description, the longest single passage asserting his ideas for the landscape architecture of Monticello, reflected his reading of William Shenstone's "Unconnected Thoughts on Gardening" (1764) through his contrast of the "shapely and wild" and Whately's *Observations* through the use of the picturesque. However, after his English garden tour in 1786, Jefferson's attitudes on the landscape of Monticello shifted: he was critical of what Shenstone created at Leasowes, calling it "not even an ornamented farm," and although he noted the pleasing effects of the temples at Stowe, he made no comment on the Chinese pagoda at Kew or the stylistically varied temples at Wotton.

Jefferson's 1771 visions for the landscape of Monticello emulated the texts he read, but his built practice at the mountaintop reflected a more discerning approach to landscape architecture. This had been formed by his travels abroad as well as the desire to cultivate a productive landscape on the mountaintop: imagined garden follies were transformed into industrial structures for the enslaved community along Mulberry Row, such as the Weaver's Cottage and the nailery. Instead of placing a temple for retreat within a winding, forested site, he situated an open pavilion within his garden terrace that allowed him to view the peaks and valleys of his property while maintaining

Fig. 24. Courtyards at Soane's house museum, from left to right: New Court, Monument Court, and the Monk's Yard (Author's diagram)

close visual and physical proximity to the activities of the plantation. The idealistic folly became a neoclassical watchtower.[27]

Without the advantage of a sprawling, open landscape, Soane had to carve spaces for nature at his townhouse. As places to escape the chaotic interiors of the home, these exterior "rooms" were tightly bound by the built fabric of the amalgamated townhomes and allowed Soane to bring natural light into other rooms of the home. Although Soane blurred the interior *parti,* he created individualized courtyards that corresponded to each of his townhouses: no. 12's New Court, no. 13's Monument Court, and no. 14's Monk's Yard (fig. 24). Each courtyard displayed Soane's increasing experimentation and eclectic tastes. The first, New Court, was established during Soane's first manipulations at Lincoln's Inn Fields in the 1790s and was a simple form, designed as an open space separating the home on the south of the site and the office on the north. The second, the Monument Court, was created between 1812 and 1819 and displayed an amplified interest in spatial manipulation through its use of framed views between the interior and exterior as well as the insertion of architectural fragments, in the form of the *pasticcio*. The final courtyard, the Monk's Yard, was crafted around 1824 to receive an unexpected arrangement of medieval ruins and architectural styles that illustrated Soane's playful peculiarity: it was a retreat for Padre Giovanni (Father John) and a sacred resting place for the beloved family dog, Fanny. Plants were also part of each courtyard: there were cultivated elements such as the potted ferns in the New Court and Monument Court, but there were also serendipitous natural elements, such as the moss of the Monk's Yard, that added to the sublime atmosphere.

Some elements of Monticello and Soane's Museum were fanciful, but it would be incorrect to classify the exterior spaces as entirely serene and solitary sanctuaries. Select features of the exterior design of the homes were crafted to provide zones for retreat; nonetheless, some of the design decisions were driven by very utilitarian concerns. Joseph Ellis's *American Sphinx* asserts that Jefferson's home was designed to "make slavery almost invisible," yet Jefferson's plantation was propelled by an enslaved community of up to two hundred at any given time.[28] The sights, smells, and noises of Monticello would have been inescapable, forming a notable component of the sensory experience of any family member or visitor on the mountaintop plantation. The cacophony from the nailery as well as the carpenter and blacksmith shops on Mulberry Row would have resounded on the mountaintop. Although industrial production on Mulberry Row slowed during Jefferson's retirement, the atmosphere of the plantation would have been filled with the commotion of animals and enslaved laborers on the Row, in the terrace garden and orchard, and around the dependencies. The smells from the smokehouse, dairy, and kitchen would have permeated the Garden Pavilion, upper roundabouts, the main house, and flanking pavilions. Even the vast plane of south terrace, which provided Jefferson and his family with a stable walking platform and sweeping views of the valley below, was punctured with chimneys that vented the aromas of the home's famous Franco-Virginian cuisine, all produced by enslaved cooks. The Garden Pavilion was as much a retreat for Jefferson as it was a functional panopticon for monitoring the plantation's activities, melding shelter and surveillance.

The excavated dependencies at the home were not a means of literally burying views of the enslaved community within the landscape, as suggested by Ellis, but rather a reference to the working farms that Jefferson studied in Palladio's *Quattro Libri:* symmetrical wings were connected to the main home to visually unify the composition and conveniently provide shelter from the elements when transporting materials and food from one end of the farm's wings to the other. With extensive knowledge of surveying and landscape architecture, Jefferson took advantage of Monticello's sloped site to create dependencies that connected the services of the home in section with an experimental manipulation of views. From the terrace level of the home, the excavated dependencies provided uninterrupted vistas of the mountaintop's landscape, and beneath the ground was an equally captivating space. Jefferson owned a copy of Castell's *Villas of the Ancients* (1728) that contained a plan and elevation of the cryptoporticus of the Laurentine Villa, an appropriate precedent for Monticello in reference to Pliny the Younger's description of the site's impressive views, mulberry trees, and garden walk.[29] Although Jefferson never walked through a Roman cryptoporticus, he did have firsthand experience in the subterranean passage at Pope's Grotto. Monticello's "all-weather passage," therefore, reflected Jefferson's integration of scholarly studies and travels with his interests in efficiency. His design also fostered a distinctive experience: the passage provided protected access to key areas of the home, and the rusticated, slate-paved tunnel was illuminated by fourteen lunettes, complete with glazing and cast iron frames.[30] Both the enslaved and free residents of Monticello used the passage, and this unusual intersection of plantation hierarchy further dispels the notion that Jefferson's architecture tried to hide slavery at Monticello. The architecture was, on the other hand, completely indicative of Jefferson's preoccupations with organization and control for all within his designed landscape.

Certain elements within the landscape and architecture of Monticello did, however, operate as screens, such as the Dining Room's dumbwaiters and revolving service door. Once again, Pliny was a precedent since he described separations in circulation and view between servants and the served. Like Jefferson, Soane studied Pliny, and his earliest library inventory recorded his ownership of Orrey's *The letters of Pliny the Younger* (1752). Pliny's descriptions may have also influenced Soane's use of courtyards as screens between the picturesque intentions and utilitarian needs of the home.[31] From certain rooms of the home, such as the Breakfast Rooms of nos. 12 and 13 and his cabinet, the courtyards provided beneficial light and air, but the courtyards simultaneously functioned as essential spaces for the domestic operations of the home. The Pasticcio in the Monument Court and the Westminster arcade ruins in the Monk's Yard were intriguing historical artifacts that also acted as screens to shield direct views of pumps, coal boxes, the scullery, and the entrance to a servant's privy. Like Jefferson, these exterior manipulations were not employed as illusionistic measures to hide those who served the home; they were architectural devices used to enhance views and the functionality of the home's outdoor rooms.

TRANSPORTED LANDSCAPES

Without the ability to freely travel and satisfy their curiosities for foreign landscapes and architecture, Jefferson and Soane both created spaces in their house museums for outdoor retreat and contemplation that not only reflected elements from their travels but also responded to the immediate context of their house museums. Set within a working farm, Jefferson's Garden Pavilion was a predominantly transparent object in the landscape that offered a place of retreat but also served as a functional shelter to monitor the activities of a bustling plantation. Soane's courtyards were individualized, carved spaces that contained fictive, ruined landscapes, and served as privatized versions of the London square typology. As spaces for escape, these exterior "rooms" were elements within the architectural topography of the homes that blurred the boundaries between inside and outside, frivolity and function. These exterior rooms allowed the architects to remain near the daily activities of the home but also provided places for obsessive observation of domestic operations and precious, out-of-doors areas for cerebral wandering.

CHAPTER 8

Libraries

The general effect of these rooms is admirable; They combine the charac-
teristics of wealth and elegance, taste and comfort, with these especial
riches which belong expressly to literature and art.
— Barbara Hofland, 1835[1]

During the Enlightenment, silent study was no longer reserved for the clois-
tered as it was in the age of humanism, and the practice of solitary reading,
once prevalent in the ancient world, was revived.[2] The growing acceptance of
independent study and scholarship impacted design: purpose-built libraries
were constructed as new subscription societies, and libraries became more
common in private residences, especially for members of the Transatlantic
Design Network. Monticello and Soane's Museum were sites where the architects created dynamic spaces for their large collections of books. Jefferson is
arguably America's most famous bibliophile who acquired works for different
libraries during his lifetime, and multiple volumes have been written about
the vast scope of his libraries, overcoming frustrations from the limited book
collecting spheres of early America.[3] Soane's library also represented a significant scholarly legacy: the only entirely preserved library of a Georgian
architect. Soane's lifetime of collecting reflected his interests in not only
painting, sculpture, and architecture but also literature, music, and contemporary trends such as publications related to the spoils of Napoleon's conquests.[4] Overall, the libraries represented the variety of interests held by the

architects, lifelong dedication to self-education, and their desire to cultivate reference libraries for their fellow countrymen; the libraries at Monticello and Soane's Museum still function as active sites of research for scholars. Beyond the sheer volume of their collections, there was also a sentimental aspect to the libraries of Jefferson and Soane that was not replicated in the collections of their contemporaries: additional copies of certain texts were sought after or retained because of their connections to friends, mentors, and respected figures in history.

The design sensibilities of Jefferson and Soane were clearly informed by the act of reading. For example, the Tulip Poplar trunks, which supported the portico of the famous west facade of Monticello until 1822, were structural placeholders for stucco-covered brick columns, but they may have also been a Virginian homage to the primitive hut rendered on the frontispiece of Laugier's *Essai sur l'architecture,* and Soane explored this rustic form of classicism in his designs from 1783 for a diary at Hamels Park (fig. 25). Additionally, the physical and scholarly compositions of their libraries were highly reflective of Pliny the Younger's descriptions of the Laurentine Villa, embellished in Castell's text, as a place for retirement and study where "the walls are contrived a sort of cases, containing a collection of authors who can never be read too often."[5] An online table (see http://www.archdsw.com/tdn .html) that cross-references nearly three hundred titles from the architectural libraries of Jefferson and Soane makes it possible to understand how Jefferson's holdings were comparable to that of a professional architect who was cultivating an unparalleled center for the study of the arts and architectural experimentation.

THE COMPOSITION OF THE COLLECTIONS

Both gentlemen began collecting books at a young age despite their limited resources. At the age of twenty-eight, Soane started to actively collect architectural texts, building his professional library, but at the same age, Jefferson experienced the devastating loss of his first library due to the Shadwell fire. This tragedy helps explain Jefferson's lifelong obsession with fireproofing that led him to specify the insertion of a layer of bricks within the floors of

Fig. 25. An elevation from Soane's office illustrating a design for a dairy at Hamels Park (1783), with partially hewn tree trunks as columns and ivy overgrowth in the tympanum. (©Sir John Soane's Museum, London, SM 68/7; photo by Ardon Bar-Hama)

his designs, an unconventional practice in American residential construction. Soane, too, was interested in fireproofing, corresponding with Dance in 1796 about "incombustible floors" and designing incombustible vaults for the Bank of England.[6]

The two architects composed their first library catalogs around the same time: Jefferson's in 1783 and Soane's a year earlier. Although Jefferson's library holdings were fragmented into four distinct collections, his cataloging was substantially more complete than Soane's attempt to inventory his concentrated holdings. Soane's sons were especially unsuccessful in their charge to catalog the library at Lincoln's Inn Fields, and a comprehensive catalog of Soane's holdings was completed only recently.[7] Since Soane's library never moved to a different residence or repository, it is easy to imagine how the architect continued to amass books without being fully aware of his inventory.

Jefferson, on the other hand, frequently moved between sites, but as the obsessive memorandum maker, he kept quite a complete listing of his holdings.

Jefferson and Soane shared several practices related to the acquisition of books. They were both attracted to volumes previously owned by significant figures, and they went through certain periods of avaricious book collecting. The funds Soane's wife inherited gave Soane a flexible income to begin seriously assembling his library in the 1790s. Just a few years earlier, Jefferson was avidly buying books during his tenure abroad: he was enthralled with the selections of European bookstores, and during those five years he purchased more than two thousand volumes.[8] In a letter, Jefferson explained to Washington journalist Samuel H. Smith that during two of his summers abroad, he spent every "disengaged" moment scouring the book stores of Paris and later at the "principal book-marts, particularly [in] Amsterdam, Frankfort, Madrid and London."[9] While in London in the spring of 1786, he browsed the titles on sale at I. and J. Taylor's architectural library at 56 High Holborn, just a short distance northeast of Lincoln's Inn Fields. Here, and at neighboring booksellers, he acquired twenty-three works on architecture that were not yet available in America. By the early 1800s, the bibliophilic tendencies of Jefferson and Soane were well known within their respective circles; consequentially, the architects started receiving books from friends and catalogs from booksellers.

As architects who were inspired by ancient texts and publications of the Enlightenment, some of the intersections within their personal libraries are not surprising. With shared interests in archaeology, they both owned Desgodetz's *Les edificies antiques de Rome* (1779), Perrault's *Ordonnance des cinq especes de colonnes selon la methode des anciens* (1683), Potter's *Archaeologia Graeca* (1824), and Stuart and Revett's *The antiquities of Athens* (1762). They consulted aesthetic theory in Hogarth's *The analysis of beauty* (1753), and they also explored works outside of western architectural traditions through Chambers's *Designs of Chinese buildings* (1759) and Mitford's *Principles of Design in Architecture, Traced in Observations on Buildings Primeval, Gothic, Arabian, Chinese, and Modern English Domestic; in a Series of Letters* (1809). As architects who were actively engaged in the construction aspects of their projects, they both owned practical building books: Halfpenny's *Practical Architecture* (1724), the *Builder's Dictionary* (1734), and the works of Nicholson, *The carpenter and joiner's assistant* (1797) and *The carpenter's new guide* (1797). Both gentlemen also held a large collection of books related to landscape architecture and gardening. For example, Soane acquired Thomas Whately's *Observations on modern gardening* (1770) in 1784; two years later, Jefferson used this text as a guidebook while traveling through the English countryside. The works of architectural masters such as Alberti, Palladio, Serlio, Scamozzi, Vignola, and Vitruvius were predictable entries in any architect's catalog, but as scholars, Jefferson and Soane studied texts comparatively by consulting multiple editions and translations.

The breadth of Jefferson's collection in America, where it was more diffi-cult and expensive to obtain specialized publications outside of urban cen-ters such as Boston or Philadelphia, was impressive. For example, in 1804 Jefferson wrote to his carpenter at Monticello, James Oldham, that the na-tion's capital was devoid of a copy of Palladio until he brought his London edition, *The first book of architecture* (1700).[10] Although Jefferson had the largest architectural library in America, his collection paled in comparison to that of Soane: the professional architect owned a copy of every architec-tural and artistic book in Jefferson's collection, with the exception of the few titles printed exclusively in America.[11] Soane typically had multiple copies of key titles since his collections served as a reference library for his students.[12] However, Jefferson's library was more varied. The extent of his political and historical texts spoke to his career as statesman, and the editions on natural science captured his technical interests; those on botany and the mechanical arts informed his operations at his plantation.

Although Soane's collection was largely dominated by titles in the fine arts, he also possessed volumes on science and philosophy that Jefferson prized. For example, Soane had the works of Francis Bacon, Sir Isaac Newton, and John Locke, the three men Jefferson called "the three greatest men that have ever lived, without any exception."[13] In honor of their accomplishments, Jefferson charged Trumbull "[to] form them into a knot on the same can-vas."[14] For this trinity, Jefferson proposed that the men would be represented as life-sized busts; the project was not actualized, but if it had been, the com-position would have been a gigantic undertaking of approximately twenty-five square feet. Within Soane's natural history collection, he owned a text by a gentleman Jefferson did not hold in such esteem: George Louis Leclerc, comte de Buffon. In his *Histoire naturelle* (1785), the French naturalist argued that the humidity of the New World would foster weaker and inferior plants, animals, and even people.[15] This concept infuriated the scientific and nationalistic sensibilities of Jefferson to the point that the avid patriot sent Buffon the entire skeleton of an American moose to prove the vast diversity, and even superiority, of American species in relation to those of Europe.[16]

THE ARCHITECTURE OF THE LIBRARY

Even from a small sampling of books, Jefferson and Soane operated in the same intellectual circles and were consulting some of the same texts. They actively built scholarly repositories that rivaled, and even surpassed, the collections of booksellers, large institutions, and even universities in terms of not only the number of volumes they amassed but also the functional architecture of their personal libraries. The libraries at Monticello and Soane's Museum were not isolated rooms, furnished with plain shelves, but were, instead, part of the ever-evolving collections and spatial experiments of the house museums. Both Jefferson and Soane dedicated certain areas to their books, but their scholarly collections occupied shelves, mantles, tables, and spare places on the floor throughout the homes. The varied placement of books displays that the libraries were not exhibits, merely showcasing an investment, but were active collections used by the architects, other occupants of the home, and, with permission, visitors to the house museums. At Monticello, Jefferson's fascination with gadgetry even pervaded his library: a custom-designed revolving bookstand, made by enslaved carpenters on Mulberry Row sometime between 1780 and 1810, allowed Jefferson to view five books open at once.[17] For a scholar interested in several languages and wary of translations, this device would have been convenient to compare editions and reference dictionaries. satisfying his claim that he would never "read translations where I can read the original."[18]

Where bookshelves were used in the houses, they were not additive pieces of furniture but were, instead, integral to the architecture. Monticello's custom-fabricated bookshelves were book boxes, individually stacked for easy removal: with the attachment of a piece of wood, each book box became a traveling case that allowed the peripatetic Jefferson to take a portion of his collections with him. These book boxes were crafted in differing heights to accommodate the variety of volumes in his collection, ranging from pocket-sized texts to folios. Once stacked upon one another, the individual units fit perfectly within the architecture of the undulating walls of Monticello's library. Soane's bookshelves contained a similar dynamism: behind and embedded within the frames of the bookshelves, mirrors multiplied the parallel shelves and provided visitors with the illusion of an infinite extension to the Library. In the yellow Upper Drawing Room, the bookcases worked as piers to frame the hippodrome-shaped room. Here, knowledge literally fortified the architecture. Soane originally designed and built this portion of the home as a loggia that provided an elevated, exterior view of the common fields to the south, but he sacrificed this porch in 1834 to accommodate his growing library.

At both residences, the architects applied categorization systems to both the collections and the physical placement of books. For example, Soane kept select volumes in the ground floor Library to show to clients before taking them on a tour of the house museum. The museum's first curator, George Bailey, continued this practice when touring Jefferson's granddaughter in 1839, an excursion that is explored further in "Visitors." Jefferson's organization system at Monticello was much stricter, and his compulsion for cataloguing fueled a three-prong system of classification for the library: reason, memory, and imagination. These classifications applied to the subjects of history, philosophy, and the fine arts, respectively. Within these categories, Jefferson specified the further subdivision of topics, and he was consistent in these classifications from the initial 1783 catalog of books to the 1825 compilation of books he wanted for the University of Virginia's burgeoning library.

Like Soane, Jefferson granted certain people access to his collections but was very specific in the etiquette he expected in the library. He kept his collection locked when he was away from the plantation, but in a letter from 1806, he informed his grandson's tutor, Scottish immigrant and schoolmaster James Ogilvie (1775–1820), that the key could be obtained from his carpenter, an Irish immigrant named James Dinsmore whom Jefferson met in Philadelphia. The fact that Jefferson left his precious library keys with Dinsmore signified a change from the architect's attitude just a decade earlier.

In 1797, Jefferson wrote the comte de Volney, a longtime correspondent on travel and climate, that the builders at Monticello suspended their work in his absence because the plan was "too little like what they have seen to trust them with its execution."[19] In the early 1800s, with much of the house completed, Jefferson finally permitted construction in his absence, supervised by trusted carpenters Dinsmore and John Neilson as well as the enslaved joiner John Hemings. Dinsmore, if not the others, was probably granted access to the library to consult architectural books for the home's moldings and entablatures.[20]

Jefferson allowed Ogilvie to borrow texts with the condition that he leave a note listing the titles and "blot it out when returned. the object in this is that should I want a book at any time when at home [from the presidency], I may know where it is."[21] Jefferson also provided a descriptive map of the library's organization: "the arrangement begins behind the partition door leading out of the Book room into the Cabinet, & proceeds from left to right round the room; then entering the Cabinet it begins at the Eastern angle, & goes round that room." If Ogilvie had weak skills in spatial awareness, the directions would have been substantially disorienting, but Jefferson accounted for this, stating that any books pulled from the shelves need not be replaced but, instead, should simply be left on a table for Jefferson to reshelve properly.

Although Jefferson spent nearly a lifetime collecting his ideal library, he parted with much of the collection in 1815 when he sold 6,487 volumes to the Congress of the United States for $23,950 to replenish the government's scant collection lost during the War of 1812.[22] At the end of his life, Soane's library totaled 6,857 volumes, only a few hundred books more than the shipment Jefferson sent to Washington. So, the collections at Soane's Museum provide a useful visual reference for the sheer volume of titles owned by the respective architects.[23] In a letter to a journalist in Washington, Jefferson's description of his library could easily apply to Soane's own bibliomania: "I have been fifty years making it, and have spared no pains, opportunity or expense, to make it what it is."[24]

A substantial curiosity of the Library of Congress sale is that Jefferson included some of his most precious books in the shipment: forty-nine works on architecture. As a young man, he spoke of the difficulty of obtaining certain architectural books and praised the wealth and bargain of European bookstores. However, he parted with carefully acquired texts to broaden the collections of the nation, and, arguably, his collection of books on the fine arts was the most impacted by the sale. For example, when Jefferson was designing the University of Virginia, he was forced to look outside of his own library for even the most essential architectural references. His letter to Madison from November 15, 1817, noted they were "sadly at a loss here for a Palladio" and inquired if Madison's copy could be borrowed "for a year to come."[25]

A PERSPECTIVE ON MONTICELLO

Jefferson may have known of Soane's architectural work through Latrobe, who had apprenticed in London in the late eighteenth century, or through newspaper articles that described significant projects such as the Bank of England. Soane's knowledge of Jefferson's architecture through books is more difficult to trace since the statesman was not truly credited as an architect in published works until the early twentieth century. However, Jefferson was well known in England as the primary author of the Declaration of Independence and a politician. Soane even owned a copy of Cyrus R. Edmond's *The Life and Times of General Washington* (1835) that contained a facsimile of a draft of the Declaration, and Soane's library also contained copy of the *Catalog of the Library Company of Philadelphia* (1835) that listed a few holdings about Jefferson, such as his American Philosophical Papers. The source that would have provided the most complete description of Jefferson and, more importantly, his work at Monticello was a Frenchman's published travel journal.

François-Jean de Beauvoir, Marquis de Chastellux, came to the United States in 1780 to serve as major-general in the Colonial Army with the French troops under the command of the comte de Rochambeau. During his three-year tenure abroad, he traveled and wrote a narrative on life in the newly formed nation. His journal was originally published anonymously as *Voyage de Newport à Philadelphie, Albany, & c.* (1781), and the first enlarged and authorized versions of the text was renamed *Voyages de M. le Marquis de Chastellux dans l'Amérique septentrionale, dans les années 1780, 1781 et 1782* (1786) (fig. 26). Soane purchased a copy of this two-volume edition, printed

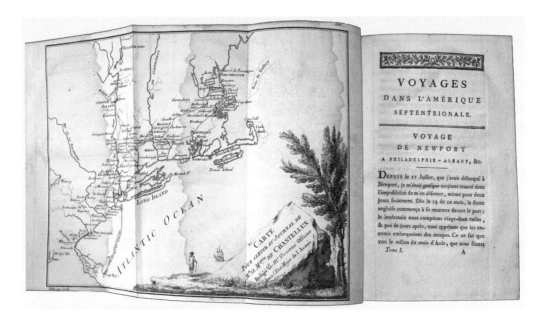

Fig. 26. The map of Chastellux's travels in Soane's copy of *Voyages dans l'Amérique Setentrionale dans les annés 1780, 1781 & 1782* (1786). (Author's photo, courtesy of Sir John Soane's Museum)

in Paris, on May 19, 1802, from John Cumming. The possession of the book in Soane's library does not necessarily mean he read the text, especially considering Soane kept nearly every book, pamphlet, and piece of paper he encountered.[26] Nonetheless, the placement of a bookplate and a pencil inscription on the front free endpaper denote some use. Other clues demonstrate that Soane, or one of his students, examined the text: there is water damage on one of the maps, showing that the page may have been open for a period, and the silk bookmark has uneven folds and fading patterns that indicate it was moved to different pages, then stored, several times. The maps within the second volume, the book that contains Chastellux's account of his visit to Monticello, have irregular creases, and this indicates that they were opened and refolded multiple times, whether by Soane, a student, or later readers.

Had Soane read Chastellux, he would have discovered the earliest internationally printed descriptions of Monticello and Jefferson as its architect. After spending seven days at Monticello and discussing Jefferson's plans for the home, Chastellux concluded that the planned revisions would give Monticello ranking among "the most pleasant mansions in France and England." During Chastellux's visit, the home was very much a work in progress:

[Monticello] of which Mr. Jefferson was the architect, and often the builder, is constructed in an Italian style, and is quite tasteful, although not however without some faults; it consists of a large square pavilion, into which one enters through two porticoes ornamented with columns. The ground floor consists chiefly of a large and lofty salon, or drawing room, which is to be decorated entirely in the antique style; above the salon is a library of the same form. . . . It resembles none of the others seen in this country; so that it may be said that Mr. Jefferson is the first American who has consulted the Fine Arts to know how he should shelter himself from the weather.[27]

Chastellux also revealed that in Monticello's initial configuration, the library was on the second floor; in the 1790s, Jefferson changed this arrangement, moving his entire apartment to the ground floor. Chastellux stated that the design of Monticello was superior to all other houses in America, so if Soane read the commentary, he may have found the self-trained architect and bibliophile across the Atlantic quite intriguing.

CHAPTER 9

Cabinets

These rooms are the smallest in this mansion, but they are not the less worthy of attention: on the contrary, as Nature frequently renders the smallest flowers, and the smallest animals the most beautiful, and appears to finish the most minute productions in the most elaborate manner.

—Barbara Hofland, 1835[1]

As projects, the house museums of Jefferson and Soane afforded opportunities to question and test architectural ideas. For both men, it seemed that design was continually at the forefront of their minds, and in his famous "head and heart" letter to Cosway, Jefferson revealed his heart's annoyance that the head was "eternally getting us to sleep with your diagrams."[2] Monticello and Soane's Museum evolved through a series of drafts, first executed in the quickly drawn sketches and marginal notes and then, more boldly, in three dimensions, treating their house museums like full-scale models that could be constructed, edited, deconstructed, and rebuilt.

Most experimental were the working spaces: these multiroom zones within the homes were dedicated to the personal explorations of the architects, bridging the residential and educational programs. These were also the areas where Jefferson and Soane crafted much of their correspondence that traveled within the Transatlantic Design Network. Over several decades of development, the form of the cabinets changed to address the needs and interests of the occupant, especially their shared desires to acquire knowledge through solitary study and maintain their correspondence. Designs executed early in their respective architectural and professional careers were substantially altered to become well-developed studies that provided comfort, quietude, and natural light. The location of their cabinets also shifted, transitioning from detached rooms to faceted spaces, intimately placed within the cores of the house museums. This afforded the architects with the opportunity to be near the operations of the home while being able to work in a semi-secluded area with premium views to the exterior, such as the terraces and gardens of Monticello and the Monument Court and Monk's Yard of Soane's Museum.

MOVING HOME AND ARCHITECTURAL INTERRUPTIONS: MONTICELLO

Jefferson and Soane worked on their respective residences for over forty years, but the process of development at these two sites was very different. Except for Soane's inhabitation of Pitzhanger Manor, his primary residence was his townhouse on the north side of Lincoln's Inn Fields. Although his office moved locations several times, Soane perpetually inhabited his experimental house museum from 1792 until his death, only taking excursions in and around London and two brief trips to Paris. Jefferson, however, seemed to be in a constant state of transit from the foundation of the nation in 1776 until his eventual retirement in 1809. Jefferson's travels and inhabitation of no fewer than eighteen residences informed his opinions on domestic architecture and the desire to craft spaces dedicated to the personal interests and ambitions of the occupant.[3] Jefferson was constantly observing and redesigning his environments: extant architectural drawings reveal that he surveyed and proposed revisions to at least half of his residences, not including Monticello and Poplar Forest, where he was the primary architect.[4]

Besides his native Charlottesville, Jefferson called several other sites home, and this extensive list covers the localities where Jefferson resided for various durations, ranging several months up to a few years. By occupying different types of residences, such as plantations, townhouses, and shared rooms that were constructed in diverse styles, Jefferson experienced assorted climatic conditions in Europe, the mid-Atlantic, and the Eastern Seaboard.

Although many scholars attribute Jefferson's architectural training purely to his bibliophilia and brief time abroad, little attention has been given to Jefferson's inhabitation of so many residences that experientially informed his architectural education.

As a young Virginian, Jefferson's explorations of the colony, and later commonwealth, began when he left his birthplace of Shadwell to live with relatives at the James River plantation of Tuckahoe outside of Richmond. He then attended university in the colonial capital of Williamsburg and later returned to this city that he said was filled with "rude, mis-shapen piles, which, but that they have roofs, would be taken for brick kilns" when he served as governor.[5] Perhaps it was Jefferson's architectural aversion to Williamsburg that led him to move the commonwealth's capital to Richmond in 1780. During his tenure as minister to France, he had long-term rentals at three different Parisian townhouses, spending three months, a year, and nearly two years at the respective residences. His return to the United States came with the immediate appointment of secretary of state, leading Jefferson to the nation's then capital in New York City and later to the relocated center of government in Philadelphia. After a brief interlude at Monticello, Jefferson spent the final eight years of his political career in the new President's House of Washington before finally retiring at his mountaintop home.

Jefferson began his drawn studies at Monticello in 1767 with loose, unlabeled sketches. These drawings were created a year before he started leveling the mountaintop for construction, but by 1768 he started to add labels for individual rooms at the plantation. From the onset, Jefferson developed a series of utilitarian south-facing rooms to accompany his modest one-room, two-story pavilion. But at one point, he posited a long and narrow two-story structure that blended domestic and utilitarian working spaces: stables, a fattening room, and the chariot room were to be built into the slope of the mountain while a central, covered staircase led to an upper story that housed six rooms and a loggia. This plan also illustrated his interest in developing rooms for his own study, including a laboratory, office, and *solitudini votum* next to a shop, lumber room, and his bedchamber.

The term *solitudini* was used in both the texts of Pliny the Younger and Palladio to describe a place of solitude for quiet study, like a *studiolo,* and the term *votum* refers to a temple offering. Although the precedent for Jefferson's phrase is unknown, the drawn symbol in the room resembles a latrine, so the Latin phrase may have been a bit of excremental humor. In a later plan, the label for the *solitudini votum* in the south wing of the home was replaced with p, possibly an abbreviation for privy, considering there appear to be two latrines in the space.[6] On the north side of the home's dependencies, a room labeled "solitude" contains a latrine symbol as well. These labels illustrate that Jefferson was considering issues of sanitation and privacy before his trip to Europe, and this was a significant departure from the standards in colonial Virginia that consisted of chamber pots and outhouses. The divided privies may also denote a hierarchical separation at the mountaintop: the pair of privies on the south side, adjacent to the spaces dedicated to cooking and the laundry may have been intended for enslaved workers, and the solitary privy in the northern dependency may have been for the family, visitors, or the paid workers residing in the adjacent octagonal "servants" room.

By March 1771, Jefferson was working on a different configuration for Monticello and had turned his attentions from occupying the small southern pavilion toward crafting a larger, symmetrical residence. The U-shaped plans of the Wren Building and Governor's Palace in Williamsburg, as well as his courtship with Martha Wayles Skelton, a widow with a young son, influenced his plans for expanding the mountaintop home. However, John died of fever six months before Jefferson and Martha married. The pair moved into the South Pavilion and the construction site of Monticello that Martha would call home for the rest of her brief life.

By the early 1770s, Jefferson was evolving as a self-trained architect and moving toward more consistent and sophisticated forms of architectural representation where window apertures were depicted as true-to-scale openings and all walls were given thickness and poché. In earlier plan drawings for Monticello and other structures, he commonly used messy, architectural shorthand: windows were shown as thumbnail elevations and walls were represented with single lines.[7] The complexity of his designs was changing as well. The 1772 plan for the U-shaped, semi-subterranean dependencies of Monticello contained twenty-nine rooms, some of which were octagonal, three sets of staircases, and a shelf-like system for collecting water that would also provide natural light to the buried rooms of the plantation.[8] The stables were vastly expanded, as were the utilitarian rooms of the plantation, now divided into specific functions such as a smokehouse, two dairies, laundry, kitchen, "servant" rooms, wine room, rum cellar, wareroom, beer cellar, and various other store rooms. Jefferson's specialized "office and laboratory" for study, however, disappeared from the plan.

Although Jefferson's only time abroad was busily occupied by his political appointment and active cultural tourism, his drawn record illustrates his continual interest in reconfiguring his personal environment. During his time in Paris, Jefferson stayed in three different rented accommodations: the Hôtel d'Orléans on the Left Bank on the Rue des Petits-Augustins, Hôtel Landron in the Cul-de-sac Taitbout, and the Hôtel de Langeac at the corner of the Rue de Berri and the Champs-Elysées.[9] At his last residence, unfortunately demolished in 1842, Jefferson surveyed the home and its adjacent park before remodeling portions of the ground floor and adding bull's-eye windows between rooms on the upper story. This was, perhaps, because he intended to return to this quirky residence with its elliptical entrance hall, chamfered walls, and skylights once he fulfilled the diplomatic obligations that necessitated his return to the United States in the fall of 1789. However, following his return to politics on the other side of the Atlantic, he arranged for eighty-six crates of his European purchases to be shipped to Philadelphia, and within these collections was an acquisition that would greatly influence his later architectural investigations: one-sided graph paper from Paris.

While serving within the nation's first cabinet, Jefferson made time to pursue his architectural interests by proposing changes to his townhome in New York City. When a new, permanent capital was proposed for Washington, the government moved to Philadelphia from 1790 to 1800 to provide easier access to the developing city. Familiar with the Pennsylvanian city from time spent during the American Revolution, Jefferson continued his residential explorations by creating several plans for his temporary accommodations. He even documented his rented house along the Schuylkill River, near Gray's Ferry and the botanical wonderland of fellow scientist Bartram. Jefferson resided there for a few months in the summer of 1793 to escape the confines of his urban residence, 247 High Street, where a heat wave and yellow fever were plaguing the city.[10] Jefferson drafted an unannotated plan of this small residence in pen and then added a sketch in pencil of a hemispherical addition, akin to the spaces found at the Hôtel de Langeac. Instead of immediately returning to the city, Jefferson took up residence in Germantown for a few months before moving into a series of rented accommodations and hotels along the city's *decumanus maxiumus,* Market Street. Here Jefferson continued his explorations of alternative configurations for several of Philadelphia's signature long and narrow row houses, an urban typology like those of London but lacking the irregular party lines that Soane was wrestling with at his townhouse.

In the spring of 1794, when Soane was newly entrenched in the redesign of no. 12 Lincoln's Inn Fields, Jefferson was finally able to focus his architectural attentions on his mountaintop. His December 31 resignation as secretary of state allowed him to return to Monticello for the first period in nearly ten years. With plans for substantial renovations that were strongly informed by time spent abroad and in two of America's largest urban centers, the building program at Monticello was once again booming by 1796. Jefferson's withdrawal from politics, however, was brief. In 1797 he was elected the nation's second vice president, and he returned to public service for another twelve years, deferring his retirement until 1809.

Jefferson's plans for remodeling Monticello illustrated his desire to craft a retreat for convenience and personal study, consisting of a more conscientious separation between the service and family spaces of the home and his own working space. His drawings from 1796 show that the southern wing, initially part of his designated working area, was reprogrammed for entirely utilitarian functions. These rooms were now the dependencies, filled with both the services and sleeping rooms for the enslaved obligated to manage dining at the plantation.[11] Jefferson's dedicated rooms were relocated to the central block of his U-shaped plan, now featuring compound shapes and connective passages.[12] Although his structural plan of the ground floor from 1796 does not have room labels, the drawing delineates, with little variation, the configuration that Jefferson would ultimately settle upon for his interconnected working spaces: library, cabinet, bedchamber, privy, closet, and greenhouse (fig. 27). Transitioning from his simplified plans for rectilinear rooms along a shared corridor, Jefferson crafted a more complex arrangement of rooms for study and solitude; in plan and section, Jefferson's dedicated spaces were the most experimental at the home.

Fig. 27. A sectional perspective of Jefferson's side of the home, overlaid on Jefferson's structural plan of Monticello (1796). (Author's diagram)

Ultimately, Jefferson's personal retreat and study at Monticello were crafted as a series of spaces that unfolded, employing complex geometries and unexpected connections between interior and exterior. This configuration was very different than the rest of the home that used enfilades and carefully coordinated axes, such as the cryptoporticus, the north and south terraces, or the processional axis running through the East Front, Entrance Hall, and Parlor before terminating on the West Lawn. With these discrepancies in mind, Jefferson's working spaces were more like the modus operandi of his landscape design than his established architectural style. Jefferson's cabinet was filled with educational objects and instruments for experimentation that were naturally illuminated: the architect reserved the rooms at the home with the best solar orientation for himself. Besides the ample light from windows, a skylight, and mirrored reflections, these spaces served as

atmospheres for discovery that enlivened the senses: the fragrance of seasonal flowers and citruses in the greenhouse permeated his cabinet, and the
chimes of clocks and calls of Jefferson's mockingbird echoed through the
interconnected spaces. Because of the refined configuration of his cabinet,
when Jefferson was "drudging at the writing table," he was surrounded by a
rich architectural space that still allowed him to experience the sights, aromas, and stippled light found in the gardens and on the roundabouts of his
plantation.[13]

MOVING HOME AND ARCHITECTURAL INTERRUPTIONS: SOANE'S MUSEUM

At Soane's residence on the north side of Lincoln's Inn Fields, plans, sections,
and perspective views chronicle over thirty years of the evolution of spaces
dedicated to working and studying. Soane's drawings for the residence also
revealed an interesting discrepancy in both secondary source material and
the interpretation of the museum. The townhouse at no. 13 Lincoln's Inn
Fields is described, in detail, as a house museum, but publications to date
have largely glossed over the fact that Soane's house museum also served as
his primary architectural office from 1794 to 1801 and from 1810 until his
death in 1837. Although today's visitors to Soane's Museum are presented
with abbreviated references to the office, the house museum would have been
filled with students sketching, drafting, and modeling. Additionally, the door
on the northern wall of the museum, the key point of access for the students,
has been blocked.

The office of Soane's townhouse had three major components: entry and
circulation space for clients, workspace for students, and workspace for
Soane. The first architectural office was isolated from the domestic spaces
of the house, but by the 1820s the office was completely interconnected
with the house museum. Drawings also reveal a second spatial transition:
Soane went from occupying an office space with the students to developing
his own, isolated working area that gave him visual and auditory command
of both domestic and professional operations. Today's visitors can walk
through Soane's private cabinet configuration, consisting of Soane's Study

and Dressing Room, that serves as a physical bridge between the programs of home, museum, and office.

As an energetic bachelor, fresh from his travels to Italy, Soane began his first architectural office in early 1781. He built an independent architectural practice while renting rooms at 53 Margaret Street, just east of Cavendish Square Gardens. Soane occupied the first floor and upper front room of the residence with his wife Eliza and their two young sons, one of whom did not survive infancy. The home was also shared with John Sanders, Soane's first student, who began work at the office in September 1784 to assist with the increasing number of residential renovation commissions. Between the office and growing family, the quarters must have been cramped: Sanders received room and board instead of wages. If Soane made any alterations to the space at Margaret Street during his three years of occupation, the details and layouts have been lost, but it is more likely that the Margaret Street office and residence was occupied in an as-built condition since Soane did not yet have an expendable income to support substantial changes, and alterations may have been prohibited by the terms of his lease.[14]

In 1787, Soane moved his home and office just a few blocks west to 77 Welbeck Street, where he was able to purchase the leasehold. If Soane wanted to make changes to the property, he was now legally able to do so, but the configuration of this residence was also untouched because Soane was commuting between two offices. Upon his appointment as architect of the Bank of England on October 16, 1788, he was given an office at the bank that was a shared with the other clerks of works. This was not a space where Soane could explore other architectural commissions or sponsor students, so he maintained his home office for independent practice. This partitioned working environment changed when Soane's wife inherited a sum from her uncle in 1790 that was so substantial Soane could have retired from practice.[15] Instead of abandoning his profession for a life of leisure, he used this newly inherited wealth to elevate his practice and fund his bibliomania as well as a lifetime of collecting casts, antiquities, and drawings. In early 1790, he also established an architectural office on part of the family's newly inherited property at Albion Place, Blackfriars. This marked the first time that Soane's personal office was divorced from his residence.

Soane purchased no. 12 Lincoln's Inn Fields from Mrs. Barnard on June 30, 1792, for £2,100 and immediately began redesigning the layout of the townhouse.[16] A series of fourteen preserved drawings trace Soane's early intentions for the office space at the home, and a flurry of design work from July through October of 1792 focused on streamlining the layout and functionality of the ground floor plan.[17] While redesigning the home, he relocated his office to Great Scotland Yard, where he practiced until his new, purpose-built office at Lincoln's Inn Fields was ready. The largest challenge presented to Soane in this endeavor was the fact that the home at no.12 Lincoln's Inn Fields had oddly shaped party walls, resulting from the medieval plot lines that once defined the site. The east edge of the site was drastically skewed, creating a very narrow northern facade. Additionally, the northern edge of the site that bordered Whetstone Park, the lane that still runs between the parallel streets of High Holborn to the north and Lincoln's Inn Fields to the south, was also angled. With few right angles or elements of symmetry, Soane needed to apply an inventive approach to the irregularities of the site as well as keen attention to the sectional character, circulation patterns, and decoration of the office space.

Early in Soane's conception for the designs of no. 12, the house and the office had separate entrances: the office was accessible from the north, along the utilitarian Whetstone Park, and the residence's entrance faced the more enticing, enclosed fields. Soane's plans reveal proposals to connect the residence and office at two different levels (fig. 28). At the mezzanine level, a narrow corridor ran along the eastern edge of the party wall, labeled "Passage" and "Lobby," linking the upper story of the office with the residence. This proposal for a narrow, elevated office was illustrated in multiple drawings, and sketches demonstrate three critical points in Soane's early spatial arrangements for the office. Firstly, the office was conceived as an exploratory space in section. The office's floor was below that of the Parlor, creating some level of variation within the home's floor plan and physically signifying a shift between the residential and professional zones. Additionally, Soane's sketches illustrate his interest in manipulating the home's roofline to illuminate the north-facing office. A clerestory window and a skylight were proposed for the office since ground-level windows facing Whetstone Park would

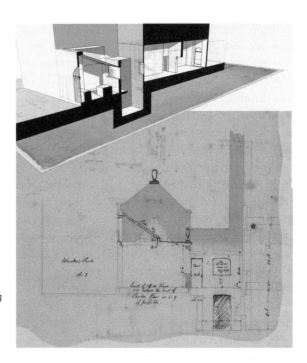

Fig. 28. Speculative model depicting Soane's scheme for no. 12, from August 1792. (Author's diagram with Sir John Soane's Museum 32/2A/12v)

have conveyed unwanted dust and noise. Secondly, the office was a hierarchical space: the mezzanine may have been intended for Soane's use since it was directly connected to the private upper story of the home and provided a supervisory position, physically above the students. Thirdly, Soane conceived the office in a highly practical manner, considering the residence and office space were joined by a combined water closet and dressing room that faced a courtyard, carved within the narrow confines of the site. This connective joint occupied approximately one-fourth of the ground floor plan: Soane willingly sacrificed space in the residence and office to separate the two functions and bring more natural light into the structure. Following a summer of the concentrated design work, he moved the practice to the north side of the townhouse, and a year and a half later his residential renovations were complete. By January 18, 1794, once again Soane's home and architectural office were reunited.[18]

Since the early 1800s, both Monticello and Soane's Museum have served as inspirational structures for aspiring and practicing architects. Like Soane, Jefferson offered young students of architecture the opportunity to visit and study his house museum and its collections. In 1803, Robert Mills (1781–1855), the first American-born professional architect, visited the home.[19] It is likely that Jefferson met Mills in 1801 or 1802 in Washington while Jefferson was serving as president and the Charlestonian transplant was working for Hoban at the President's House.[20] Through Jefferson, Mills obtained an apprenticeship with Latrobe between 1803 and 1808, and Jefferson invited the young designer to Monticello to see the house under construction and consult the architectural library.[21]

Sometime after the visit, Mills created two drawings of Monticello: a rendered elevation and a composition that reenvisioned Jefferson's Monticello as a Francophile villa (fig. 29). Although Monticello was still very much in progress during Mills's visit, neither of his drawings illustrated the home as the active construction site that was described by the wife of doctor-architect Thornton and Washingtonian socialite, Anna Marie Brodeau, in September 1802:

The house is of brick but in an unfinished state, tho' commenced 27 years ago; the ground plan is a good one, & the elevation may look very well if ever completed, but Mr. Jefferson has so frequently changed his plan, & pulled down & rebuilt so often that it has generally more the appearance of a house going into decay from the length of time it has been erected, than an unfinished building . . . . The whole is in a state of rude nature. There is something rather grand & aweful, than agreeable or convenient in the whole place, a situation you would rather look at now & then than inhabit.[22]

Presenting a finished home, Mills's rendered elevation is a well-known drawing within his oeuvre; however, his reimagined scheme for Monticello has received little consideration. This drawing, composed of a ground floor plan and corresponding elevation of the western facade, presents a building in the style of Ledoux rather than the Jeffersonian experiment that melded

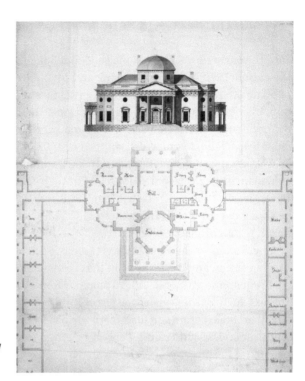

Fig. 29. Monticello, as reinvented by Robert Mills, ca. 1803. (Massachusetts Historical Society N155)

elements of Virginia's vernacular architecture with an English country house and a French townhouse. Looking beyond the irregularities of Mills's reimagined plan, his depiction of the ground floor may reflect conditions that he observed while visiting Monticello. In the drawing, Jefferson's dedicated working space, labeled as the "Library," occupies approximately one-quarter of the ground floor plan, and this was, perhaps, a reflection of Jefferson's growing collections that were already spilling into other rooms of the house. In Mills's design, the only bedroom that occupies the ground floor is Jefferson's since the guest rooms on the northeastern side of the home were reassigned as a "Tea-room" and "Parlour." This arrangement bisected the plan, with Jefferson's private rooms and working spaces occupying the entire southern side of the home, and the public rooms to the north of the central east-west axis. If Mills's drawing reflected what he saw at Monticello, the re-configuration of the ground floor illustrates a home where the architect and his extensive working spaces had the largest dedicated square footage and the best natural light.

While Mills was exploring Monticello and Jefferson was serving two terms as president, Soane was turning his attentions away from Lincoln's Inn Fields and toward two other endeavors. His work as architect to the Bank of England had increased, and he had recently purchased Pitzhanger Manor. Conse-quentially, the layout of home and office at no. 12 remained largely unchanged from the turn of the century until 1808; this was to be the longest period when the townhouse's configuration was untouched during Soane's lifetime. In the early 1800s, Pitzhanger captured his personal design attentions since the site was a new laboratory for his architectural aspirations. Instead of using the same techniques employed in his early manipulations of his townhouse, where the office and residence were only barely connected and had separate entrances, the watercolors by Soane's student C. J. Richardson illustrate that Pitzhanger integrated the family and working areas. In Richardson's sketch, Mrs. Soane is shown in silhouette, writing in front of a window, and in his later watercolor, a table cluttered with architectural drawings and notebooks occupies the central area of the library.[23] At Pitzhanger, the assimilation of areas for living, studying, and designing significantly shaped Soane's later work at the townhouses, but the country residence did not achieve its ulti-mate ambition of cultivating a Soanean architectural dynasty.[24]

Moving his hopes toward the establishment of a public architectural leg-acy, inspiration struck Soane in summer of 1808, and he began envisioning a different life for the newly purchased no. 13 Lincoln's Inn Fields. He drew a series of plans and had his students work on several perspective views that were mainly concerned with expanding the office on the northern side of no. 12 and establishing a museum area at the back of no. 13. Soane moved the location of the office door along Whetstone Park further to the east to correspond with the new location of the enlarged office, and this explains many of the scars on the home's northern wall, details that typically escape visitors to Soane's Museum (fig. 30). The old office, located on the northern side of no. 12, was turned into a library. Here Soane was beginning to develop his individual working space, a *studiolo;* the library was for his use, and al-

Fig. 30. The north facade of Soane's Museum, along Whetstone Park. (Author's photo)

though it was set apart from the students, it was connected to their portion of the office through a small, top-lit vestibule that also provided access to a storage closet to the north and the passage to his L-shaped Dressing Room to the south (fig. 31).

In 1810, Soane's plans for Lincoln's Inn Fields took a bold turn. A watercolor of the Museum Dome, executed by then student George Bailey, was one of the first drawings of the house museum that illustrated a visual cacophony of casts, artifacts, and ruins within a dynamic triple-height space (fig. 32). The watercolor has been published numerous times; however, little attention has been given to the small plan in bottom right corner of the drawing. Unlike the actual site, the plan is highly rectilinear and imagines perfectly square corners and a straight party wall between nos. 12 and 13. The labels on the plan denote Soane's intended use of the spaces: the family retained no. 12 as a residence, no. 13 was entirely taken over by a "gallery," and the office disappeared from the site. The newly designed rooms and collections at no. 13 would be a public architectural academy in an urban context that could rival

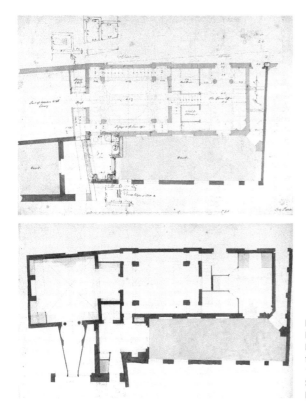

Fig. 31. A comparison of the 12/13 LIF Ground Floor Plan of Rear buildings as proposed by Soane from July 4, 1808, and August 18, 1808. (©Sir John Soane's Museum SM 3/2/41 and SM 32/3/51; photos by Ardon Bar-Hama)

the collections of the Royal Academy, the British Museum, and other house museums. Shortly after its proposal, Soane dismissed his plans for the Lincoln's Inn Fields Academy, and this may be related to his sale of Pitzhanger in 1810. After moving both the family and the contents of the country residence back into the city, he may have discovered that inhabitation of no. 12, alone, could no longer accommodate the family's needs. As rendered in Bailey's plan, the symmetrical and rectilinear arrangement of Soane's proposed academy pales in comparison to the spatial complexity found at the site today, so it is of some relief that Soane abandoned his ambitions for the academy in favor of the unexpected angles, chamfered walls, and honeycomb spaces that responded to the existing irregularities of the site.

Fig. 32. No. 13 LIF View of Various Architectural Subjects belonging to John Soane Esq. R.A. as arranged in May MDCCCX (1810) by George Bailey. (Sir John Soane's Museum 14/6/3)

REFINING THE CABINET

Soane's private working spaces for no. 13 were not delineated in plan until the summer of 1812 when the reorganization and rebuilding of nos. 12 and 13 were well underway. In January 1812, Soane persuaded no. 13's longtime tenant, George Tyndale, to move into no. 12 so he could fully renovate the property. By the summer of 1812, he was steadily focused on designing an interconnected house, museum, and office. Working though the challenge of designing circulation between these spaces, Soane retained the office's separate entrance on Whetstone Park and divided the office space, elevating the students' room above the main museum corridor and adding a new, lower office on the east. Soane then envisioned a luxurious Dressing Room on the west side of the Monument Court, the location of the current no. 13 Breakfast Room, and east of the Monument Court he labeled a long, thin corridor as his "cabinet."

By 1822, the cabinet amalgamated Soane's Study and Dressing Room. For Soane, this private working area formed a path between the domestic and professional sides of the home, and it served as an intimately designed space for study. As a long, thin space suspended between the Monument Court to the west and the Monk's Yard to the east, Soane's cabinet is an example of an occupiable poché within the home where the definition of a wall and a room were blurred. Within his cabinet, Soane surrounded himself with a drastically different working atmosphere than what he provided for his students in the Upper Office: the walls of Soane's cabinet were adorned with rich paint colors, faux finishes, and three large windows with colored glass and louvers to provide views of the courtyards. The students, on the other hand, were fully surrounded by paneled walls, casts, and artifacts that were largely monochromatic, and they worked tirelessly for twelve hours a day, six days a week beneath two long, parallel skylights of clear glass.

Soane, like the students, was surrounded by inspirational elements. In his Study, Roman casts adorned the walls; in the Dressing Room, Soane's own designs furnished the architectural environment: shelves held small models of his projects, such as the facade of no. 13, framed plans and elevations of his projects were mounted to the walls, and the skylight in the room was capped with a model, rendered in stained glass, of his design for the dome of the nearby Freemason's Hall. In his cabinet, classicism met Soanean style. He was also surrounded with technological comforts that were not afforded to the students' Upper Office: his cabinet had a water pump for the washing basin, one of six in the house, a water closet, and artificial illumination from an Argand lamp.[25]

The movement away from an architectural office where Soane and the students worked together but were disconnected from the domestic spaces of the home to a configuration where Soane's cabinet served as a bridge between the residence and office illustrates Soane's changing attitudes toward the use of his townhouse. When needed, Soane could use large portions of the home as an advertisement of his knowledge of the arts and command of design. He could also isolate himself within his cabinet, a space surrounded by objects, drawings, and gadgetry that could spark his imagination. Like Soane's Museum, Monticello's entire site often served as a spectacle for students, guests, and even uninvited visitors to explore Jefferson's accomplishments, collections, and architectural innovations. Jefferson's cabinet, too, was a microcosm, providing the architect with a space that was conducive to private study and was filled with his most treasured books, gadgets, and accoutrements.

Jefferson, Soane, and their curious homes were known attractions, and although Jefferson lived in a relatively rural part of Virginia, he had to take greater measures than Soane to escape the bustle of his house museum. Soane could simply close his cabinet's doors and retreat to a space with books, areas to write, natural and artificial light, heat, water, and even a privy. Jefferson, too, had these conveniences in his cabinet and even employed various devices for sound dampening throughout the home to reduce noise and distraction, ranging from the insertion of soft surfaces to reduce resonance, such as oilcloths, carpets, and drapes as well as the use of nogging in between the wythes of the brick walls and between the joists. This principle was similar to the "deafening" strategies that were later encouraged in the Architectural Publication Society's 1889 dictionary. Nonetheless, for peaceable retreat from visitors, some so brazen that they broke windows at the home to obtain better views of the former president, Jefferson had to travel to his other residence.[26] In the summer of 1811, Jefferson wrote Philadelphia doctor Benjamin Rush that only at Poplar Forest could he enjoy "the solitude of a hermit" to attend to his letters and "absent friends."[27]

CHAPTER 10

Laboratories

Architecture is not only a science but an art, that is capable of producing simple, beautiful, and sublime scenes.
—John Britton and Augustus Pugin, 1825[1]

In the eighteenth century, scientific organizations such as American Philosophical Society, Lunar Society, and Royal Society fueled the international circulation of theories and investigations within natural history and medicine. Experiments within architecture, however, were largely left out of the discussion, even though certain designers of the era were members of such organizations and using their constructions as exercises in applied science. The scientific community is, generally, dismissive of the concept that architecture could be an act of applied science prior to early twentieth-century modernism, assisted by mechanization, mass production, and health reform between the two world wars. However, with shared interests in optics and mechanical operations, Jefferson and Soane both treated their homes as architectural hypotheses: refining variables as needed to achieve spaces that were functional, adaptable, and interesting.

THE SCIENCE OF ARCHITECTURE

Select architects were part of formal scientific organizations, such as the Royal Society but, oddly, membership in the society was not among the many commonalities between Jefferson and Soane.[2] Although Jefferson was never elected a member, several of his fellow Americans were elevated to the society, such as Franklin (elected 1756) and Francis Fauquier (1703–1768; elected 1753), the governor of colonial Virginia from 1758 to 1768 and one of Jefferson's collegiate mentors. A few Americans were elected after the Revolution, such as astronomer David Rittenhouse (1732–1796; elected 1795), but there was a severe decrease in transatlantic members following the American Revolution, which may explain Jefferson's exclusion. Other notable figures were omitted, such as Benjamin Rush, the doctor who promoted inoculations and groundbreaking approaches to mental health; Peale's work in paleontology was overlooked, and so were the engineering innovations of Robert Fulton (1765–1815) and Eli Whitney (1765–1825). Yet, the Royal Society had members in the early nineteenth century, such as Soane, who never recorded an experiment. Soane's involvement with and contributions to the society's activities were minimal: his attentions were clearly attuned to the Royal Academy as one of the few architects heavily involved. The perceived boundaries between the arts and science were even made physical at Somerset House: the organizations occupied the same building but were accessed through different doors.[3] Nonetheless, Soane and Jefferson challenged these divisions, and it is possible to read both Monticello and Soane's Museum as structures that blurred the established boundaries between science and design.

As a series of unfolding forms that are filled with innovative building technology and objects for critical investigation, their house museums exist somewhere between the picturesque and the scientific. Beyond serving as repositories for ever-growing collections, the house museums were exercises in applied science: optics, structure, and thermal manipulation. In their work and letters, both architects referenced the work of Nicolas Le Camus de Mézières. His text, *Le Génie de l'architecture* (1780), as well as the Halle au Blé exemplified the use of *lumière mystérieuse* and structural innovations to facilitate the creation of soaring, light-filled interior expanses that had only been imagined by architects such as Boullée. At Monticello and Soane's Museum, the architects applied the principles of de Mézières to domestic architecture by experimenting with form and new glazing methods to facilitate the diffusion of natural light and flow of air through the homes.

In 1808, Soane translated the first section of *Le Génie de l'architecture* in preparation for his Royal Academy lectures, and later he would experiment with his own mysterious luminosity at the house museum through the use of colored glass in primrose and amber tints, varied skylights, and imbedded grates in the ground floor to bring light to the Crypt.[4] The effects of clear glass were also tested by the use of handblown panes that distorted light and view in contrast with the clarity of cutting-edge plate glass. Unlike Jefferson's symmetrical roof plan at Monticello, the aerial view of Soane's Museum resembles a city of glass where large domed spaces are complemented with long, angular lights and external vitrines that were designed to protect delicate glass, such as the model of the Freemason's Hall's dome in Soane's Dressing Room. The Age of Enlightenment marked the first use of the word "atmospheric," and Soane's Museum may offer one of the best illustrations of this principle.[5] With more than thirty skylights and various colors of glazing, the house museum is a spectacle in sunlight. Conscientious of his created environment, Soane was known to dismiss visitors on dreary days in preference of their return on a day with optimal natural lighting conditions.[6]

In lecture 8, Soane noted that "windows must be of dimensions suitable to the particular climate."[7] At Lincoln's Inn Fields, he emphasized the profundity of his strategy for illumination in the house museum by mentioning the term "light" no less than thirty-two times in his *Description:* dome-light, lantern-light, moonlight, skylights, and the changing character of light from different cardinal orientations. Soane's *Description of the House and Museum, on the North Side of Lincoln's Inn-Fields, the Residence of Sir John Soane* (privately printed 1830, 1832; revised 1835) paired spatial narratives with the architectural language of orthographic projection and perspective engravings. Therefore, the *Description* set forth an agenda about the museum's arrangement and Soane's intentions. Beyond the repetition of "light" in the *Description,* Soane also used the phrase "powerful effects of light and shade" repeatedly.[8]

Whereas Soane's glazing was more experimental in form, Jefferson's was more innovative in the functional details of fabrication. For the Dome Room, he specified an incredible handblown oculus measuring four feet in diameter, and for the windows and other twelve skylights of the home, Jefferson ordered nearly 1,000 sheets of glass from Philadelphia glazer Joseph Donath, ranging from 12″ square panes to 18″ x 24″ panes.[9] To span the large openings for the skylights, sheets of glass were stacked together, leaving a small air space between and 2.5″ of overlap. This layered design illustrated Jefferson's understanding of capillary action since the air space essentially provided a drip edge. Jefferson did, however, experience problems with the skylights, especially in severe weather. While serving as president in Washington in 1801, he learned that a hailstorm destroyed two skylights at Monticello that had been "left uncovered," inferring that he had a system in place to protect the precious glass on the mountaintop.[10] An exterior closure system for the skylights would have been akin to the rest of the home since there were interior and exterior shutters on the majority of the vertical apertures, and Jefferson installed shutters on the long skylight of Poplar Forest's dining room.[11] At Monticello, a counterweight system was attached to at least five of the skylights. This could hold the laminated panes open, when desired, and both staircases benefited from this system that paired natural illumination with air circulation. Located along key corridors, stretching from the basements to the upper floors, the staircases functioned as vertical ventilation shafts.

Besides the use of skylights and oculi, Soane and Jefferson had other, similar glazed elements that brought light into the house museums through unexpected means. Jefferson inserted fenestration into the language of classical architecture when he replaced the solid planes of three metopes in the home's south facade with square, pivoting windows. These illuminated a small semi-octagonal room on the second floor, located directly above Jefferson's cabinet, which served as a nursery for his many grandchildren. The apertures, with their sloped sills to reflect light, and the lower ceiling height created a space thoughtfully composed in relation to the scale of a child. Although Soane did not incorporate metope windows into his house museum, he toyed with the idea in his design for Holy Trinity Marylebone.[12] For Jefferson and Soane, the ultimate source of inspiration for the metope window may have been Ledoux's work for the Director's House at the Royal Saltworks of Arc-et-Senans, a project that Soane knew from drawings and Jefferson knew from his travels.

In Royal Academy lecture 3, Soane noted that architecture, unlike painting and sculpture, was not purely modeled on nature because it was "an art of invention" that owed its origins to necessity.[13] This concept of responsiveness in the built environment reflected Soane's connection to an established vein of architectural theory that had roots in the writings of Vitruvius and had been tested by English predecessors such as Wren: architecture could not be understood from the perspective of Platonism because buildings needed to respond to their climates and the existing conditions of the site. Melding architectural practice with Lockean theory, the house museums of Jefferson and Soane were ultimately derived from their experiences and knowledge of the site, bolstered by years of careful observation. For example, windows were absent from the north side of Soane's home due to the noise, dirt, and general distraction that would have resulted from apertures facing a utilitarian urban street. When he could not collect light from punctures in vertical surfaces, he placed them in the horizontal planes of the home, crafting a skyline of skylights. Many of Jefferson's architectural strategies for optimum solar orientation, the use of natural light, and the desire to create thermal comfort were inspired by a lifetime of monitoring the weather.

In Query 7 of his *Notes,* Jefferson commented on broader changes in the climate that would impact buildings, agricultural practices, and settlement patterns. Understanding climate and monitoring its changes were essential to understanding a site and, by extension, designing an advantageous architectural response. Architecture was an exercise in designed hypotheses where certain variables could be identified and ideas could be tested through trial and error. A comprehensive history of sustainable architecture has yet to be written, but Jefferson and Soane would certainly be included because of their work as architect-scientists. Their designs proved that the built environment could be a performative one that was optimized for daylight and airflow, filled with objects and operations of convenience that employed the latest advancements in materials and technology. The architects, however, were not alone in their explorations: while in the Veneto in 1779, a young Soane noted in his sketchbook that he saw "an invention of conveying a cool breeze in to their apartmnts by Pipes."[14]

Soane surrounded himself with instruments for measuring time and the climate in his home, with a particular concentration in his cabinet, and this was reflective of developments in engineering and mechanical arts in London during the early nineteenth century.[15] During his only trip to England, Jefferson, too, found the scientific side of London inspiring, and he wrote to Madame de Corny that "their mechanics certainly excel all others."[16] His memorandum books and letters reveal that he was not interested in visiting the city's churches but instead preferred exploring sites with cutting-edge engineering, such as pumping stations and places of manufacture, and shopping for scientific instruments, totaling £60. In his penultimate day in England, he made a trip with Royal Society member John Paradise (1743–1795; elected 1771): "pd. Seeing observatory & hospital at Greenwich."[17] He toured the observatory with the royal astronomer, Nevil Maskel. Here, where science and design were aligned, Jefferson discovered a true appreciation for the integration of environmental monitoring and gadgetry with architecture, as well as Wren's design work. The Octagon Room, designed around 1675 for first Astronomer Royal John Flamsteed (1646–1719), was a double height space with clocks, scientific instruments, and a series of lofty windows to provide panoptic views of both Greenwich and the firmament above the Thames. After returning from Europe, Jefferson designed his own octagonal room for reflection beneath Monticello's dome.

PRIVATE LABORATORIES

From its inception in 1768, Jefferson envisioned Monticello as a site where he could pursue his curiosities in weather, agriculture, industrial production, and architecture. His plans for the early dependencies of the home included a "laboratory," perhaps imagining this as a working space for testing new theories or creating objects of convenience. By March 1771, Jefferson moved away from creating a cubic laboratory within the home and made a radical shift in his design thinking by exploring the concept that the entire home, and by extension the plantation, could function as an instrument for monitoring and mediating the environment.[18] During this era, Jefferson designed bold interventions for his property, such as an observatory for Montalto, the "tall mountain" that stood four hundred feet above Monticello; however, this was never constructed, nor was his scheme to relay water from the taller mountain to his plantation's grounds through a system gravity-fed pipes that would also provide water pressure to fuel garden follies within the grounds.

Work at the mountaintop was interrupted by his diplomatic appointment abroad, yet experience in Europe greatly informed his architectural sensibilities and sophistication. He saw structures abroad as well as instrumentation that strongly shaped his design interests: architecture was not just a vessel to house technological objects, but it could also perform mechanical operations and control certain environmental conditions. For example, upon his return to construction at Monticello in the late 1790s, he installed a wind plate on the ceiling of the East Portico that was connected to a weathervane on the roof that allowed him to observe the direction of the wind from within five rooms of the home. There were thermometers in almost every room of the ground floor, and where the solar orientation was not advantageous, Jefferson added elements to manipulate the environment: on the southern side of the home, where his Library, Cabinet, and bedchamber were located, he installed two Venetian porches flanking the greenhouse.[19] By folding the tall and narrow panels or removing the lunettes in the top portion of these louvered structures, one could manipulate light and the flow of air. Like the layered panels of Soane's Picture Gallery, the configuration of Jefferson's Venetian porches could change the experience of a room. In the Dining Room, situated on the northern side of the home, Jefferson used double-glazing on the triple sash window and placed two sets of sliding doors, topped by a double-glazed semi-elliptical transom, in the threshold of the adjacent Tea Room. In 1805, he even proposed a mechanical system of louvers to shade the porticos of the home (fig. 33).

Although Jefferson contended with both extreme heat and cold on his mountaintop, it seems that an overabundance of natural light, or solar gain, was rarely a problem at Soane's home. The lack of sunlight during London's long, gray winters prompted Soane to test a variety of heating methods, transitioning from coal-burning fireplaces and moveable stoves to a mechanical system using steam, and later to hot water that provided centralized climate control.[20] The mechanization of conveniences in the home also extended to the privies: adjacent to his Dressing Room was a "Patent Water Closet" with a flushing mechanism. In a country where in-house privies were rare in the early 1800s, Jefferson installed three conveniences in Monticello that were illuminated by a skylight on the tin-shingled roof, and Jefferson referred to them in his building notebooks as "air-closets." Additionally, there were two privies located in the subterranean "all weather passage" and a stand-alone

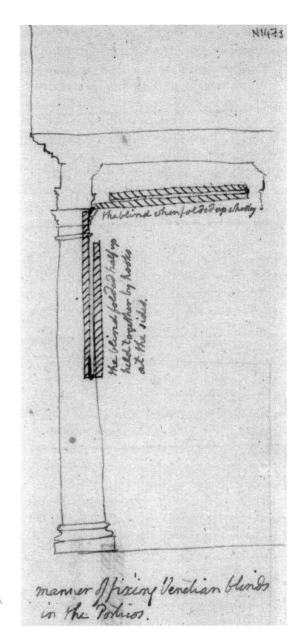

the blind when folded up wholly

the blind folded half up
held together by hooks
at the sides.

manner of fixing Venetian blinds
in the Porticos.

Fig. 33. Jefferson's designs for portico louvers at Monticello, 1805. (Massachusetts Historical Society N147S) "necessary house of wood" on the industrial alley of the plantation, Mulberry Row.[21] Using a much more simplistic sanitation system than that of Soane's conveniences, the privies of Monticello required manual cleaning, but mid-nineteenth-century restorations revealed that the home's three privies were each connected to a vertical ventilation shaft that reached to the subfloor of the home's basement. This may have accommodated a dumbwaiter of sorts to lift a chamber pot into place and lower it to be emptied.[22] Jefferson knew of plumbed toilets from his time abroad: there was a flushing mechanism at the Hôtel de Langeac through its connection to the city's municipal water system, but the installation of such a system at Monticello would have been difficult since water was constantly in demand on the mountaintop, and Jefferson's home, unlike Soane's system, operated without municipal services. Soane's water supply came from a local contract with the New River Water Company, an established but unreliable system that served Lincoln's Inn Fields, as well as series of supplemental cisterns and wells.[23] As an instrument for efficiency, Jefferson installed four cisterns at Monticello that collected rainwater from the roof of the home and two pavilions as well as the large terraces that covered the dependencies. Like many other architectural experiments at the home, Jefferson's cisterns were not without fault: his cement mixture was flawed, and the reservoirs often leached the collected water back into the earth.

OPTICAL EXPERIMENTS

Using architectural design as a form of applied science, Jefferson and Soane demonstrated shared interests in the study of optics, perhaps inspired by keen awareness of their own eyesight. Jefferson corresponded with a Philadelphia optician on the design of clear and tinted glasses, and from the year 1806 he wore spectacles for reading. His sight, unlike Soane's, was relatively consistent throughout his life, and just a few months before his passing, Jefferson wrote to architect Robert Mills that his vision was the least "impaired" of his faculties.[24] Much has been written about use of glass and mirrors at Soane's Museum; however, the hypothesis that Soane drastically increased the use of reflective surfaces in the 1800s because of his diminished eyesight has not yet been fully explored.[25]

Initially, Soane's urban residence functioned as a retreat from the polluted and crowded city, but it later became an architectural experiment in atmospheric escapism.[26] In the latter portion of his life, Soane added more mirrors to his house museum and punctured its roofline with more skylights. The number of reflective surfaces increased, employing convex mirrors as well as looking glasses placed on the backs of doors and interior shutters as well as mirrored panels set within cabinetry. These techniques were not paralleled within any of his other built works; therefore, it is plausible that Soane's use of mirrors at the house museum was an attempt to not only "dissolve the appearance of support" but also to amplify light within his dimming world.[27]

In 1815, Soane began to experience problems with his eyesight. That year he also lost his wife, so the architect was faced with the prospect of not only a life in solitude but also a creatively crippling future in the dark. On December 24, 1824, without the aid of anesthesia, Soane underwent cataract surgery. Although he never fully lost his eyesight, Soane's weak eyes forced the architect to use the secretary of the Royal Academy, Henry Howard, as a reader for his lectures from 1821 onward, and his record of correspondence diminished in his later years due to his eyesight.

Other members of the Transatlantic Design Network, such as Trumbull and Cosway, experienced severe eye troubles that impacted their later years, but it was only Jefferson and Soane who fully took on the charge of studying physical and geometric optics through architecture. In both of their house museums, Jefferson and Soane had instruments to measure and augment the properties of light through reflection, refraction, and magnification. Their collections included microscopes, telescopes, and prisms as well as volumes on perspective written by artists and scientists ranging from da Vinci to Malton, Priestly, and Ferguson. In 1794, only two years after he purchased no. 12 Lincoln's Inn Fields, Soane recorded the purchase of two convex mirrors from P. and J. Dolland.[28] This was the very same merchant that Jefferson used to purchase various "instruments" on five different days in the spring of 1786.[29] Jefferson also made purchases from London "optician" Mr. Cary on the Strand, and upon his return to the United States he continued pursuits of the latest scientific tools by obtaining "European catalogues of Optical, Astronomical &c. Instruments."[30] Jefferson's interest in optics and how they could distort architectural space even impacted other close friends who were not artists or designers: in 1806 he ordered a convex mirror from London for future president and fellow Virginian James Monroe.[31] By its opening in 1825, optics would even be listed as a primary course of study at the University of Virginia, and Jefferson employed a subtle optical trick at his academical village. Moving away from the central Rotunda, the distance between the individual pavilions increases to compensate for the effect of foreshortening; to a visitor standing on the steps of the Rotunda looking over the Lawn, the pavilions look evenly spaced.

Beyond gadgetry and the scholarly studies of optics, Jefferson and Soane integrated visual devices and even illusions and trompe l'oeil in material treatments into the architecture of their homes. At Monticello, the wooden facade of the East Portico was painted and textured to resemble ashlar block, and dozens of pine doors were grained by Richard Barry to look like mahogany with boxwood inlay, a project so thorough that even the inside panels of attic doors were painted. In the Library and Dining Room, Soane had the moldings and ornaments painted to look like bronze, and visitors described the "porphyry-painted walls" of the stairway.[32]

At both sites, concave and convex mirrors provided unique distortions of space. In Jefferson's bedroom and the Dining Room, he placed arched mirrors purchased in France directly across from triple sash windows, thereby reflecting the landscape of his rambling, west-facing flower garden. In the Parlor, he used a similar device: pier mirrors, also purchased in France, flanked the Parlor's "self-operating doors" and reflected views of the garden. At both homes, the careful placement of mirrors could also internalize space. In the no. 13 Breakfast Room, mirrors were placed on the backs of all the doors. When open, the room was a golden threshold between the deep red Dining Room and the tonal gray casts naturally illuminated beneath the Museum Dome; when closed, the complex geometries of the Breakfast Room, capped by one of Soane's signature canopy domes, were reflected like a hall of mirrors. An abundance of reflective surfaces adorned the no. 13 Breakfast Room, the cabinet, and the Museum Dome, as per Soane's design. But a number of mirrors, especially those in stairwells and the Crypt, were added for security by Bolton when he served as curator; these were so well integrated within the home's composition that many scholars have mistaken these for Soane's design work.[33]

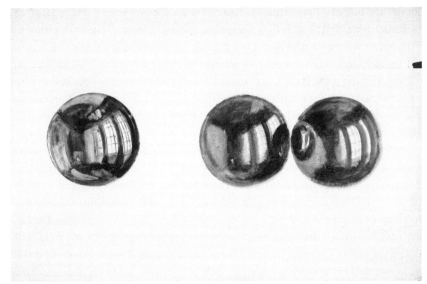

Fig. 34. J. M. W. Turner's lecture diagram, Reflections in a Single Polished Metal Globe and in a Pair of Polished Metal Globes (ca. 1810). (Tate D17147)

Through artistic works and discussions with friends, both men found inspiration for the edification of their house museums. For example, in preparation for a series of lectures as the professor of perspective at the Royal Academy (1807–1837), Soane's close friend and fellow Academician J. M. W Turner crafted five drawings around 1810 that depict the reflective properties of glass and metallic surfaces. These drawings illustrate Turner's interest in optics and ambient radiance through their rendered distortion of space and light. In the catalog for the exhibition "Illuminating a Friendship," Dorey noted that Turner's studies in optics may have influenced Soane's work at the house museum, particularly the use of convex mirrors.[34] This source of inspiration is particularly evident when looking at Turner's drawings of metal and glass spheres reflecting an architectural space; the fascinating rendering predate Soane's ownership and subsequent manipulation of no. 13 Lincoln's Inn Fields (fig. 34).

In Monticello's Dome Room, Jefferson used mirrors to solve a challenging design problem. Half of the windows of the octagonal room faced the home's roofline, whereas the other half had pristine views of Montalto and the flower garden to the southwest and the valley of Charlottesville to the northwest. To conceal the less than desirable views of Monticello's tin roof, Jefferson placed mirrors on the bottom half of his east-facing bull's-eye windows and in the lunette above the room's door. This reflected views back into the luminous, centralized room and gave the illusion that the Dome Room was an isolated perch, a domestic lighthouse, instead of a slightly asymmetrical and irregular space tightly nested against the home's roof.

For both residences, mirrors were used prolifically in the spaces that were more architecturally experimental, in rooms that were filled with a concentration of collections, and in common areas. Their cabinets were also adorned with mirrors, but looking glasses were not simply for vanity: mirrors were inserted to reflect the architecture, amplify light in their primary working spaces, and complement their collections of ocular instruments. There is a noted absence of mirrors in the Students' Room; perhaps Soane found this distracting for his apprentices and believed that their work received ample illumination from the pair of long, trapezoidal skylights running parallel to their workspace.

At the house museums, the volume of collections paired with the use of trompe l'oeil and mirrors also disguised several small architectural gaffes. For example, the skylights of Soane's no. 13 Breakfast Room have a variety of fascia boards to conceal the shims that were used to make the apertures level, many of which settled askew over the last two centuries. In Monticello's Entrance Hall, the large double doors of the Parlor were too tall in proportion to the gallery level of the Entrance Hall, an error that likely resulted from Jefferson's numerous alterations to the home's configuration. The improperly aligned section was cleverly concealed with an optical trick from Jefferson's skilled plasterers: the ceiling beneath the gallery gently curves to receive the door frame, and the deception is only discovered with careful inspection since the curve is partially hidden in the shadow cast by the gallery's floor. For Soane, the play of light, shadow, and curved edges also help conceal the irregular stair risers on the north side of no. 13, connecting the museum corridor with the Crypt.

CHAPTER 11

Pasticci

Oh what a falling off do these ruins present—the subject becomes too gloomy to be pursued—.
—John Soane, "Crude Hints toward an History of My House in Lincoln's Inn Fields," 1812[1]

Today's visitors to Monticello and Soane's Museum can find twenty-first-century re-creations of the three-dimensional *capricci,* developed concurrently by the respective architects: Jefferson's was in place sometime between 1809 and 1816, whereas Soane started developing the concept from 1808 and installed the full composition in 1819. By taking a portion of the museum's collections out-of-doors, Jefferson and Soane crafted playful exhibits that reflected, and reinvented, historical narratives. At Monticello, Jefferson created a small composition that literally amassed his interests in architecture and science. At Soane's Museum, the architect created a nine-part column, known as the Pasticcio, that mixed styles and, as a focal point visible from several rooms within the home, served as a compass rose for visitors to the museum.

The *pasticci* of Jefferson and Soane illustrate their eclectic aesthetic interests and innovative approaches to bringing Piranesi-styled compositions to life. In terms of their collections, use of stylistic references, and the precedents employed in their architecture, the entire composition of Monticello and Soane's Museum were pastiches, and the *capricci* were explicit, sculptural references to the ways in which the architects integrated history and architectural invention. These constructions were also reflections on the architects' personal lives and careers: Soane had recently lost his wife, and the renovations at no. 13 were mostly complete; Jefferson, as evidenced by the physical placement of the pasticcio, was turning his architectural attentions from the mountaintop toward the valley of Charlottesville and the design of his new university.

SOANEAN HISTORIES

Soane's creation of the Pasticcio in the Monument Court reflected his increasing interest in programming exterior spaces at the house museum. Considering that the creation and refinement of these courtyards spans the forty-year construction period of the house museum, it is possible to read the courtyards as built artifacts that showcased Soane's design evolution. Like many of the other elements of the house museum, the genesis and evolution of the Pasticcio may be read through three primary sources: the drawings by Soane's students, the evocative watercolors made by Gandy, and Soane's accounts of the arrangement and intended interpretation of the courtyards in his *Description* (fig. 35). The New Court of no. 12 and the Monk's Yard of no. 14, spaces that chronologically and physically frame the Monument Court, also provide evidence for interpreting Soane's intentions for the Pasticcio. The first courtyard Soane created, the New Court, is very stark in comparison to the later experimentations, and it housed utilitarian functions: a lead cistern that predated Soane's occupation of the home, a water closet for servants, and access to a coal cellar.[2] The Monk's Yard was designed to separate the rented spaces of no. 14 from the area of the home occupied by Soane's Picture Gallery and the Monk's Room. Unlike the cubic designs of the New Court and Monument Court, the Monk's Yard had an L-shaped plan and contained an arrangement of reclaimed medieval ruins as well as a tomb for the family dog, Fanny, capped by a small *pasticcio.* The courtyard's function and plan reflect Soane's increasingly introverted nature as well as his developing interests in the creation of a mythology revolving around

his home: Soane wrote in the *Description* that the dog belonged to "the pious Monk" and was his "favourite companion, the delight, the solace of his leisure hours."[3]

Composed of stacked and repositioned architectural elements, the reclaimed ruins in the Monk's Yard were placed in a picturesque arrangement, rather than an archaeological one that recalled their original configurations at Westminster. Soane, perhaps purposefully, accelerated the sublime effect of the ruins, considering he did not install any weatherproofing details to protect the sixteenth-century Reigate stone arcades and fourteenth-century Caen stone canopy: a survey from 1969 estimated that over 50 percent of the stone's surface had been lost, and the ruins, as well as the Monk's Grave and Fanny's Tomb, were covered in organic growth.[4] Even the floor of Soane's courtyard was a fanciful exercise. The pavement of the Yard, a patterned arrangement of aggregate, was composed of large stones and glass roundels. Upon closer inspection, one can see that the glass fragments were the tops and bottoms of champagne bottles. Acknowledging the whimsical design of the Yard, Soane quoted Horace in the *Description* (1835): "*dulce est desipere in loco* [it is delightful to play the fool occasionally]."[5]

Soane's first and last courtyards at the home can be described as functional opposites: the New Court as a utilitarian garden space and the Monk's Yard as an urban folly. The Monument Court, then, serves as a mediating construction for specific elements of the collections. As the central courtyard, the Monument Court has the largest spatial impact on the rest of the house museum: the Pasticcio is visible from fourteen rooms, on four different levels. On the north-south axis, the Monument Court is aligned, on-center, with the large tripartite window of the Dining Room. On the east-west axis, the Monument Court serves as a visual and spatial divider between the shared family space of the no. 13 Breakfast Room and the private, reflective space of Soane's Dressing Room and Study. Therefore, the Monument Court was designed as a space to frame views between the inside and outside and serve as an essential exterior "room" that provides light and air to other spaces in the house museum.

Soane first installed elements of the Monument Court's Pasticcio in 1819; however, he was contemplating, and even constructing, prototypes for the Pasticcio more than a decade earlier. An annotated sectional sketch from 1808 shows a stacked column of architectural fragments nested within a niche on the north wall of the museum. Although it is unclear if this construction was intended to be freestanding or semi-attached, using the walls of the museum as an armature, the drawing illustrates Soane's desire to create a vertical architectural collage, a form that would be repeated in Gandy's watercolor from 1811 that featured an aggregate entablature on the western wall of the museum.

Soane's Pasticcio was altered several times between 1819 and 1825, and eventually the composition reached nearly forty feet tall. At the time of Soane's death, the configuration from bottom to top consisted of: (1) an unpainted marble drum with ballast, (2) the "Hindoo" capital, (3) a stone spacer block, (4) a domical spacer block, (5) the stone "Tivoli" capital, (6) a Soanean flat dome of Portland stone, (7) a Norman capital and part of a column shaft, (8) a three-sided stone block with engaged Ionic pilasters that were later adorned with four cast iron urns, and (9) a cast iron upper element with a pineapple finial. Within this pastiche, Soane created a composition where East met West, and ancient architecture met Soanean design. However, beneath each element was an English undertone: certain sections were made in England, others used English materials, and some featured work by English designers. For example, the "Hindoo" capital (2) was a British copy of a Nasrid design from the fourteenth century, possibly inspired by the Alhambra. The stone spacer block (3) was possibly from a building by Soane's early architectural mentor, Holland. The domical spacer block (4) had a similar, albeit smaller, canopy profile to the Soanean flat dome of Portland stone (6). The former was not mentioned in any of Soane's editions of the *Description,* but it was shown in plan and elevation in a dimensioned drawing of July 1819, perhaps inserted to provide physical stability and a visual connection to the Tivoli capital.[6] As one of the most prominent examples of English appliqué within the Pasticcio, the Tivoli capital may have been a spare from the Bank of England or one carved specifically for Soane as a keepsake; it was reflective of Soane's architectural travels as a young student to the Temple of Vesta.[7] Although referencing French influence, the Norman capital (7) was made of greensand stone, a fossil-rich sandstone first identified by British geologist William Smith (1769–1839) and published in his *Delineation of the Strata of England* (1815) just a few years before Soane compiled the Pasticcio.

Like the rest of the museum, Soane reconfigured the Pasticcio several times, but the most drastic of his changes was the insertion of the marble drum at the base. The drum was originally under the statue of Apollo Belvedere, but in 1825, when the Pasticcio was already towering over thirty feet, the construction was partially disassembled and lifted to accommodate the new base.[8] Soane's acquisition of the sarcophagus of Seti I prompted the bold and structurally complex reorganization. To move the extremely heavy and large alabaster sarcophagus into the Museum, Soane removed a portion of the north wall of no. 12 and rearranged a portion of his collections, moving the statue of Apollo from the central space in the basement, directly beneath the Museum Dome, to the west side of the dome on the ground story. This allowed the newly acquired sarcophagus to occupy the most prominent location in the museum's spatial composition.[9]

During Soane's lifetime, the individual pieces of the Pasticcio did not have a unifying structural connection and were only affixed to each other with iron cramps or rods.[10] It is odd that Soane, who was otherwise fastidious in his structural attentions as evidenced by the custom-designed bricks for the Bank of England's domes, was not wary of the precarious situation that a disjointed column posed. When the Pasticcio was dismantled in the late nineteenth century, the column was in a hazardous state: "the whole structure was very insecure and swayed visibly when touched on the upper part . . . [it] was 7 1/2 inches out of the perpendicular."[11] A brick well, discovered in 1999 beneath the paving block, compounded the Pasticcio's unstable foundation.[12]

Despite its visual prominence in the house museum, the Pasticcio was not illustrated in any of Soane's three editions of the *Description,* and Soane's written depiction of Monument Court and its centerpiece was concise: "decorated with fragments of ancient and modern art . . . advantageously seen from the rooms on the ground floor."[13] The earlier publication advertising the home, Britton's *The Union of Architecture, Sculpture, and Painting* (1827), also lacked visuals of the Pasticcio and only briefly addressed its arrangement: "a kind of trophy composed of a capital of an Hindoo column and of other architectural fragments."[14] Soane's students, however, frequently drew the monument and represented its tightly enclosed environs through wide-angle perspectives. Pasticcio was used as a teaching tool for the students and a surprise for Soane's clients who visited the home, discernibly advertising Soane's talents as an architect by placing his designs directly adjacent to ancient precedents.

AN AMERICAN MONUMENT

At Monticello, Jefferson melded his fascinations with architecture and science through the creation of his own *pasticcio.* Although it was only a fraction of the size of Soane's composition and contained only three stacked elements, Jefferson's columnar creation showcased a similar theme: an architectural arrangement with nationalistic undertones. In his composition, Jefferson placed a relatively unknown scientific object, a spherical sundial, atop one of Latrobe's American Order capitals and a simple, square Doric pedestal. Placed on the corner of the north terrace, Jefferson's *pasticcio* was in a primary line of sight for visitors to the plantation: it was on axis with the North

Pavilion, the Baths of Diocletian–themed Tea Porch, and foreground the view for those peering from the mountaintop's terrace toward Charlottesville.

The spherical sundial, also known as a globe sundial, was a foreign object in America. References to similar objects do not appear within the collections of institutions such as the American Philosophical Society, Bartram's garden, the Columbian Institute, or Peale's Museum. A cousin of the spherical sundial, an open-framed instrument known as an armillary sundial, was more familiar since it was an established tool based on a mariner's astrolabe. Painted with latitude lines and a bisecting horizontal meridian, the spherical sundial was skewered by a thin iron rod, and the attached arm could be adjusted to the latitude, yielding an accurate measure of both the time at the sundial's location and the approximate location of solar noon on the globe. Jefferson's ownership of a spherical sundial further underscores his interest in contemporary scientific developments and was probably inspired by the instruments he saw on his brief trip to the Royal Observatory in Greenwich and his reading of Ferguson. Unlike the scientific objects that Jefferson imported from London, the 10.5″ sphere of black locust was made at Monticello, sometime between 1809 and 1816.[15] The wooden portion of the spherical sundial also matches the diameter and style of the spherical finials that cap the dependency privies, visually connecting, albeit subtly, two of the home's technological "instruments."

The *pasticcio's* capital was a gift from Latrobe in 1809 and represented one of the designs that the architect proposed for the new American Order, to be featured in the US Capitol. Conceived as manipulations of the Corinthian order, the designs incorporated elements from familiar American plants: corn, the magnolia, and the tobacco leaf. For Jefferson, a retired statesman, architectural enthusiast, and farmer, the concept of an American Order was exceptionally pleasing, and the correspondence between Jefferson and Latrobe proves that the capitals' designs were intended to serve as pieces of nationalistic *architecture parlante* at the federal seat.

In addition to the corncob capital, Latrobe sent Jefferson a model of the tobacco capital. Jefferson's dimensioned sketch of his *pasticcio* does not show what capital he intended to use since it is only loosely rendered as some sort of Corinthian order with vertical delineations. However, it is plausible that

Jefferson selected the corncob for his *pasticcio* because the object arrived at Monticello before the tobacco-inspired example, and he may have favored the display of corn over tobacco because of his own experiences with the plant. Although Jefferson often wrote of the agricultural issues produced by tobacco and "Indian corn," he possessed a stronger aversion to tobacco on the mountaintop. It was, originally, the cash crop of Monticello, but he eventually abandoned its cultivation in the mid-1790s due to several poor seasons and his observation that the crop disrupted the aesthetic appeal of the plantation: "my hills are too rough ever to please the eye, and as yet unreclaimed from the barbarous state in which the slovenly business of tobacco making had left them."[16] At Poplar Forest's more uniform elevation, where there were no dramatic views of mountains and valleys, Jefferson continued the cultivation of the plant.

In a letter accompanying the first capital, Latrobe accurately predicted that a visit to the plantation was unlikely because of his obligations in Washington.[17] Much like Hadfield, Latrobe found the position as architect of the US Capitol a relentless, thankless job. When Latrobe sent Jefferson the corncob capital, he was ensconced in his longest period of uninterrupted work at the Capitol, spanning 1808 to 1812. Disruptions from the war prompted Latrobe to take on work elsewhere, predominantly based in engineering; however, he returned to Washington in 1815 to help rebuild the scorched Capitol and serve as the surveyor of the City of Washington. In the winter of 1818, Latrobe left Washington for New Orleans, a port city secured under Jefferson's presidency, where he contracted yellow fever and died less than two years after his arrival.

Because of its location, Jefferson's American *pasticcio* was more than a tripartite object. On the north terrace, the stacked creation rested above two systems that, like the *pasticcio,* melded architecture and science: rooflets, the triangulated structural systems beneath the terrace's planks, and an icehouse (fig. 36). The zigzag construction of the rooflets collected water from the surface area of the terraces and funneled it into adjacent cisterns. With four layers, the rooflets also formed a structurally redundant system: the planked floor of the terraces, an air space, a series of miniature gables that ran perpendicular to the top planks, and a ceiling plane. Although a labor-

Fig. 36. Sectional collage of the placement of the American pasticcio and its adjacent technological conveniences: rooflet water collection system, cistern, privy, and icehouse. (Author's diagram)

intensive system, it was employed by Jefferson at several of his projects and provided a solution to one of the problems that continues to plague modern architects: how to drain water from a flat roof. Farther below the *pasticcio* was Jefferson's masonry icehouse, first installed at the mountaintop in 1803. In the winter, the deep, circular structure was filled with layers of ice from the nearby Rivanna River and a bed of straw for insulation. As a structure, an icehouse was not particularly innovative in America, considering Washington had one at Mount Vernon and Jefferson suggested improvements for the one at the President's House, yet the placement of Monticello's icehouse was unique. Unlike icehouses that solely relied on the earth's thermal mass for insulation and were typically outbuildings, located in disparate parts of a plantation's landscape, Jefferson nested his icehouse within both the ground and the fabric of the home, making it readily accessible. Although its sheltered location may have protected enslaved workers from the elements, ice retrieval was not a prized task in the summer since the cool, subterranean space would have been a welcome retreat for animals hoping to escape the heat and humidity of a Virginia summer.

RE-CREATING THE *PASTICCI*

Latrobe never saw his capital on the mountaintop; however, his son, lawyer John H. B. Latrobe (1804–1891), was able to see the creation when he visited Monticello in August 1832 en route to the warm springs of western Virginia. The journey from his hometown in Baltimore took him through Washington, then Orange County, where he briefly stayed at Madison's residence of Montpelier. Here, he noted, "the whole design is in bad taste, yet sufficiently imposing," but he applauded the ailing Madison's collections, ranging from paintings by American artists to portrait bust casts. Continuing to Charlottesville, John visited the University of Virginia, where Robley Dunglison (1798–1869), Jefferson's former doctor and a professor, showed him the "shabby genteel" grounds and the honorable "temple to knowledge," the Rotunda. A brief ride on horseback brought John to Monticello, now under ownership of James Barclay. Here he was met with a dismal scene: the once captivating home filled with collections and tokens of friendship from European correspondents, American compatriots, and the tribes of North America was in "utter ruin and desolation." Although critical of certain elements, John's overall impression of the architecture was favorable, and he was able to explore the tattered plantation in leisure since Barclay was not home: "the internal arrangement, so far as I could judge of it by the peeps I made into peepable place, is whimsical." While exploring, John saw his father's "somewhat mutilated" capital, toppled amid a mess of chairs, architectural fragments, and plants on the north terrace. Moved by the notion that "this spot, visited by thousands in the life of Mr. Jefferson, contained something that recalled my parent's genius," John righted the capital on its remaining pedestal before he left the mountaintop.[18] John Latrobe's diary did not mention the spherical sundial, perhaps destroyed or pilfered after Jefferson's death.

By the late 1830s, Jefferson's American *pasticcio* existed only in memory, and for visitors to Soane's Museum in the twentieth century, the remarkable Pasticcio was entirely absent. Jefferson's composition was reinstated in 2001, and a year later a conservation and reconstruction project at Soane's Museum was initiated to reintroduce the Pasticcio to the Monument Court. Less than half of the original elements survived: only the unpainted marble drum used as the base, the "Hindoo" capital, and three of the four cast iron urns that capped the composition were preserved. Although the surviving elements comprised only a fraction of Soane's composition, drawings and written accounts assisted in the accurate re-creation of the Pasticcio. A new concrete foundation received the compressive forces of the object, and a steel rod, designed to mitigate lateral wind loads, was inserted to the core of the Pasticcio. Then, on April 18, 2004, the final piece of the Pasticcio was installed, completing the void that had been left in the Monument Court since 1896.

As distinct elements of the homes that represented cultural eclecticism, blurring the boundaries of architectural history for Soane and melding form and utility for Jefferson, the *pasticci* reflected their shared appreciation of, and response to, the work of Piranesi. Both architects owned publications of Piranesi's work, and they studied how the Venetian transplant observed, recorded, and reimagined Rome's rich palimpsest through his sketches and engravings. Through Soane's travels in Italy and relatively close access to the rich publishing houses of Paris and London, he acquired nearly fifty titles, some with multiple volumes, featuring Piranesi's work. Jefferson's acquisitions were more difficult. In 1791, he asked his former secretary who was still residing in Paris to procure copies of Piranesi's publications and engravings. Jefferson wanted an edition containing various *vedute* and a "compleat set of Piranesi's drawings of the Pantheon."[19] The request was unsuccessful, and it was not until 1805 that Jefferson was able to purchase a volume from a book agent in Baltimore.

In the spring of 1807, Jefferson received a letter from Piranesi's son, Francesco, extolling the president's "reputation in the arts" and offering two new publications, as well as the opportunity for the American government to establish a commercial exchange with his new engraving shop in Paris.[20] If Jefferson responded to Francesco, the letter has not been preserved, but Jefferson's correspondence about Piranesi's work in the early 1800s certainly could have inspired the construction of his American *pasticcio*. As a piece that melded his interests in agriculture and architecture, referencing his work in Washington and correspondence with one of the nation's leading designers, the composition and placement of the *pasiticio* was intended to spark curiosity and, more importantly, a conversation about cultural eclecticism. Unlike Jefferson, Soane owned original works by Piranesi and saw other *capricci* while on his professional Grand Tour, such as the composition in the courtyard of Palazzo Farnese in Rome. Soane's mingling of diverse architectural fragments from different eras and cultures was not unprecedented; however, the large Pasticcio was structurally radical and presented a synthesis of diverse architectural styles and eras, reminiscent of the fanciful towers, monuments, and decorative objects featured in the *Hypnerotomachia Poliphili* (1499). Soane's three editions of the text were often found in the bookshelves of the no. 13 Breakfast Room, and from this vantage point, one could study the volume's intricate woodcuts of *capricci* and simultaneously gaze at Soane's construction that stretched beyond the frame of the large windows.[21]

PART III

Legacies

The Transatlantic Design Network's selected time frame of 1768 to 1838 encompasses the productive lifetimes of Cosway, Jefferson, and Soane and is bounded by several significant changes in travel, technology, and national identity. In America, this era captures the critical and ideological transitions from the colonial period to the Early Republic. By 1838, the nation was on the eve of Manifest Destiny, a massive expansion in geographical boundaries and political purview that shaped what would become the Antebellum Period. In England, the year 1838 coincided with the coronation of Queen Victoria and the inauguration of a new era characterized by drastic changes in taste, industrial production, and social hierarchies.

The selected period is also framed by several major transitions in travel and politics. Bracketed by the latter portion of the Republic of Letters and the era of the steam-driven transatlantic ocean liner that began in the late 1830s, this study of the Transatlantic Design Network examines a period of exchange when letters were still primarily conveyed through personal interactions; although oceanic travel was far easier than earlier centuries, transatlantic voyages were not yet readily accessible. In 1838, the Great Western Steamship Company established its first route between Bristol and New York. With faster and smoother travel than packet ships, the number of Americans traveling to Europe grew exponentially from one or two thousand in the late 1700s and early 1800s to over thirty thousand on the eve of the

Civil War.[1] By the middle of the nineteenth century, the offspring, students, and followers of Jefferson, Soane, and Cosway were living in a different world where travel was easier and publications were more readily available. This world, however, had been significantly shaped by the legacies and advocacy of members of the network.

The final theme, Legacies, explores the impacts that Cosway, Jefferson, Soane, and several others within the Transatlantic Design Network had upon future generations of students and travelers. "Museums" explores how architecture and display developed in concert at Monticello and Soane's Museum and why, unlike most collections in the Atlantic World, their house museums managed to survive. "Tokens" examines selected paintings and objects within the collection that were representative, transatlantic gifts. "Academies" discusses the lasting contributions of Cosway, Jefferson, Soane, and several others within the network through their localized educational entrepreneurialism. Jefferson's granddaughter, Ellen Wayles Randolph Coolidge, explored Soane's Museum in 1839, and "Visitors" addresses her perceptive narration. Overall, the lens of the Transatlantic Design Network and these final chapters reveal several rich research projects awaiting future scholars, placing overlooked sites and figures in conversation.

CHAPTER 12

Museums

I am persuaded that we shall be enabled to make a very interesting and curious volume: and one that will tend to perpetuate your name when your buildings are levelled to the dust, and to persons and countries where your designs cannot be seen.

—John Britton to Sir John Soane, April 21, 1826[1]

Wunderkammer and *studiolo* were established in the Renaissance as the accepted architectural language of the collector; but it was not until the Enlightenment that the concept of a museum as a curated and empirical endeavor flourished, which fueled the establishment of public museums. During the late eighteenth and early nineteenth centuries, there were four common types of museums in the Atlantic world: subscription-based institutions, income-driven tourist destinations, public institutions, and house museums. As house museums, neither Monticello nor Soane's Museum were unique in their program, but they were designed as distinctive experiences where art, science, and structural innovation were combined. As they developed, in terms of both the scope of the collections and the configuration the spaces within, Monticello and Soane's Museum became unprecedented experiments in exhibition design. Their collections were placed within inventive compositions of built fabric, and after forty years of development, the architecture of Monticello and Soane's Museum arguably became the most important artifact of the collection. Furthermore, the house museums were exceptional in terms of their longevity, considering most contemporary museums in the Atlantic world had short lifespans: the incredible house museums of the Cosways, Ashton Lever, Thomas Hope, the Peales, and many others were all casualties of finance and fashion by the 1840s. Despite periods of uncertainty, Monticello and Soane's Museum survived, and were revived, for their twenty-first-century visitors.

COLLECTIONS IN GEORGIAN LONDON

The British Museum was established in the year of Soane's birth, and Jefferson was able to visit the collections with John Adams on April 24, 1786.[2] He did not record his impressions of the visit in his memorandum books or letters, but for a scholar of ancient cultures and natural history, the unparalleled collections must have been impressive, and the opportunity to visit was a distinct privilege, shared by few other American compatriots, since the British Museum was difficult to access as an independent visitor. Curious tourists, however, had a range of other private cabinets of curiosity and house museums to explore in Georgian London.

In 1775, Ashton Lever (1729–1788) moved his collections from Lancashire into his Holophusicon in Leicester Square and began charging visitors a steep fee for admission. The natural history museum contained seventeen rooms, divided between two floors, filled with more than twenty-seven thousand objects that Lever had purchased as well as gifts from international explorers, such as James Cook.[3] Although it contained an arched entryway and an impressive number of glass cases, some with mirrors to provide views of objects, Lever's Museum was architecturally mundane. The Holophusicon, much like the collection's original home at Alkrington Hall near Manchester, was simply a repurposed residence. Despite the variety of objects and centralized location in London, the museum was not financially sustainable, and Lever announced a lottery in 1784. He sold less than a quarter of the tickets; however, James Parkinson claimed the winning one, with the museum as his prize. Shortly after the transfer, Parkinson moved the collections to a purpose-built space on Albion Street, Blackfriars, just a few doors from where Soane had temporarily established his architectural office.[4] Parkinson benefited from Lever's lifetime of collecting but took a more inventive approach

THE TRANSATLANTIC DESIGN NETWORK

toward curation. The new Leverian Museum had five main apartments; in the large Rotunda, cases lined the circular walls, and a gallery provided an extra level for exploration. Narration, too, improved in the reinvented museum: Parkinson commissioned an explanatory guide, the *Companion to the Museum,* and managed to successfully operate the museum for nearly twenty years before selling the contents in 1806.[5]

Like many of London's early nineteenth-century house museums, Thomas Hope's interior design collections at his Duchess Street Mansion failed to outlast its founder.[6] Purchased in 1799, the home was part of the Adam brothers' Portland Place development, and Hope established a series of thematic rooms on the upper two floors. When Soane visited in 1802, he discovered that, like his own home, the mansion was designed to set an impression for clients and to reinforce his stylistic ambitions. Hope's published description of the mansion, *Household Furniture and Interior Decoration* (1807), illustrated a highly organized atmosphere that integrated paintings and sculptures within thematic architecture. For example, the room containing Greek sculptures had coffers and fluted columns. There was, however, a disconnect between the stylized form and structural accuracy: hieroglyphics adorned the decorative frieze of the Egyptian Room, but the room also had a shallow barrel vault. Although employed by the Egyptians using adobe, evidence had not yet been discovered, and Egyptian precedent was primarily associated with trabeated form. With very few changes between 1802 and 1819, the "museum" operated more like a gallery of interior design, presenting stylistic vignettes that could be seen as the precedents for the insertion of period rooms into the collections of modern museums.

Even Soane's preeminent architectural rival, John Nash (1752–1835), had a house museum. Like Soane's, it served as a self-designed suite of rooms that were simultaneously advertisement and productive office, filled with architectural models and copies of paintings by Renaissance masters. Located at nos. 14–16 Regent Street (1818–1824), within his ambitious urban redevelopment connecting Buckingham Palace to Regent's Park, Nash designed a residence for both him and his cousin, John Edwards.[7] Like buildings on the rest of the block, Nash's house museum and office occupied the upper floor while commercial properties on the ground floor provided rental income. A series of unfortunate events in 1830, including a stroke and the death of his patron, King George IV, as well as increasingly harsh public attacks on his professional integrity, prompted Nash's sale of the property in 1834. He retreated to East Cowes Castle for the final year of his life and left no interior views of his Regent's Street hotel.

While Soane was initiating his manipulations of no. 12 Lincoln's Inn Fields, a new institution was taking shape on the south side of the gardens. The Company of Surgeons purchased no. 41 in 1797, and two years later the site became home to the anatomical collections of surgeon John Hunter (1728–1793). The collections now known as the Hunterian Museum of the Royal College of Surgeons, not to be confused with those of Hunter's brother at the University of Glasgow, had previously occupied Hunter's residence-cum-teaching-college at 28 Castle Street in Leicester Square.[8] Although depictions of the interior arrangement exist, a sketched plan by William Clift (1775–1849), Hunter's apprentice and later curator of the collections at the Company of Surgeons, reveals that the townhome had a complex circulation route, a top-lit gallery that was "warmed by hot air from house," a yard with a "great skylight," and a library with a suspended passageway between the hall and anatomical theater (fig. 37).[9] Here, architecture, display, and technology were unified. When the collections were moved to a purpose-built structure in 1813, designed by George Dance and James Lewis, Hunter's Museum no longer resembled a resourceful pastiche. The building was distilled and regularized as a decorative shell, and, inside, its repetitive domes were not responsive to elements within the collection.

The preceding examples demonstrate that although several museums had developed in London around the turn of the nineteenth century, few of these creations were actively exploring how the display of collections and surrounding architectural forms could be developed in parallel. Collections were either packed into extant spaces, placed behind uniform cabinets, or housed in purpose-built structures that did little to test architectural or experiential conventions: rooms had little interconnectivity, horizontally or vertically, and few spaces used techniques for maximizing natural light.

Although lost to history, the Cosways' residences in London featured collections and a dynamic architectural atmosphere that could have rivaled the creations of Jefferson and Soane. From 1784 to 1791, the Cosways occupied Schomberg House and then moved to Stratford Place, a residence occupied

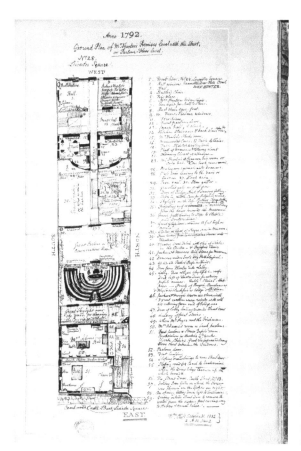

Fig. 37. William Clift's plan sketch of Hunter's townhome at 28 Castle Street in 1792, as remembered in 1832. (Royal College of Surgeons Special Collections, Hunter Album, 39)

from 1791 until June 1820, when, prompted by Richard's failing health, the estranged couple sold the property and moved into an apartment along Edgeware Road. It is difficult to fully reconstruct a picture of the Cosways' house museums since both structures were altered, and the Cosways' collections were dispersed at Christie's auctions in 1791, 1821, and 1822. Nonetheless, the sale catalogs, engravings, and a few written descriptions provide insight into the configuration of the house museums. In a letter to Jefferson, Cosway wrote that the homes once contained a "valuable & immense Collection."[10]

Fig. 38. *Richard and Maria Cosway, and Ottobah Cugoano* by an unknown engraver, after Richard Cosway (1784). The Cosways employed Cugoano from the mid-1780s until Maria's London exodus. (Fondazione Cosway, Lodi)

Within their residence in the central portion of Schomberg House, 81 Pall Mall, the visual experience must have rivaled the leading galleries in London and Paris: the 1791 Christie's catalog lists 478 "pictures" for sale from the "Great Salon" and eight other principle rooms of the home.[11] The catalog only lists paintings and drawings, providing an incomplete image of the extent of the Cosways' collections. Richard's self-portrait from 1784, however, depicted the garden of the home as a series of outdoor rooms filled with architectural elements, sculpture, fountains, and even a peacock (fig. 38).

The couple welcomed their only child, Louisa Angelica Paolina, on May 4, 1790; however, the next period was marred with turmoil for Maria, possibly due to postpartum depression, and she spent the next years traveling in Italy.[12] During Maria's time abroad, Richard moved into no. 20 Stratford Place, and his wife did not join him until 1794. If the 1821 and 1822 sale catalogs are any indication of the collections at Stratford Place, the Cosways' second residence was even more eclectic, and the home was filled with antiquities, mystical objects from the East, mirrors, clocks, occult books, and armor.[13] It was amid these collections that little Angelica was raised. After a brief "sore throat," the couple's daughter died on July 29, 1796, and, to Maria's horror, Richard had the body embalmed and commissioned Thomas Banks to create a marble sarcophagus for display in the parlor.[14]

Contemporary antiquarian John Thomas Smith (1766–1833) provided one of the only descriptions of the Stratford Place house museum: "Cosway fitted up in so picturesque, and indeed so princely, a style that I regret drawings were not made of each apartment, for many of the rooms were more like scenes of enchantment pencilled by a poet's fancy than anything perhaps before displayed in a domestic habitation."[15] This scene, paired with other contemporary descriptions that called the studio "one of the most interesting apartments we remember ever to have seen . . . [a] virtuoso's museum," reinforces the idea that the diverse arrangement of objects at Stratford Place may well have influenced Soane.[16] The architectural character of the home is, however, more ambiguous.

Soane would have been intimately familiar with the Cosways' residence since he frequently called on the couple and recorded in his notebook that on December 10, 1803, he "went to Cosway, survey'd his house" before the group went to an evening event at the Royal Academy.[17] No drawings of Stratford Place are preserved within Soane's archives, so it is unknown if Soane was surveying the home for a future design project or to augment a published description of the house museum, similar to what Soane would develop for his own residence in the 1830s. Due to the lack of evidence, key details about the home are unknown, such as the full plan, the configuration in section, or presence of skylights to illuminate the collections. Maria's letter to Soane from May 22,1823, proves that the built fabric of the home was manipulated, and that, at one point, a wall in the house failed.[18] Although it housed a well-developed and rich collection, the Cosways' London residence at Stratford Place seemed to have been crafted more as a provocative repository of curiosities with flair for mysticism than a scholarly endeavor with a developed architectural agenda.

MUSEUMS IN EARLY AMERICA

In comparison to eighteenth-century Europe, the development of museums in America was delayed.[19] This may be explained by a lack of established sponsorship: American museum founders came from diverse backgrounds, ranging from members of well-established North American families to recent immigrants, and unlike the collections of royal families, aristocrats, or established universities, the early museums of America were often entrepreneurial endeavors undertaken by designers, artists, historians, antiquarians, and explorers. Additionally, the culture of collecting was affected by the lack of concentrated urban populations in early colonial settlements and, later, by the agitations of the American Revolution. The absence of funds for collecting paired with the limited access to repositories of ancient artifacts and art explains why many early American museums focused on the most readily available subject for study in North America: natural history. Bounded by the eighteenth century's broad definition of the term, the study of natural history included archaeology, astronomy, botany, geography, meteorology, and paleontology. America provided a new lens for studying these subjects since the climate and topography yielded new and curious properties that were foreign to Europe.

In 1728, Quaker farmer John Bartram established an extensive botanical garden dedicated to the American genus at his home in Philadelphia. In recognition of his extensive travels on the Eastern Seaboard, he was appointed the royal botanist to King George III in 1765 and was elected a member of the Royal Society. Because of his correspondence and the work at his garden, which is still in operation, he is celebrated as the father of American botany. Although not a museum in the conventional sense because of its out-of-doors condition, Bartram's Garden was nonetheless a carefully curated endeavor that had a rich collection of natural specimens, both native to America and imported from his transatlantic correspondents.

Following the Revolution, several museum-like institutions were founded in Philadelphia, making the city a mecca for intellectual exploration since it was also home to the large Library Company and the American Philosophical Society. In 1782, an immigrant from Geneva, Pierre Eugène Du Simitière (1736–1784), established a natural history collection as the "American Museum," but the institution closed two years later due to the founder's death. Although there were scant examples of American museum collections that explored topics outside of natural history, such as Dr. Abraham Chovet's (1704–1790) anatomical museum founded in 1774, it was not until the work of Charles Willson Peale that America saw the development of a purpose-built museum that melded fields of study such as the arts, natural history, and technology.

Unlike many collectors abroad, the creator of America's first long-standing public museum with sponsors and widespread advertisements was not an aristocrat. Unencumbered by his humble background, Peale displayed an entrepreneurial spirit from an early age as well as an ability to garner external financial support for his endeavors. Born on Maryland's Eastern Shore, Peale spent seven years in servitude as a saddlemaker before he started advertising his services in painting. In 1766, several local patrons took notice of his work and pledged to sponsor travels and subsistence for the twenty-five-year-old budding artist to study painting with West in London from 1767 to 1770.[20] Here Peale would have been part of a large network of American colonists in London: by 1770 there were an estimated five hundred living in the city.[21]

As one of the first transatlantic students, Peale studied under West for twenty-eight months but never formally joined the school or exhibited at the Royal Academy. Originally Peale expressed interest in painting miniatures; however, one of his patrons, Charles Carroll (1723–1783), advised Peale that he should instead study a "Branch of the Profession that would Turn out to Greater Profit here."[22] Promising to advance the impoverished Peale additional funds to support his studies, this Annapolis barrister with no art training essentially steered the course of Peale's career by urging him to explore portraiture and history painting.

PEALE'S MUSEUM

Peale's time in London was predominantly occupied by the arts, and there is no evidence that he visited a museum during his time abroad.[23] Peale was not consciously avoiding collections: the London that he experienced in the late

1760s was not yet full of private museums and commercial ventures in didactic display. It does not appear that he was unable to gain entry to the British Museum, William Bullock had yet to found his Egyptian Hall, and collectors such as Charles Townley had not yet established their private salons. Nevertheless, without much firsthand experience in museums, Peale led the appeal for public institutions in America in the years immediately following the country's establishment. Several authoritative texts have examined Peale's Museum, and its varied incarnations between 1784 and 1827, from the perspectives of scientific method and Peale's contributions to the establishment of museum culture in America, but the ways in which the collections and architectural spaces developed in concert have not been fully addressed.[24]

When Peale returned to America in 1770, he quickly became a significant figure in the artistic community by capturing some of America's foremost founding fathers in portraiture. For example, his 1772 painting of George Washington is the only existing pre-Revolutionary image of the commander. Just prior to the adoption of the Declaration of Independence, Peale moved his family to Philadelphia and then spent three years serving in the Continental Army. Following the Revolution, he began to explore the idea of creating of a museum within his home on the corner of Lombard and Third Streets, where he could capitalize on both America's independence and his artwork by charging admission to see his portraits of Revolutionary War figures. Shortly after opening in 1784, he added an "Exhibition of Perspective Views, with Changeable Effects; or Nature Delineated, and in Motion." This exhibition used lamps, screens, and transparencies to simulate movement and changes in natural light.

By 1786, he started advertising an even larger program for "rational amusement": natural specimens, arranged by class, joined his art collections. Unlike *lusus naturae,* the "whims of nature," that often characterized the monstrous collections within European cabinets of curiosity in the Renaissance and early Enlightenment, Peale's Museum employed Linnean taxonomy.[25] By moving away from exhibiting provocative oddities or collected "trophies," Peale introduced a more professional approach to museum culture that was largely influenced by his studies at the American Philosophical Society that provided access to texts such as Buffon's *Historie Naturelle* (1749–1788) and George Shaw's description of the Leveran Museum, *Musei*

Leveriani explicado, anglica et latina (1792).[26] Over the course of a few short years, he created a museum within his simple saltbox house that, unlike most of the established museums of Europe, simultaneously showcased science, technology, and the fine arts. As an entrepreneurial curator, Peale also established tenets for the safety and security of both the collections and his visitors, installing some of earliest signage that cautioned against touching because the taxidermic displays had been treated with arsenic.[27] The museum eventually advertised not only Peale's paintings and taxidermy but also his technological experiments, including a self-regulating, columnar fireplace, capped by a bust. Although innovative, Peale's "smoke-eater" was never put into operation outside of the museum (fig. 39).

Peale initially founded the museum to supplement his income, but his intentions changed in the late 1780s. Although the nation had yet to ratify the Constitution, he hoped that his museum could become a national institution. This ambition, however, was never actualized. Nonetheless, Peale named the museum his principal occupation in 1792 and solicited an elite group of twenty-seven citizens, including Jefferson, to serve as the museum's "Inspectors." Shortly thereafter, in 1794, the collections of his house museum moved to a rented space within the American Philosophical Society's home, Philosophical Hall. It was here that English antiquarian Henry Wansey visited the collections and published his reflections in *The journal of an Excursion to the United States of North America in the Summer of 1794* (1796), stating that he was "entertained for two or three hours." To enliven the overall atmosphere of the collections, Peale and his sons painted backgrounds for the mounted birds and quadrupeds and added evening hours to allow visitors to inspect the museum in lamplight. To create an even more engaging and interactive space, Peale experimented with trompe l'oeil: *The Staircase Group* (1795), a double portrait featuring his sons Raphaelle and Titian was framed by an actual door jamb and grounded with a protruding stair. Inspired, others tried to replicate Peale's profitable museum venture but found little success. For example, in 1811 Caleb Boyle tried to establish a permanent "National Museum" of Gilbert Stuart's works in the artist's Latrobe-designed studio in Washington, occupied 1803 to 1805, but the project failed after just a few weeks.[28]

The collections and the museum's popularity grew exponentially in the first decade of the nineteenth century, prompted by the reception of eth-

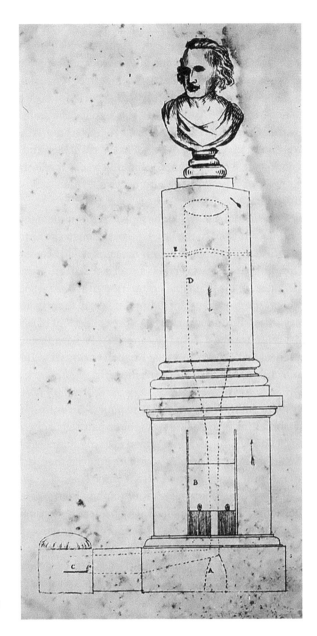

Fig. 39. Sketch of the "smoke-eater," a decorative brick stove for the museum by Charles Willson Peale, 1798. (American Philosophical Society, *The Weekly Magazine,* vol. 2, no. 25 [July 21, 1798])

nographic objects and natural specimens from the Lewis and Clark expedition as well as Peale's involvement with the exhumation and reassembly of mastodon fossils. In late 1801 the museum became the first institution in the world to display the massive skeleton of an "Incognitum." In a letter to Jefferson in 1809, Peale explained that the creature had been recently identified as a new genus and named the mastodon by a scientist across the Atlantic, Georges Cuvier (1769–1832).[29] Later, while serving as a curatorial consultant of sorts for Napoleon, Cuvier tried to acquire a mastodon skeleton as a pièce de résistance for the emperor's collections, but his efforts were unsuccessful.

With growing collections, Peale's Museum moved to the State House, Independence Hall, in 1810 and remained in place until Peale's death in 1827. A sketch from 1822 shows that Peale united the collections and architecture on the upper floors: the abundance of windows provided ample natural light to illuminate more than 250 portraits, situated within an oversized frieze, and the cabinets that housed natural history specimens framed thresholds and created thematic rooms within rooms. Peale's self-portrait of *The Artist in His Museum* (1822) best represents the spatial and programmatic boundaries that Peale severed through his work: gallery and museum were combined (fig. 40). Although not a federally sponsored museum, Peale's Museum established a new model in America and was formally incorporated on February 1, 1821, with a board of trustees and instructions that the museum could not be moved from its home in Philadelphia without compensation.[30] Looking toward the museum's future, Jefferson suggested that Peale's body be deposited in the museum's center, "under a Mausoleum, light as tasty," where his contributions could be immortalized.[31]

As a business model, the museum inspired two of Peale's sons to start their own enterprises: in 1825 Rubens founded a museum at 252 Broadway in New York City, and in 1814 Rembrandt established the nation's first purpose-built museum at Holliday Street in Baltimore. At the latter, Rembrandt created a central, open-plan room to house the collections. This three-story space had stacked galleries and clerestory windows to flood the museum with indirect, natural light, much like Soane's Dulwich Picture Gallery (1811–1814). By the late 1820s, it appeared the Peale family had created a multistate dynasty of museums. Yet all three institutions disbanded by 1842; the collections were dispersed in various sales, and the sites of the Peale Museums

Fig. 40. *The Artist in His Museum* (1822) by Charles Willson Peale.

were either destroyed or drastically altered. Today, only the facade of the Baltimore Peale Museum remains, and it has been recently reinvented as The Peale Center for Baltimore History and Architecture.

DISPLAY AT MONTICELLO AND SOANE'S MUSEUM

During his only tenure abroad, Jefferson wrote lengthy epistles to two young Americans, Thomas Lee Shippen (1765–1798) and John Rutledge Jr. (1766–1819), who were embarking on a European tour. Jefferson's letters predated by four decades the first tour book published exclusively for Americans traveling abroad, Putnam's *The Tourist in Europe* (1838). Although sent to the young men separately, Jefferson's advice was identical: he provided recommendations on the specific places to visit, where to get certain currencies, where to stay, how much time to devote to select sites, and what local fare should be sampled. He also offered cautionary advice on tourism:

When you are doubting whether a thing is worth the trouble of going to see, recollect that you will never again be so near it, that you may repent the not having seen it, but can never repent having seen it. But there is an opposite extreme too. That is, the seeing too much. A judicious selection is to be aimed at. . . . [T]ake care particularly not to let the porters of churches, cabinets &c. lead you thro' all the little details in their possession, which will load the memory with trifles, fatigue the attention and waste that and your time. It is difficult to confine these people to the few objects worth seeing and remembering.[32]

Jefferson's advice to the young men was reflective of his own experiences in Europe, and it may explain why, despite his seemingly limitless curiosity, Jefferson's memorandum books reveal that he made only a few visits to museums and established cabinets.

Jefferson encouraged a type of productive tourism: collections could overwhelm and even confuse; therefore, it was best to explore foreign lands independently, searching for knowledge and experiences that could be of use at home. His eight suggested "objects of attention for an American" were agriculture; mechanical arts, lighter mechanical arts and manufactures; gardens; architecture; painting, statuary; politics; and courts. Within each category he explained what specific elements should be studied, ranging from the plants that could be imported to the American continent, architectural models that could be replicated in the rapidly growing nation, and how issues of personal liberty were addressed in diverse nations. Although worthy of attention, he warned that studying painting and sculpture was not particularly useful as it was "too expensive for the state of wealth among us."[33] As a foreign ambassador surrounded by a rich history of art and architecture, Jefferson saw America as a nation that should not strive to rival the established collections of Europe but should instead focus on cultivating new research and talent. The nation could exploit its natural advantages and celebrate its independence from monarchical traditions, odd rituals that he likened to watching "beasts of prey" at the menageries of London and Versailles. Jefferson's 1788 letter also demonstrates the development of his philosophy on didactic display: his desire to celebrate "recent" history and innovation, as well as his encouragement of the study of the atypical natural conditions in North America, illuminates the shared rationale behind the development of some of America's earliest museums.

When compared to contemporary public and house museum endeavors in London and America in the late 1700s and early 1800s, Monticello and Soane's Museum possessed several commonalities that were not shared with other transatlantic counterparts. Unlike the museums of Lever or Peale, neither Jefferson nor Soane charged for entry. During the lifetimes of the architects, Monticello and Soane's Museum were independent of institutional or governmental sponsorship, yet these house museums welcomed more visitors than similar, fee-charging endeavors. And although Soane's Museum mirrored Hope's in that the structure served as an active advertisement for his designed taste, Soane constantly changed the configuration of spaces and the arrangement of objects within his museum. Aside from the privately printed *Descriptions* of the museum that were produced at the end of Soane's life, the house museums of Jefferson and Soane did not employ narrative guidebooks or object labels. By avoiding organizational systems of chronology, classes, or stylistic categories, Jefferson and Soane placed authentic objects next to casts, and examples of classicism were situated next to the vanguard. The pairing of disparate items next to each other spurred unusual conversations and unexpected parallels.

In his letters to Shippen and Rutledge, Jefferson warned the pair about the disadvantages of taking curator-led tours in house museums; therefore, the variety and arrangement of objects that Jefferson presented to his visitors, displayed without descriptive texts or an accompanying guidebook, reflected his preference for self-driven study and analysis. Much like Soane's Museum, visitors were able to independently judge the concepts, forms, and cultures presented. Unlike the arrangement of many modern museums, where collections are presented to visitors as rigidly framed historiographies with tight interpretive constraints that are managed by signage on the walls or audio tours, the museums of Jefferson and Soane presented viewers with natural and man-made objects ranging from ancient to modern times, all within a single vantage point. Within a dynamic physical environment, they created collages in three dimensions for visual and intellectual exploration.

Although Jefferson had architectural instruments as well as a select number of prints and models, the architectural collections at Monticello were largely confined to representations in wood and plaster. Each of the rooms of the home were adorned with an order from a different classical building or architectural treatise, and Soane provided visual references to many of the same structures in his home. The frieze of Jefferson's Entrance Hall held plaster casts of the griffins from the Roman Forum's Temple of Antoninus and Faustina; Soane had a cast of the same frieze hanging under the Museum Dome. The reign of Emperor Antoninus Pius was known as a period of peace, and the building served as his personal treasury, so the use of the building's frieze in prominent locations within the house museums may have been a shared allusion for Jefferson and Soane: the griffins cast their watchful gaze over some of the most cherished objects in their collections.

The order of the Temple of Fortuna Virilias, a building modeled in cork in Soane's crypt, adorned Jefferson's bedroom. One of Soane's other cork models illustrated the Temple of Vespasian in the Forum; Jefferson referenced this structure, albeit incorrectly, for his Parlor's ornamentation. When selecting the order, Jefferson consulted *Desgodetz's Édifices Antiques de Rome* (1779), a text much criticized by Soane for the "inaccuracy of this celebrated architect."[34] Unlike Soane, Jefferson did not have the opportunity to see, let alone measure, the buildings of ancient Rome; therefore, he often referenced the detailed drawings of Palladio and, later, Desgodetz, for his work at Monticello. While in Philadelphia, Jefferson instructed his former secretary who was still residing in Paris, William Short, to acquire a copy of the text.[35] Here he found an example of the Corinthian order the text cited as the Temple of Jupiter Tonans, complete with a diverse ribbon of objects in the frieze such as urns, weapons, and bucrania. By the 1820s, the temple had been further excavated and received its proper attribution in several British publications that would have been familiar to Soane. Jefferson consulted texts that had some proportional inaccuracies, yet the editions of Desgodetz and Palladio, beneficially, illustrated structures with full sections. This informed Jefferson's abilities to design in three dimensions, unlike many of his gentlemen architect peers who relied primarily on the works of Morris, Benjamin, or Biddle that displayed buildings in only plan and elevation.[36]

Soane, in his third Royal Academy lecture, stated architecture was "an art of invention," so by extrapolating the drawings found in treatises, Jefferson demonstrated his inventiveness in the ornamentation of the interior of his home, especially the Dome Room. Here, he used the order from the Temple of Nerva Trajan, but instead of simply using the height of the room to define the scale of the order, he made a design decision that illustrated his understanding of both section and proportion: the Dome Room's moldings are in proportion to the distance from the floor of the Parlor, directly below the Dome Room, to the zenith of the dome. The moldings and the bull's-eye window frames of the Dome Room are almost mannerist in their boldness, and Jefferson used another source of inspiration for the stacked profile of the dome's exterior: the Temple of Vesta. As arguably Soane's favorite building of antiquity, the Temple of Vesta in Tivoli was given a dedicated recess in his home. It was also represented in several models and was partially reinvented for capitals at Soane's Bank of England.

As a professional architect, Soane assembled collections that were principally related to buildings. His earliest designs from 1792 for the first townhouse at Lincoln's Inn Fields, no. 12, note that the corridor along the eastern party wall should be "ornament'd with plaster casts."[37] The small notes on his plans were the first signs of Soane's desire to develop a working museum in concert with his architectural office. Soane was interested in giving both students and clients immediate access to examples of architectural inspiration, and this interest in didactic display was further emphasized in his tenth Royal Academy lecture: "it is from the associations of ideas that Ruins excite in the mind that our feelings are aroused."[38] Like Soane, Jefferson expressed his desire to include a museum at Monticello in the home's earliest drawings. A rough sketch from the early 1770s identified a semi-octagonal "museum" in the space now occupied by the Tea Room.[39] When sketching his first museum plan, Jefferson had yet to acquire many works of art, books, casts, or scientific objects: his collections grew substantially during his European shopping sprees and then again during his tenure as president due to diplomatic gifts as well as the receipt of specimens from the federally sponsored westward expedition of Lewis and Clark.[40] Within the forty-year development of

Monticello, Jefferson came to realize that his museum could not be contained within a small corner of his home, but instead the entire home could operate as a space for display.

For more than forty years, Soane acquired a range of fragments and casts from ancient buildings, models, drawings, and architectural instruments, but his collections were diversified with sculptures, paintings, gadgetry, and natural history samples. Jefferson's Parlor at Monticello had less than half of the number of works displayed in Soane's Picture Gallery and contained copies, whereas Soane's art collection largely consisted of original works, gifted from friends and collected at estate sales. Nonetheless, the art collections of both men were some of the largest private holdings in their respective countries, and the thematic categories of their art collections were autobiographical representations of their careers and interests. Jefferson displayed people and events that were critical to the development of the young nation as well as pioneers in intellectual discourse, science, and discovery. Soane's collected works showcased a lifetime of design development: the sites he visited as a young man, the masters who influenced his interests, the buildings he constructed, and the buildings that came to life only in the renderings of Gandy.

In letters and publications, Jefferson and Soane frequently displayed serious, and often somber, attitudes toward their work, yet a playful side emerges when assessing their collections, considering both men placed portrait busts of themselves in their house museums (fig. 41). Both architects had several portraits and busts of themselves in the house museums, but the placement of two works highlights how Jefferson and Soane paid special attention to the spatial arrangement of their collections. As noted in "Ambassadors," Jefferson's larger-than-life, Roman-style bust by Guiseppe Ceracchi was placed in the Entrance Hall across the room from a life-sized bust of his political nemesis, Alexander Hamilton.[41] Crafting a literal representation of the "union of architecture, sculpture, and painting" beneath the Museum Dome, Soane placed his own Roman-clad bust above smaller sculptures of the Renaissance masters Michelangelo and Raphael. Beyond the hierarchy in scale, with Soane's life-sized bust looming over the two figurines, he further elevated the prominence of architecture within the triumvirate of creative subjects since both the sculptor and painter he selected as representatives

for their arts were also practiced architects. Since the Entrance Hall of Monticello and Soane's Museum Dome were key rooms for the public to explore the collections, they were apt spaces for Jefferson and Soane to place themselves, perhaps in jest, amid their assembled artifacts.

For Jefferson and Soane, their ever-growing collections may have satisfied a sense of wanderlust. Too occupied with their own work to travel, the act of crafting their house museums may have satisfied their curiosity and desire for constant intellectual incitement. As creators, collectors, and curators, Jefferson and Soane were exceptional examples of the Enlightenment spirit: personal intellectual exploration matched with a desire to disseminate information and cultivate curiosity in others. Their house museums contained diverse collections that spanned cultures, contemporary tastes, and expansive time periods. The varied objects of their collections occupied every surface, and breaking the conventions of larger museums, their displays were crafted without labels or prescriptive paths for visitors that followed chronology or a particular theme. Authentic objects from antiquity and some of the most celebrated artists of the day were placed adjacent to reproductions and casts. Their house museums were evocative, affording visitors the opportunity to appropriate a wide range of lessons and inspirations.

CHAPTER 13

Tokens

Tho I remember Your vast collection, I took the liberty to add a drop of water.

—Maria Cosway to John Soane, February 19, 1831[1]

Members of the Transatlantic Design Network served as agents for one another, buying and sending gifts across countries and bodies of water: books, marble pedestals, music, and architectural models. These gifts often recalled shared experiences: as recorded in a thank-you letter from Jefferson composed on Christmas Eve in 1786, Cosway sent Jefferson, who played the violin, a series of songs she composed for him, a gift in response to the transcribed aria from Antonio Sacchini's *Dardanus* that Jefferson sent Cosway in October.[2] The gifts moving within the network, however, were not always artistic commodities: a shared journey, whether in person or through the prose of a long letter, or even a letter of introduction to a new acquaintance could be a benevolent token between friends. Cosway, like many of the members of the network, was talented at maintaining close friendships for extended periods of time, despite separation by vast distances and camaraderie characterized by more time spent apart than together. Members of the network were able to build trust through transactions, whether by the exchange of objects, shared woes, or the revelation of sensitive financial matters. These became the binding agents for lifelong friendships.

Tracing some of the gifts shared between Cosway, Jefferson, and Soane, it is possible to understand the precarious nature of sending transcontinental, let alone transatlantic, gifts. In a letter to Soane on May 22, 1823, Cosway expressed her concern about mail lost in regionalized postal systems: "what can be the reason of the miscarriage of letters? for several have had this fate."[3] Therefore, when possible, members of the network tried to convey packages through mutual friends. Jefferson and Cosway's rich history of exchange predated the gifts that passed between Soane and Cosway. For most of Jefferson's tenure abroad in the late 1780s, the diplomat was based in Paris, and Cosway resided in London. Separated by four traveling days, the pair exchanged letters and tokens of friendship through friends, such as Trumbull and Church, traveling between the two cities. Once separated by an ocean, the gifts between many of the members of the network waned, but their letters continued: histories, portraits, and landscapes were conveyed through the art of words. In an early letter to Jefferson, Cosway wrote that the most precious exchange of all was simply the "gift of a long letter."[4]

TOKENS OF FRIENDSHIP

In April 1822, Cosway wrote to Soane from her temporary residence on Duke Street at Manchester Square; London was no longer her home and had not been for twenty years.[5] Educational and etching projects in Paris, Lyon, and Lodi had lured her away from London, a city where she was an estranged wife to Richard Cosway, a grieving mother to a deceased child, and an out-of-fashion artist. It was only because of Richard's failing health that she returned to the city, briefly, in 1815 and again in 1817. After his death on July 4, 1821, she stayed in London to settle his affairs. Before she departed London for the final time in July 1822, she had two sales at Christie's auction house to discharge her husband's collections and artwork. Soane assisted with these sales, as well as three previous ones dealing with Richard's collections, and the depth of his friendship with Cosway was underscored by his service as the executor of her estate in London, along with Prince Hoare, from 1830 until he had to resign the position in 1834 due to his failing eyesight.[6]

Anxious to return to Lodi, the small Italian city southeast of Milan that she called home for the remainder of her life, Cosway spent her last years in London trying to distribute the remnants of her own possessions and artis-

tic works that had been left in the English capital. Cosway's April 1822 letter to Soane was related to this dispersal and was accompanied by Cosway's *A Persian Lady Worshipping the Rising Sun.* The painting had been exhibited at the Royal Academy in 1784 and had been gifted to Cosway's friend Lady Lyttelton. The painting returned to Cosway under the stipulations of Lyttelton's will, and once again Cosway gifted the image, this time to Mrs. George Hardinage. In a moment of déjà vu, the painting returned, several years later, after Hardinage's death. For the third time, Cosway presented her painting to a dear friend, but this time she was sure it would stay in the possession of the recipient. Soane's collections had been steadily growing for the past twenty-five years, and Cosway must have been confident that Soane's house museum would be preserved for visitors, even after its creator's lifetime.[7] In her letter, Cosway wrote that she had no room for the image and that the painting "has received its value from tokens of *friendship.*"[8] For Cosway, the painting was a sentimental exchange and one of the many gifts she would bestow on Soane and his museum. Soane eventually placed the painting in his Picture Room, at the back of no. 14, and it is the only image by Maria Cosway in the house museum. However, it was not the only token of friendship exchanged between the two. Soane was gifted three drawings by Richard Cosway, and he purchased several lots at the 1821 and 1822 Christie's sales that would eventually be showcased in the house museum: bronzes, terra cotta fragments, mirrors, ancient and medieval weapons, drawings by Raphael, and even a mummy.[9]

In many ways the most interesting item exchanged between the two friends also has the most obscure history and vague provenance within the otherwise well-documented collections of Soane's Museum. Hanging in a prominent location on the southern wall of the Breakfast Room of no. 13 Lincoln's Inn Fields is one of the first known portraits of Napoleon from the Continent (fig. 43). The portrait, a small piece of oil canvas glued to a constructed timber panel measuring only 12.2 inches by 10.6 inches, is still in its original nineteenth-century gilded frame and was recently inspected for conservation.[10] It was commissioned by Cosway when the young general was on his first series of conquests, the campaign of Italy. It is unknown how and when Soane acquired the portrait since it is not documented in a letter between the two friends, Soane's notebooks, or the Christie's sale catalogs. The painting does, however, appear in Soane's first edition of the *Description* (1830) with the short explanation that it was "a Portrait of Buonaparte in his twenty-ninth year, painted by a Venetian artist, and esteemed an admirable likeness." Subsequent editions of the *Description,* issued in 1832 and 1835, however, included a lengthy description of the painting and a transcription of the artist's letter. The details of the portrait occupy three pages of Soane's *Description,* and it was the first piece delineated in the book, directly following the list of plates and artists included. No other single item or even architectural space in the museum received such attention. Yet, Soane's careful presentation of the painting and the letter were not set alongside an account of how the artwork came into his collection, an odd exclusion for Soane, considering his otherwise meticulous attention to provenance. More-

Fig. 43. Portrait of Napoleon (1797) by Francesco Cossia, hanging in the Breakfast Room of no. 13, Lincoln's Inn Fields. (Author's photos care of Sir John Soane's Museum)

over, the text presented in the *Description* completely disregarded the fact that Cosway commissioned the portrait, and consequentially the *Description* set forth a series of assumptions and misunderstandings that muddled the interpretation of the portrait. It took the pioneering work of a young intern, Salomon Xavier, and several researchers at Soane's Museum in the early 2000s to correctly identify the portrait's artist as well as its connection with Cosway. Nonetheless, there are still several outstanding questions surrounding the portrait of young Napoleon, not least of which is why Soane was interested in a figure who was considered so threatening to his nation and why his text in the *Description* seemed aimed to obscure the painting's origins, despite its preserved packaging and explanatory letters, and the circumstances of its arrival to the museum.

The painting came with a three-page letter from the artist, written in an irregular Venetian dialect, to art dealer Signor Borghini. Dated March 17, 1797, it gave a detailed account of how the painter contacted Napoleon and was given permission to paint while he was in Verona. At the time when the painting was created, Napoleon had been on a yearlong mission as the général en chef de l'armée d'Italie. Marching from Nice through the Piedmont, he entered Milan and eventually drove the Austrian Army north in the Battle of Lodi on May 10, 1796. By the time the artist met Napoleon in Verona, the general had already made his way through Castiglione and Arcole and was now marching toward Venice. According to the letter, the artist was received "with great politeness and goodness and told me he was very sorry that his immediate departure would not allow him to do justice to my abilities."[11] Due to the general's ambitious campaign plan, the artist was given just half an hour before and after dinner to sketch. Realizing his need for additional time, he accompanied the general to San Bonifacio the next morning to steal a few moments after breakfast to finish the portrait. The artist's descriptions of the noises from the constantly moving cavalry and distant skirmishes illustrate that he was unnerved by his time, albeit brief, with the military campaign. His abilities, however, were not dampened by the atmosphere, and he noted that he was able to "paint with good spirits because I saw that they were much please'd with the work already done." Although his letter is apologetic for the rushed nature of the commission, he believed the work to be "a great resemblance." With a downward gaze and a simple rendering of the general's clothing, the artist's depiction of Napoleon looks nothing like the conquering hero of Antoine-Jean Gros's works or the arrogant emperor later depicted in the paintings of David. Instead, the young Napoleon appears contemplative and introspective, a calm contrast to the brazen military leader that emerged during later conquests.

Misreading a blurry signature in red at the bottom of the portrait and the smeared signature in ink on the artist's letter, Soane attributed the painting to Francesco Goma.[12] The artist, however, was Francesco Cossia, a painter from the Veneto who had no other major commissions. First misattributing the artist, Soane then misidentified the person who commissioned the image. Perhaps it was his misreading of the broken Italian in the letter, composed of run-on sentences with little attention paid to forming a cohesive narrative, or Soane's own fascination with Napoleon's wife that led him to write in the *Description* that the painting was commissioned by Madame Beauharnais, the Empress Josephine.[13] Indeed, considering the softer, almost romantic image of Napoleon, it is possible to understand why Soane could persuade readers of the *Description* and his visitors that the painting was commissioned by Napoleon's bride to commemorate their first year of marriage. In his letter to art dealer Borghini, Cossia stated that he "sent him [Napoleon] the packet of Madame le Général," and in the *Description* Soane used this reference as evidence that the painting was commissioned by Josephine. In truth, Cossia simply delivered a letter from Josephine during his visit with Napoleon.

Soane's *Description* overlooked the second letter accompanying the painting that identified both the true artist and his patron. Francesco Ricardi's one-page letter to Cosway reveals that she had been asking for a painting of Napoleon for several months, and her requests had been conveyed to Ricardi by Borghini, who had been in contact with both Cossia and the newlywed Madame Bonaparte. Cosway and Josephine may have interacted at the Parisian court in the late 1780s; however, Cosway's primary connections to the young Napoleon predated his marriage. Napoleon's father, Carlo Buonaparte, was a military aide to Pasquale Paoli during the Corsican revolt against the French invasion in the late 1760s. Unlike Paoli, who was exiled to London, Carlo Buonaparte stayed in suppressed Corsica to continue his law practice and raise his family. Cosway and Paoli were introduced in London at the Cosways' home at 4 Berkeley Street in 1783, and the two were apparently fast friends as Mediterranean transplants in the English landscape.[14] Through his stories and friendship, Paoli likely inspired Cosway's early interest in Napoleon.[15]

Within the letter, Ricardi explained to Cosway that the painting was made by Cossia and that he enclosed a letter from the artist that detailed "the difficulties that he had, and his keenness and his interest in working on this flattering commission."[16] He explained that the painting was almost lost when it fell into the River Adda at Cassano, a town near Milan, but it had been recovered and would reach her after a trip through Switzerland to Hamburg, where another art dealer would ensure the painting made it to London. Based on Ricardi's letter and estimated travel time, it is possible that the Cossia portrait arrived at Cosway's Stratford Place by late spring 1797.

Soane started calling on the Cosways regularly after 1801, so it is likely that he saw the portrait during one of his visits. Like the Cosways, Soane was also fascinated by Napoleon. He found the emperor's reconstructions of

Paris inspiring, praising this model of urban renewal in his Royal Academy lectures, and he acquired several other items connected to Napoleon: a series of 140 commemorative medals issued by the Paris Mint between 1798 and 1815 that Soane believed belonged to Josephine and a miniature of Napoleon by Isabey that was supposedly painted during the emperor's exile on Elba. Soane even had a gold mourning ring created to hold a lock of the emperor's hair.[17] Within a growing collection of Napoleonic treasures, it is clear why Cosway may have bestowed the Napoleon portrait on Soane as another "token of friendship."

As demonstrated by the contents of Cosway's letters to colleagues and friends that were sent after her departure from London in the 1820s, it is unlikely that she would have gifted the Napoleon portrait to Soane without an explanatory note. Even after Cosway took up permanent residence in Lodi, she frequently corresponded with her remaining London contacts, especially when disseminating her collections and the work of others. For example, from Lodi she continued her relationship with the Royal Academy by writing to then president Sir Thomas Lawrence at his Russell Square residence, extoling the talents of an associated engraver who was hoping to sell his publication of prints copied from the gallery in Bologna.[18]

Beyond the continuance of her institutional connections, Cosway maintained her personal correspondences with close friends in London, such as Soane. In a lengthy letter from 1831, Cosway regaled him with a curious description of an excavation in the neighboring Roman era town, known as Lodi Vecchio:

The most extraordinary thing I ever heard, and which made me almost faint, was this: two peasants found a skull with a golden bandage, like a crown round it (here stop); they threw the skull away, and one ran to a silversmith and sold it for silver, for which he received 30 livres; his companion was angry and said it was gold and ran to the silversmith, but had in answer it was already melted, which they always do for fear of being discovered. God knows who's skull it was, but a golden bandage with an inscription![19]

Motivated primarily by the monetary potential of their find, the robbers apparently melted the gold of their discovery to generate a quick sale, causing

Cosway to lament what a "precious curiosity" the crowned skull would have been in a museum. In other letters, Cosway wrote to Soane about the discarded fragments from Italian palaces, "here fine objects of art are dispersed and lost" and described the sad disintegration of homes with antique ornamental gates and fine "freese."[20] Clearly, Cosway and Soane shared preservation and curatorial aspirations. Therefore, it seems unlikely that she would have left Soane without some record about the Napoleon portrait.

It is plausible that Soane's notes on the Napoleon painting in the *Description* were just another fictionalization about his home and its collections since the obscured provenance is perfectly aligned with his penchant for the eccentric and imaginative, especially in the later years of his life. In the summer of 1812, he crafted a curious manuscript adopting the voice of an archaeologist who was attempting to decipher the ruins of the townhouse at Lincoln's Inn Fields.[21] A little more than ten years later, when adapting the northern portion of the newly acquired no. 14, Soane crafted a cavernous study for the fictive Padre Giovanni (Father John), complete with a courtyard composed of salvaged ruins from the Palaces of Westminster. If the painting of Napoleon entered Soane's collections in early 1820s, when Cosway was the most active in the dispersal of her collections, Soane may have crafted a mythology to accompany the painting, crafting a romantic tale about the young general and his bride.

DISPLAYING EGYPT

In a letter to Soane in the late summer of 1830, Cosway requested that the architect send "a catalogue of your extraordinary Museum" to a friend in London who could directly deliver the parcel to Cosway during one of his frequent voyages to Italy.[22] Soane had anticipated this request since earlier that summer he began the process of sending a copy of the *Description* to Cosway.[23] In February 1831, Cosway "received, late last night, Your precious book," and she displayed the richly illustrated *Description* within her circle of Italian compatriots, an act that may have been the first dissemination of Soane's work in Italy.[24] Although Cosway received a copy of the 1830 edition of the *Description* from Soane, it is unclear if she ever received, or viewed, the subsequent editions where Soane dedicated three precious pages to a discussion of the Napoleon portrait.

Would Cosway have taken offense to read her absence in the recounting of the portrait's commission, or would she perhaps have played along with the conceit? Either way, she was not shy in correcting her friend: after reviewing the 1830 *Description,* she noted in a letter to Soane that his Italian translation in one section was grammatically incorrect.[25] In the same letter, she also revealed that she was sending two small objects "to add a drop of water" to his vast collections:

When I was at Paris, my friend, Monsieur Denon, whom you must know by reputation, was just returned from Egypt, with B [Belzoni?]. He gave me two small Egyptian figures he found himself, they are in perfect preservation, and tho small, the work is with much taste and beauty, and the hieroglyphics perfect and clear. I even left the Egyptian dust on them. These I put in a small box with Mercury and a Minerva found here at Lodi Vecchio, and consigned them to a person who is going to England, but I am afraid they will be long on the road, but hope will be safe.

Like many of her contemporaries, Cosway preferred to send letters and gifts with personal acquaintances who were traveling between nations rather than relying on national or privatized mail services. This, perhaps, explains why she never sent Jefferson a token of friendship during the 1820s when she was dispersing her collections. Without a personal acquaintance to guard a parcel against the perils of the transatlantic journey, Cosway may have been wary of conveying anything precious; nonetheless, Jefferson would have enthusiastically welcomed Napoleonic collections and objects from Egypt.

Sometime before 1815, the former president acquired a bust of Napoleon in Carrara marble that he displayed in the Parlor of Monticello.[26] It was placed alongside the tall, mahogany French doors, where visitors to the Parlor could view the bust of the emperor and then, appropriately, look outside to the west. The bust and the vista were choreographed reminders for Jefferson's visitors of the significance of the Louisiana Purchase that was ratified by the Senate in October 1803 and leveraged upon a loan from London's Barings Bank. Less than a year later, Jefferson launched the Corps of Discovery, led by Meriwether Lewis and William Clark, to scout and map the newly acquired territory for the purposes of navigating a trade route to the West Coast and establishing diplomatic relations with American Indians. During their two-year expedition, the team sent several natural specimens and diplomatic gifts to Jefferson, and he eventually displayed these items in the Entrance Hall of Monticello. When he returned east, Jefferson implored Lewis, an Albemarle County native, to direct his route to Monticello so that Jefferson could show the Matootonha chief traveling with Lewis "Big White," the ever-growing collections "from other Indian friends" on display at the house museum's "Indian hall."[27] Using the very same phrase Cosway penned in her letter to Soane, Jefferson described the diplomatic gifts from the west as "tokens of friendship" and displayed various pelts, shields, and pipes alongside European works of art and maps of the known continents, consequentially crafting a room of cultural juxtapositions.

Like Soane, Jefferson displayed various elements of Napoleona in the public rooms of the home, illustrating a shared interest in a complex leader who had revived public art and architecture in France. Both men overlooked many of the more complex political and social associations of the emperor, focusing on his more favorable contributions to global knowledge and design. It was not Napoleon's conquests that led Soane to investigate the chateaux at Malmaison and St. Cloud during his 1819 visit to Paris, but rather his interest in the architectural surroundings that were home to Napoleon and Josephine during their contented years. With this understanding that a military agenda was not part of Soane's collections, it is easy to understand why Soane had no items related to Napoleon's contemporaries in England, such as Nelson. At Monticello, Jefferson's display of Napoleona and related tokens of friendship were carefully placed gestures that referenced the wonders opened to Americans because of the former president's acquisition of new western territory, a purchase that some considered an unconstitutional and ill-fated move by a Francophile president. In Jefferson's interpretation, Napoleon's place within the collections at Monticello was that of an explorer and innovator. In their senior years, the two leaders even shared the welcome ease of domesticity: Jefferson tending to his plantation on horseback and cultivating new hybrids in his terrace garden, while Napoleon, rising with the sun and donning a straw hat, tended to his garden at Longwood in St. Helena.

Moving beyond the figural representations of Napoleon at Monticello and

Soane's Museum, one finds that the collections of Jefferson and Soane also reflected interests in the broader scope of Napoleon's career. Again, their focus was not military prowess, but rather his desire to disseminate information about the cultures of Egypt and Libya as part of the Armée d'Orient campaign from 1798 to 1801. Although it was a strategic campaign of imperial proportions, historically reminiscent of the conquests of Alexander and Ptolemy, Napoleon's interests in northern Africa were also fueled by his curiosity in ancient Egypt, especially its architecture.[28] Artists, scientists, and historians were specifically solicited to travel on the campaign. The Rosetta Stone was discovered in 1799 during engineering excavations associated with the construction of a fort, and Napoleon commissioned a series of publications, *Description de l'Egypte* (1809–1828), to illustrate the travels and findings of the campaign. Acknowledging new discoveries, both Jefferson and Soane highlighted objects from Egypt within their collections, showcasing contemporary efforts in exploration and excavation.

In Monticello, Jefferson crafted an entire "Egyptian corner" that was composed of a map of Africa, a cork model of the Great Pyramid, and a statue that he originally identified as "Cleopatra in marble."[29] This Egyptian corner occupied a critical area in one of the most public rooms of Monticello, the Entrance Hall, and was situated in the circulation path between Jefferson's private chambers and the Parlor.[30] As described in the memoirs of one of Jefferson's great-granddaughters, this was a key area for family as well as invited and uninvited visitors to the home:

The lofty hall of entrance with its Indian trophies—its gallery decorated with enormous antlers—its walls covered with relics from all lands and climes, was today relieved of its sombre aspect: a sleeping statue of Ariadne on the rocks of Naxos [the original Cleopatra] had been removed to another part of the hall: a fire place had been revealed in which burned a cheery wood-fire, produced a somewhat incongruous effect, for projecting over the mantel piece was a model of the Pyramid of Cheops, the base so contrived as to contain a portion of the sand and pebbles of the desert! What a spot this was for a tete-a-tete of a moment—the more valued because sure to be interrupted—many were the brief snatches of talk in front of this blazing fire, for this was a comer of the hall between a door opening to Mr. Jefferson's suite, and the door leading to the suite occupied by the family.[31]

Within the Entrance Hall, Jefferson placed maps and objects related to each of the known continents, and he crafted an experience to stimulate the minds of philosopher farmers, fellow educators, and lifelong students. In terms of America's public, he aspired to cultivate a level of knowledge that was both contemporary to and competitive with Europe. Jefferson was particularly sensitive to the possibility that the oceanic divide between the Old and New Worlds could create educational discrepancies, and he asked a fellow transatlantic traveler, the Marquis de Chastellux, "whether those in America who have received such an education as that country can give, are less improved by it than Europeans of the same degree of education."[32] Written in 1785, before Jefferson substantially transformed Monticello as an experimental house museum, the question expressed his motivations for importing publications and objects, as well as gifts from friends abroad, to maintain current perspective on the world at his rural house museum.

On an entirely different scale, but with similar intentions, Soane populated his museums with Egyptian items such as bronzes, Ushabti and stone figures, stele, a mummified head, the wooden lid of a coffin, and a massive alabaster sarcophagus. Several of these items were acquired in the early 1800s, corresponding to the surge of Egyptomania that swept England; however, the largest Egyptian artifact within Soane's collection was not acquired until 1824: the sarcophagus of the New Kingdom pharaoh Seti I. Soane purchased the sarcophagus from explorer Giovanni Belzoni for £2,000 after the British Museum refused it.[33] Although many of the major spatial additions and alterations to the amalgamated townhouses of Soane's museum had been completed by 1824, he entirely rearranged the museum's dome area to make room for the sarcophagus. In celebration of the acquisition, Soane issued over nine hundred invitations and opened his home to the public on the evenings of March 23, 26, and 30 in 1825 to view the then translucent sarcophagus by candlelight.[34] Underscoring the importance of the piece in his collection, Soane dedicated a few plates to the sarcophagus in the 1835 *Description,* illustrating the artifact's interior and exterior through precise orthographic drawings. A short transcription of Belzoni's *Narrative of the Operations and Precedent Discoveries in Egypt and Nubia* (1820) also appeared in the *Description:* "I cannot give an adequate idea of this beautiful and invaluable piece of antiquity, and can only say that nothing has been brought into Europe from Egypt that can be compared with it."[35]

SHARED GIFTS

Jefferson and Cosway reveled in a shared love of nature and dramatic landscapes, and in a letter to Jefferson, Cosway affirmed that she had recently "be[e]n reading with great pleasure your description of America," revealing that Jefferson gave Cosway one of the few published copies of his *Notes*.[36] Since a copy of *Notes* was not listed in the Christie's sale catalog, and a copy of the book appears within the archives of Lodi, it is likely that Cosway retained her volume. In 1787, Jefferson hoped that Cosway would travel to America to visit some of the sites featured in his *Notes,* and when Cosway mentioned an upcoming trip to Italy, the diplomat wrote: "But why go to Italy? You have seen it, all the world has seen it, and ransacked it thousands of times. Rather join our good friend Mrs. Church in her trip to America. There you will find original scenes, scenes worthy of your pencil, such as the Natural bridge or the Falls of Niagara. Or participate with Trumbull the historical events of that country."[37] Jefferson hoped that he could put Cosway's talents to use in the nation as a landscape and portrait artist who could help broaden the world's understanding of America by illustrating some of the country's natural wonders as well as critical scenes of the nation's foundation.

Had Cosway made the journey to America, her connection to Jefferson would have been essential to obtaining commissions. Trumbull's travels from the late 1700s until 1815 prove that consistent work as a transatlantic artist was difficult to come by: commissions in early America were rare, his portraiture commissions in France and England slowed due to the Napoleonic Wars, and his work in London from 1808 to 1816 was interrupted by tensions over the War of 1812. Trumbull's governmental appointments, such as serving as a secretary to John Jay and a commissioner abroad, subsidized his artistic ambitions, and it was not until the federal commission for the painting of the Capitol dome, initiated in 1816, that Trumbull was able to fully dedicate his attentions to art. Nonetheless, Jefferson's patronage and encouragement of

Trumbull's artistic work was steadfast. Since his years in Paris and through diplomatic introductions, Trumbull was able to meet and paint many of the French veterans of the American Revolution.

During her independent Parisian visit from late August until late November in 1787, Cosway saw Trumbull's studio in action at Jefferson's renovated Hôtel de Langeac. In addition to portraiture, Trumbull was working on two other paintings in his American Revolution series, *The Battle of Bunker's Hill* and *The Death of General Montgomery in Attack on Quebec.* Trumbull's plentiful commissions were, however, a point of contention for Cosway: in December 1787, she wrote to Jefferson that another trip to France in the near future was unlikely because "you have given my dear Sir all your commissions to Mr. Trumbull."[38] Cosway's aggravation subsided, and in her later years, she displayed both of the aforementioned images by Trumbull as engravings in the *saletto* of her Collegio in Lodi, in fond remembrance of her time in Paris with the creative American colleagues that she still called friends through their continued transatlantic correspondence. Both engravings are still on display in the Collegio, and, ironically, Cosway probably did not know that Jefferson had a matching set on display in his Library of Monticello.

Cosway possessed one other, dearer artistic piece connected to Jefferson and Trumbull: a miniature portrait of Jefferson that Cosway commissioned in 1788. Trumbull made three of these portraits: one for Cosway, one for Church, and one that he presented to Jefferson, who then gifted it to his daughter (fig. 44).[39] Although the portraits are approximately the same size, from the same era, and depict Jefferson in the same position, the execution and detailing of each image were different. Jefferson's version of the portrait depicted the American patriot with his famous red hair and simplified dress, whereas the ladies' portraits, much like Brown's portrait, showed Jefferson in the "foreign veneer" of diplomatic dress, with a powdered wig.[40] Church playfully chided the discrepancies, writing Jefferson in the summer of 1788: "Mr. Trumbull has given us each a picture of you. Mrs. Cosway's is a better likeness than mine."[41] Church was well acquainted with Cosway's version of the portrait, and Cosway was staying with the Churches at Down Place when she wrote Jefferson. In reply, Jefferson noted that the portrait was "the most worthless part of me. Could he paint my friendship to you, it would be something out of the common line." He concluded that in the following spring,

Fig. 44. John Trumbull's miniature portraits of Jefferson (1788) for, left to right, Angelica Schuyler Church, Maria Hadfield Cosway, and Martha Jefferson. (© The Metropolitan Museum of Art/Art Resource; White House Collection/White House Historical Association; ©Thomas Jefferson Foundation at Monticello)

Church should cross the Channel so that they could sail to America "in concert" from Le Havre.[42] Despite the fact that Jefferson wrote several other letters to both Church and Cosway urging them to make plans, the group was never able to coordinate a transatlantic voyage together. Nonetheless, they continued their correspondence and circulation of gifts. During his final years abroad, Jefferson served as a book agent for Church in Paris, sending her two volumes of *Les Antiquitiés d'Herculanum* (1781) by conveyance of his secretary, William Short.[43] Cosway probably had the benefit of examining the gift with Church since, due to their proximity, the women spent a significant amount of time together at Down Place.

Shortly before his departure to America, Jefferson lamented the lost opportunity of shared travels, writing to Cosway, "We would have travelled a great deal together, we would have intruded our opinions into the choice of objects for your pencil and returned together fraught with treasures of art, science and sentiment."[44] Jefferson was fully unaware that his journey to America in the fall of 1789 would be his last trip across the Atlantic, and he had even written to Cosway that "my absence may be as short as five months, and certainly not longer than nine."[45] However, while in New York City in the summer of 1790, serving as secretary of state, he realized that a return to Europe was unlikely. He wrote to Cosway, "I am now fixed here [in America], and look back to Europe only on account of that circle. Could it be transferred here, the measure of all I could desire in this world would be filled up."[46] Now separated by an ocean, Cosway continued to express her desire to "surprize you on your Monticello! I have Your picture by Troumbel on the side of my Chimney always before me, and always regret that perhaps never can I see the Original."[47] Cosway's version of the miniature remained in the private quarters of the Collegio until 1976. Upon America's bicentennial, the Fondazione Cosway, on behalf of the Italian government, gifted the piece to the collections of the White House.

"SUBLIME OCCUPATIONS"

Although Jefferson never returned to Europe, his interconnected group of designers, art enthusiasts, and inquisitive travelers that consisted of figures such as Church, Cosway, and Trumbull continued to circulate letters through the early 1800s. The group, however, had to rely on mail systems instead of personal conveyance since the coterie that once operated between London and Paris was now widely dispersed, with members moving between three countries and disparate sites: Albany, New York City, Philadelphia, Washington, London, Paris, Lyon, and Lodi. These distances and the lack of an assured delivery may explain why they did not exchange tokens of friendship in their later years. Many in the group were also busily engaged in long-term projects: the cultivation of house museums, the foundation of educational institutions, large-scale painting projects, and activities as patrons. With a considerably shorter distance to traverse, Cosway and Soane continued their transcontinental exchanges, and on March 20, 1834, Cosway wrote Soane thanking him for the "beautiful drawings," noting that she would place them, once framed, in her drawing room.[48] With no Soanean masterpieces preserved at Lodi, the subject of the drawings is unknown, but it is possible that they featured his house museum since Cosway noted that the drawings represented "your last work." Soane and Cosway continued writing through 1835, and unlike her correspondence with Jefferson that was eventually impeded by distance, her letters to Soane stopped due to their mutual "want of sight." In her May 16, 1835, letter to Soane, the last preserved in the museum, she wrote that she would not "prolong my letter for consideration of your eyes" but promised that her next epistle would contain the gift of a description of her recent trip to Rome, detailing all its "changed embellishments." The letter never arrived.

CHAPTER 14

Academies

The time, not distant far, shall come
    When England's tasteful youth no more
Shall wander to Italia's classic shore,
    No more to foreign climates shall roam
In search of models better found at home.

—Thomas Francklin, qtd. by John Soane while lecturing to the Royal
Academy[1]

Many members of the Transatlantic Design Network were educators who
not only instructed students but also attempted to shape educational policy
through their writings and entrepreneurial ambitions to establish new institutions. Of the members of the network who wrote about or founded institutions, the majority situated academies within their immediate vicinity,
underscoring the importance of local sites for education that were accessible
to a wider audience, not just those in developed urban areas. By recognizing
that not all students were afforded the opportunity or had the finances to
undertake educational Grand Tours, members of the Transatlantic Design
Network set forth a collective agenda: social class or geographic location
should not define academic pursuits. Additionally, they experimented with
ways that their academies could be constructed as rich architectural atmospheres: they posited designs for structures and curricula to entice students
to explore their surroundings, physically and intellectually. Within the network, the belief that new instructional models could cultivate the next gen-

eration of civically engaged and design-minded citizens was widespread, and discussions of their new institutions dominated the final letters of Cosway, Jefferson, and Soane.

It is possible that the shared educational interests of members of the network were inspired by their status as, largely, self-made men and women. Consequently, they opposed the accepted institutional practices that reserved formal education for the wealthy and elite. Additionally, certain members of the network, such as Hadfield, Thornton, Jefferson, and Cosway, rejected the notion that productive academies had to be situated within established, densely populated urban centers. They believed that training in design and aesthetic theory should be disseminated to a wider audience to cultivate the potential of young designers and stir the interests of future patrons. Through these goals, new educational institutions could also foster the development of broader systems of personal interconnectivity that countered the established practices of closed intellectual groups and facilitated new artistic, philosophical, and social circles. The three educational sites established by the key triumvirate of the Transatlantic Design Network best illustrate the rhetoric, physical manifestations, and legacies established by the educational endeavors, but beyond Jefferson's University of Virginia, Soane's Museum, and Cosway's Collegio delle Grazie di Lodi there were a few institutions and curricular aspirations blossoming within the network in the early 1800s.

EDUCATIONAL AMBITIONS

In 1801, Hadfield attempted to establish an architectural academy in Washington, elevating scholastic pursuits in the developing nation's capital since there was not yet a single institution in the city dedicated to formally training architects. In the first two decades of the 1800s, Godefroy tried to establish his own educational legacy by serving as an independent drawing tutor and, concurrently, an instructor of design and the mechanical arts at St. Mary's. Here students learned in spaces constructed to his architectural specifications. After Godefroy migrated to England, he designed a Catholic school in the Somerstown area of north London in the 1820s, a commission connected to his previous work with the Sulpicians in Maryland and Kentucky. The order, like many members of the network, was charged with dedication to lifelong learning.

Others in the network used discourse rather than built practice to assert new education initiatives. In the late 1790s, Thornton and his wife wrote a "Treatise on National Education."[2] Much like Jefferson's personal and legislative writings on education, the Thorntons' treatise ambitiously extolled educational equity: "the children of the rich and poor . . . would be nurtured in the consciousness of equality, the dignity of nature receive no humbling check from the caprice of fortune."[3] The treatise stipulated that each state was to have primary and "high" schools (above the age of ten) as well as colleges that would send their most promising students to the National University in Washington, which would teach the sciences and languages in addition to liberal and mechanical arts. Condemning L'Enfant's urban scheme for its lack of a "seat of learning," the Thorntons' proposal stated that the National University would attract talent to the nascent city through a series of academic buildings and classrooms out-of-doors: "botanical gardens, a national museum, printing offices, libraries, an observatory, forrest of the different trees of America, and all that can be desired to accommodate the learned and unlearned."[4]

The treatise did not specify materials or an architectural style, but the proposal melded functional buildings and didactic landscapes. This, in the Thorntons' opinion, was in direct opposition to the development of sites in the capital. William Thornton condemned federal constructions, such as the President's House, for their frivolity and connections to monarchical precedents: "Avoid palaces and the gardens of palaces. If you build a palace I will find you a king."[5] Although the treatise was unfinished and never published, many aspects of it could be applied to Jefferson's later foundation of the University of Virginia, shaped by Jefferson's correspondence with Thornton on the design. The treatise, as well as the architectural assessments found in her correspondence and diaries, illustrate that Anna Thornton also actively participated in dialogues about design. In her household accounts, she detailed that she produced many of the working drawings that Thornton used in his practice as a busy gentleman architect in Washington.[6]

The Thorntons' treatise addressed selected elements of the conceptual and physical architecture of education. Yet the final endeavors of the trium-virate that form the core of this book best extolled the importance of a na-tional interest in the architecture of education. As educators, they redefined and expanded the audience for formal instruction within their respective nations, and from the 1810s, the establishment of their academies domi-nated the rest of their lives. The fact that these educational endeavors were concurrent expresses their shared interest in the creation of an educational legacy. These academies still function, and elements of their original design are remarkably preserved. As institutions for exploration, architectural engagement, and the cultivation of civic spirit, their work left an endur-ing legacy.

With no offspring to directly pursue the interests they championed, Cosway, Jefferson, and Soane turned their attention to the foundation of public institutions. Jefferson had no direct male heir to further his politi-cal and architectural agendas, and although he was grandfather to twelve, none of his grandsons pursued architecture, or any field of design or the arts, as a career. In the family's realm, Jefferson's granddaughter Ellen was his aesthetic surrogate. However, in the realm of Virginia's exclusively male-dominated government and educational systems, Ellen was unable to act as her grandfather's heir.[7] At the end of his life Soane, too, found that he had no architectural heirs: his namesake died in 1823, and he was estranged from son George. Therefore, he created an architectural dynasty through his stu-dents. For Cosway, Jefferson, and Soane, the students of their institutions could be seen as extensions of their families, and this concept was most suc-cinctly, and sentimentally, expressed in Cosway's letter to Soane from Feb-ruary 6, 1832: "You will laugh when I tell you I am a grandmother, of almost three hundred children."[8]

Despite the failing eyesight experienced by Soane and Cosway, and Jef-ferson's crippling rheumatism and financial woes, these three dedicated the last decades of their lives to the demanding, politically trying, and unpaid occupations of establishing an educational legacy. The drive to pursue such a task in the face of adverse conditions was, in part, driven by their experi-ence within the Transatlantic Design Network. For Cosway, Jefferson, and Soane, international experience proved transformative to their respective interests and career trajectories, cultivating a broad experiential knowledge of the arts while building their diverse personal networks. The meetings they had during these travels, and the resulting introductions to new friends and associates, inspired a lifetime of epistolary exchange and helped expose the members of the network to new sites, buildings, discoveries, and ideas. For the triumvirate, the formulation of educational institutions exclusively for erudition in situ was not academic xenophobia, nor a critique of travel or multinational education. Instead, the foundation of the Jefferson's university, Soane's Museum, and the Collegio reflected the shared desire to instruct a broader group of citizens, locally, in preparation for their later endeavors, whether at home or within international communities of scholars. An analysis of Soane's famous poem from his first Royal Academy lecture, quoted at the beginning of the chapter, illuminates how the triumvirate's academies were models for localized education and practical instruction. When read with an understanding of Soane's architecture as applied science, the verse was not a dismissal of the Grand Tour, important for forming an understanding of history and culture, but rather a cautionary note that the architecture of the Mediterranean should not be transplanted to England: these two areas had distinctly different climates, material resources, and opportunities, especially considering London was at the center of developments in industrial production and technology. Through immediate access to architectural training and rich repositories of knowledge, England could produce architects with the ability to craft designs responsive to the English landscape and, perhaps, create new models that would attract their own set of curious visitors from abroad.

Early in his career as a statesman, Jefferson championed the "general diffusion of knowledge," and three years before his university was established, first chartered as Central College in 1817, Jefferson wrote to a friend that he hoped an "Academy or College" could be "established in our neighborhood."[9] A year earlier he had been in contact with the Trustees of East Tennessee College and wrote to them, "No one more sincerely wishes the spread of information among mankind than I do, and none has greater confidence in it's effect towards supporting free & good government."[10] In this letter, he also first expressed his belief that a new educational institute could be designed as an "academical village" that was "friendly to study," and through its configuration of independent classrooms, professorial lodges, and student

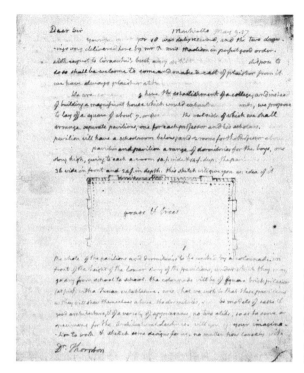

Fig. 45. Jefferson's letter to Thornton from May 9, 1817, with a plan sketch of his U-shaped "college" framing "grass and trees" in the center. (Public domain and from N300, "The Thomas Jefferson Papers," Albert and Shirley Small Special Collections Library, University of Virginia)

barracks with covered means of conveyance between, the institute could be constructed in parts, as funds were available (fig. 45).

Jefferson described the founding and designing the University of Virginia as the "hobby of my old age."[11] Although architecture was not one of eight proposed professorships (ancient and modern languages, mathematics, natural philosophy, natural history, anatomy and medicine, moral philosophy, law), it was a core subject for students, listed as one of the nine key topics of study in the curriculum plan cited in minutes of the Board of Visitors and letters to the Virginia Literary Fund Board in 1824.[12] Architecture was also an implied subject through the innovative arrangement that Jefferson described to Cosway: "Varieties of the finest samples of architecture, has made of it a model of beauty original and unique."[13] He further explained that the university's library would be housed in the building still under construction, built "on the principle of your Pantheon." Students at the university had dedicated dormitories, and here Jefferson enacted his "light rule," a mathematical formulation, adapted from the concepts of Palladio and William Pain, that he believed would ensure the optimum natural illumination for study. In his building notebook Jefferson wrote: "Light. Rule for the quantity requisite for a room. Multiply the length, breadth, & height together in feet, & extract the square root of their product. This must be the sum of the areas of all the windows."[14] Exercising this calculation for a student's room at the university, Jefferson included the area of the room's entry door in the equation, and this alludes that, whenever weather and circumstance permitted, Jefferson intended his students to leave their doors open to the Lawn.

The U-shaped composition was also designed to frame views. In one direction, the key structure, the Rotunda, was designed as a temple to knowledge that housed the library, an observatory, and various laboratories. In the other direction was nature, a westward view toward the Blue Ridge Mountains and figurative Manifest Destiny for the developing nation. Overall, the University of Virginia was a manifesto for the application of science in architecture: it provided unity, tranquility, and, of the utmost importance, security against fire and infection.[15] Jefferson the naturalist designed exterior classrooms in the form of gardens for botany lessons and hoped that the didactic architecture of the site would improve "the virtue and science" of Virginia.[16] For the classrooms, Jefferson proposed an extensive list of "Instruments for the classes of Nat. Philosophy & Mathematics" that included tools for experiments in mechanics, hydrostatics, optics, acoustics, electricity, astronomy, and devices for the "application of Science to arts." Although Jefferson did not see his university completed, he was able to supervise construction through his final years, often from a telescope mounted on Monticello's north terrace that was trained on the university's grounds.[17] When Jefferson died in 1826, key structures such as the Rotunda and the Anatomical Theater were still under construction. Nonetheless, the specificity of his plan, in terms of its architecture and curriculum, enabled the fulfillment of the scheme as envisioned.

In the last letter Jefferson received from Cosway, dated September 24, 1824, she asked her "transatlantic friend" to send an image or further descriptions of his "fine Seminary": "I have had my great Saloon painted, with the representation of the [. . .] parts of the world & the most distinguished objects in them I have at a loss for America, as I found very few small prints— however Washington town is marbd & I have left a hill barren, as I would place Monticello, & the Seminary."[18] Jefferson's response to the request is un-known, and he was, perhaps, too ensconced in the pressing efforts to secure funds and complete the design. In an earlier letter to a fellow Virginia states-man, he wrote: "It is the last act of usefulness I can render, and could I see it open I would not ask an hour more of life."[19] After a delayed opening due to the arrival of foreign professors, the University of Virginia welcomed its first sixty-eight students on March 7, 1825; Jefferson was eighty-two years old.

Cosway's first plans for the Collegio were dated around the same time as Jefferson's letter to Tennessee College, and a full history of the design and de-velopment of the Collegio, founded in 1811, is a rich project awaiting a future scholar. Like Jefferson, Soane, and others in the network, Cosway believed that the physical location of her institution was critical to its significance, writing to Soane that "here [in Lodi] the want of good education was more in need of than in England."[20] Using a third of her revenue from the sale of Rich-ard's collections to help establish the Collegio, Cosway founded an institute to foster the intellects of young children, described to Jefferson as "growing tender plants."[21] At the Collegio, Cosway designed curricula that included the formal instruction of math and science alongside artistic studies in drawing and music. As a school for girls, this charter was unprecedented in Italy.[22]

The Collegio was founded on the site of a fifteenth-century monastery, directly adjacent to a Baroque church and the medieval walls of Lodi; the site, like that of Soane's Museum, provided only one significant facade (fig. 46). The architecture and spatial arrangements were, therefore, rationalized through a series of courtyards, wide arcaded spaces that could be used for outdoor classrooms, with a range of interior enfilades connecting vaulted classrooms, bedrooms, and the other utilitarian functions of the school. Plans showed a new passage to the church, slipping behind the apse, and even a Soanean space in an auxiliary chapel where the students could watch mass from arched openings in a gallery. In a letter to Soane, Cosway wrote: "It was a poor miserable Convent, and now it is a very respectable building."[23] From 1811, a redesign transforming the convent into the Collegio occupied Cosway's time, and it appears that a small, personal project on the adjacent

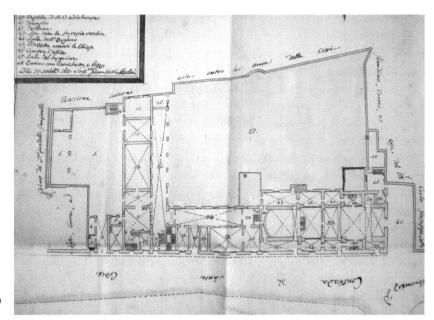

Fig. 46. Plan of the Collegio delle Grazie, Lodi, ca. 1812. (Archivio Storico, Milan 49741)

site captured her attentions, too. A survey from 1822 shows a *"caseggiato e cortile rustico"* next to the Collegio, and this may be the small house that Cosway wrote to Soane about in 1823. She had recently purchased the property and noted its poor arrangement, but with only scant funds to make it "habitable," she would have to make changes *"poco a poco,* the most necessary, in short something every year."[24]

Soane's Museum, like those of his peers, experimented with new models of educational accessibility since he opened the museum's doors, for free, to students of painting, sculpture, and architecture. Soane also asserted a pioneering piece of legislation with his advocacy for the Soane's Museum Bill, passed on April 1, 1833, and entered as an Act of Parliament on April 20, 1833.[25] This preserved the house museum and had a key provision that stated that the objects within could not be moved to another museum. The records of Parliamentary Debates reveal that there was a proposition to transfer the collections to the nearby British Museum; however, this was overturned: the collections could not be divorced from their innovative, custom-designed architectural armature. The fact that Jefferson did not attempt to preserve his house museum reflects his personal financial situation at the end of his life as well as the absence of American governmental intervention in preservation.[26] These conditions also help explain why Jefferson used the university as his legacy. A congressional act similar to the Soane's Museum Bill would have been unprecedented in any of America's courts during Jefferson's lifetime, and following his passing in 1826, the future of the nation as a union was becoming more and more perilous.[27] In a letter from 1833, former president Madison wrote that the "torch of discord" was intensifying between the "North and South."[28] Discussion of the "North and South," used as proper nouns, was part of the political and social rhetoric that had been developing since the Missouri Compromise of 1820, foreshadowing the Civil War and underscoring that by the end of the Early Republic, two distinct geographical identities were evolving in the United States. They were sharply distinguished by differences in demographics as well as labor and industrial practices. When Parliament moved to preserve Soane's house museum in 1833, the United States had little power to save the house museum of a founding father because it was simply trying to preserve itself. The bifurcation of the American governmental system into state and national branches, however, facilitated the foundation of Jefferson's university.

In the early nineteenth century, a national university, as proposed by the Thorntons, would have been an impossible project; however, Jefferson's university, sponsored by the Commonwealth of Virginia, could operate as a semi-autonomous, regional institution. Virginia's government and its local citizens were, however, not without reservations in terms of funding the ambitious plans for the university. Some were skeptical of Jefferson's charter that opened the university to all white males, removing the condition of land ownership that was requisite for entry into all other American colleges, except the University of North Carolina. With the desire to cultivate support for the public lottery and justify the architectural arrangement that some deemed "extravagant," Jefferson wrote a letter to the *Richmond Enquirer* in 1817 that demonstrated a narrative approach similar to Soane's manuscript, "Crude Hints towards an History of My House."[29] In the letter, published by the newspaper, Jefferson adopted the fictionalized voice of "a correspondent of the Editor of the Enquirer" who had recently traveled through Charlottesville on his return from the Warm Springs of western Virginia.[30] Here he reported that he had "good confidence in their success" because the overall design was "very remarkable," and the college's location in the "central and healthy part of the country" would afford "our sons the benefits of education . . . that the future destinies of their country will depend."

Cosway was less of a self-promoter for the "usefull occupation of my dear College at Lodi," but her work, nonetheless, received commendation from local and regional authorities and became a model for other institutions in the area.[31] In 1830, she purchased the deed and later brought other "English ladies" to the school to take charge of the day-to-day operations. In her will, the administration of the Collegio passed to the Commune di Lodi, ensuring its operation after the founder's passing.[32] Although the girls' school closed in the 1970s, the site still operates as a primary school, and the Fondazione Cosway was established to manage the Collegio's archives.

Although located in three different countries, the academies of Jefferson, Soane, and Cosway exhibit critical similarities. Students were educated in unparalleled environments where they could explore, both indoors and outdoors, and forward the pursuits of their institution's founder. Of the many academies proposed by members of the Transatlantic Design Network, several floundered, and few ever transitioned delineations in pen and ink to built experiments. However, Cosway, Jefferson, and Soane were able to actualize and maintain their academic creations. Elements of their institutions, such as responsiveness to both the site and the conditions of learning in the "modern" world, were echoed in the text and images of British gentleman architect Charles Kelsall's *Phantasm of an University: With Prolegomena* (1814).[33] In self-promotion, Kelsall sent President Madison a copy of his educational treatise in early 1817 in hopes that it might prove useful for "raising an University worthy of the American States."[34] The newly retired Madison penned a response in October 1817, noting that a "Central Institution [Jefferson's university]" was currently underway in Virginia, and it would "embrace an extensive circle of Sciences" through its organization and architectural plan.[35] Although it was not yet completed, Jefferson's university was already cited in international conversations about architecture and education.

CHAPTER 15

Visitors

Like all private houses in London this house is small, but it contains a great number of casts, fragments of antique statues and buildings, vases, sarcophagi, little panels and bronzes, all exhibited in the most ingenious way, in the smallest of spaces lit from above and the side, often only 3ft wide. Medieval, antique and modern works are intermingled at every level; in courtyards resembling cemeteries, and in chapel-like rooms, in catacombs and drawing-rooms, ornamented Herculanean and Gothic styles. Everywhere little deceptions.

—Karl Friedrich Schinkel, *The English Journey*, 1826[1]

The figure who provides an exceptional lens on the transatlantic exchange of ideas and an unmatched reading of Monticello and Soane's Museum in conversation is Ellen Wayles Randolph Coolidge (1796–1876). As one of Jefferson's granddaughters, she spent her formative years in the domestic and diplomatic chaos of Monticello. When Jefferson retired from public service in 1809, his daughter, Martha, and the rest of the Randolph family moved to the mountaintop. It was here, amid the constant construction, diverse collections, a vast library, and the attentiveness of her grandfather, that Ellen's interests in the arts, science, and nature were cultivated.[2] The saturated academic and social atmosphere of Monticello, truly unparalleled in the nation, was a productive one for Ellen: she interacted with the mountaintop's countless visitors and met many of the transatlantic guests who traveled to see the house museum, even acting as the host of Monticello in Jefferson's absence. She also frequently traveled to Poplar Forest with her grandfather, and in the rooms of the octagonal retreat the pair would read and write and in the evenings would sit "some time after dinner, in conversation on different subjects."[3] Like her "grandpapa," she delighted in exploring the sublime scenes of Natural Bridge and shared a love of gadgetry, lamenting in a letter to her mother in 1817 that she lost her prized pocket telescope on one such journey of rural exploration.[4]

As a young woman, Ellen's educational experiences transcended many of her peers: she was better read due to studies guided by her mother, a product of the Parisian convent school Abbaye de Panthemont, and Jefferson. She was also perceptive and demonstrated attention to architectural detail in her letters, writing to her mother that Poplar Forest was looking "more dismal than usual" after a period of extended absence: "wilderness and desolation of everything around, the weeds growing to the very door of the kitchen, as high as your head, the planks of the terrace torn up in places by the violence of the winds, the front of the house offering nothing but the sashes of its windows, except where they were protected by the portico, the dining room darkened by the boarding up of the skylight, and the floors stained and moulded by the entrance of the rain water."[5] Ellen's skills in observation and evocative narration would prove useful in her travels. By the time she was twenty-one, she had explored Washington, Baltimore, and Philadelphia, cities that Jefferson did not reach until his forties. While in Washington, she visited the charred remains of the Capitol, wandering through the substructure that was designed by Hadfield and noting in a letter to her sister that "vaults [were] so dark and gloomy that you may almost fancy yourself in the castle of Udolpho or some other place of the kind." In Philadelphia, she sought the townhomes where Jefferson resided as secretary of state and vice president. She also made trips to see the collections of both the Academy of Fine Arts and a museum where she had her silhouette made to send the family at Monticello. The latter was mostly likely Peale's Museum, and she wrote that she hoped to visit again before her departure.[6]

JEFFERSON'S GRANDDAUGHTER AT SOANE'S MUSEUM

Ellen and Joseph Coolidge married in Monticello's Parlor on May 27, 1825. In July 1838, they traveled to London for what they anticipated to be a six-week layover before continuing their travels to China for Coolidge's business.[7] The stay, however, lasted ten months, and Ellen's notebooks form a copiously descriptive journal that chronicles her time in the newly Victorian city. The London that Ellen experienced in 1838 and 1839 was certainly different than the one Jefferson saw in 1786, but both transplants were highly critical of the city's architecture. Jefferson wrote: "Their architecture is in the most wretched stile I ever saw, not meaning to except America where it is bad, nor even Virginia where it is worse than in any other part of America, which I have seen."[8] Ellen's critiques were no less severe: "Nothing seems to me more mistaken in architecture than useless columns, pillars out of place; but it is one of the commonest mistakes of false taste. In the United States many honest edifices are made simply ridiculous by such appendages. Here in London they stand every where like unprofitable servants."[9] Like Jefferson, she softened her initial and unfavorable opinions when she sought refuge outside of "the mud and filth and smoke and noise, of dirty, dark London" by visiting gardens and estates in the city's environs, and even traveling north to Scotland.

The latitude of Ellen's travels in and around London were bolstered by her relationship with the American ambassador, fellow Virginian and Albemarle County native Andrew Stevenson (1784–1857). Besides general advertisements or word of mouth, it is possible that Ellen learned of Soane's Museum directly from Stevenson since Soane sent him at least one copy of the *Description* (1835) following its private publication, and Stevenson forwarded the volume to the Library Company of Philadelphia.[10] According to Soane's notes, the architect directed only a few copies toward an American audience: one to the Philadelphia Academy and another to the Washington Academy. The specific institutions that Soane refers to are unclear, but the likely candidates were the Library Company or the American Philosophical Society in Philadelphia and the Library of Congress, Columbian Institute, or Columbia College in Washington. Curiously, another copy of the *Description*

(1835) with a handwritten inscription "To His Excellency Andrew Stevenson, Esqre/ From the Author, with sentiments of respect" exists and is now held within the University of Virginia's Special Collections.[11] Stevenson, perhaps, retained this copy and brought it with him upon his return to the United States in 1841. He eventually retired to his Albemarle estate, Blenheim, but remained active in Virginia politics and the affairs of the University of Virginia.

Ellen's London diary, although extensive in its daily record of events and full of candid observations, does not contain many explicit parallels between her recollections of Monticello and what she encountered abroad. There were, however, many opportunities to record commonalities. For example, at Chiswick Ellen thoroughly described the layout and annotated a small plan with the observation that the site was ideal for a "good game of Hide & Seek," but she made no mention of her grandfather's visit to the site or the resemblance of the octagonal dome to the design at Monticello. Of the few instances Ellen specifically referenced Monticello, the majority were in in relation to the natural landscape: she noted that the foliage of Regent's Park reminded her of the tree below her window at Monticello, and that "the view from the [Stirling] Castle is more like that from Monticello than any thing I have seen in my travels."[12] Considering that Ellen did not regularly compare life at Monticello and the sights of London, it is not surprising that her diary entry from her visit to Soane's Museum does not contain a lengthy passage about the commonalities between the constructions of Jefferson and Soane. Nonetheless, her other activities in London and recorded observation reveal that her years at Monticello inspired curiosity in history, the arts, and museums. She also possessed a keen architectural eye. During her travels abroad, she visited several galleries, studios, and auction houses and visited Thomas Hope's collection on December 28, 1838, noting that the rooms gave more of an "air of a magazine, a storehouse, a Bazaar, rather than a dwelling house, a home where a family live and move, having their wants, their occupations and their habits."[13]

She also made multiple excursions to sites such as the British Museum and the National Gallery in order more carefully examine specific rooms or see new exhibitions. Throughout her ten months in the city, Ellen visited both the vogue sites of Victorian London as well as those farther afield from

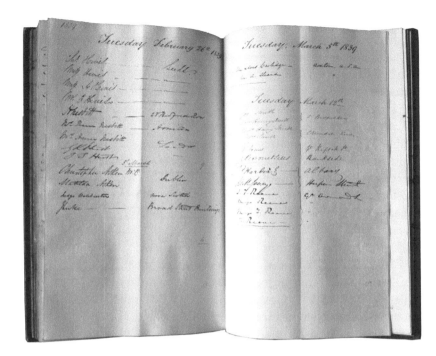

Fig. 47. The visitors' book from Soane's Museum, marking Ellen Wayles Randolph Coolidge's attendance on March 5, 1839. (©Sir John Soane's Museum, London; author's photo)

the typical path of the foreign tourist, such as the East India Museum. Following the advice of her grandfather's hints to Americans traveling in Europe, she did not strictly follow the recommendations of a guidebook or local touring agents but instead followed her own interests. Ellen's visit to Soane's Museum on March 5, 1839, was, like most of her museum visits, with her husband Joseph Coolidge. Augustine Heard (1785–1868), Coolidge's fellow trader and business partner, accompanied the couple, and the curator's book notes that they were the only visitors for the day (fig. 47).[14] Heard had just accompanied the couple's youngest son, Thomas Jefferson Randolph Coolidge (1831–1920), across the Atlantic, but the young man, just shy of his eighth birthday, did not join the family on the visit to Soane's Museum.

Directly following Soane's death, his museum was closed for nearly a year while the first curator, George Bailey, cataloged the contents. Visitor numbers varied during these first few years, but "Open Days" typically yielded thirty visitors.[15] On quiet days, such as the spring afternoon of Ellen's visit, only a handful of spectators wandered the house museum, and as Americans, Ellen and her touring party were fairly unusual visitors.[16] In the early years of the museum's operation, the majority of visitors were locals, and consequentially the visitors' book reads like a local address book: Gray's Inn Road, Southampton Row, Bedford Place, Woburn, Fitzroy Square, Tottenham Court Road, and Long Acre. Although there were foreign visitors, from places such as Dublin, Vienna, Constantinople, Rome, Paris, and The Hague, American visitors were rare: in the available records from 1835, 1838, and 1839, only seven groups of American visitors, including Ellen's party, were recorded. Therefore, Stevenson's connection to Soane through the architect's self-promotion of his text or Ellen's own architectural curiosity inspired her visit to the museum.

Ellen's party was the only set of visitors for March 5, 1839, and the curator's diary does not expose any additional insights, noting only, "The Museum [was] open. Attendan[ce] as usual." Ellen's diary reveals that "Mr. Baillie, the Curator" was "pleasant & polite," and after their introduction in the Library, he showed the party around the museum, drawing their attention to a few specific items. In the Library, he selected three books to show to the visitors: a first edition Shakespeare folio, a large edition of Josephus on parchment, and a "grand folio" of Palladio. It is unclear which edition of Palladio Bailey showed the group; however, it would have been a familiar text to Ellen since Jefferson had at least four copies of the *Quattro Libri*.[17] Ellen's diary entry recorded, in detail, her observations on the paintings in the home, paying particularly close attention to the allegorical series *Rake's Progress* by Hogarth. Although Ellen's description predominantly focused on the art of the home, she made a few animated observations about the architecture, writing that the home was "intricate & endless in its divisions. It has as many cells as a piece of honeycomb, & some of them not a great deal larger than those made by the Bees."[18] Ellen's poetic phrasing bears a striking resemblance to a passage from Britton's *The Union of Architecture, Sculpture, and Painting* (1827):

As the construction and arrangement of the honey-comb manifest the instinctive sagacity of its uneducated builder—as the position and formation of the dwelling of the beaver evince a degree of skill and foresight almost rational—as the geometric symmetry of the spider's suspended and outstretched web shows the cunning of its wily weaver—so does the house of the Architect, the gallery of the Painter, and the library of the Author, exhibit some prominent characteristic trait of its respective owner.[19]

Ellen's evaluation of the home, like Britton's, may allude to the observance that the home was an accretion, built over many decades. Soane's Museum was an architectural apiary, where pieces were added or changed when needed, and this process of never-ending construction certainly would have been all too familiar to Ellen from her time at Monticello. Although her uncanny use of the term "honeycomb" may illustrate that she read Britton's text, it is also possible that her organic analogy was entirely original considering her scholarly studies, architectural discussions with Jefferson, and experiences growing up at the mountaintop.

The guided tour moved from the Library through the Cabinet to the Museum Corridor and then into the Picture Gallery. Proceeding through the museum, beneath the Students' Room, Ellen was able to identify casts and models of several buildings before the group stopped to peer into the Crypt to see the sarcophagus of Seti I. Overall, she found the museum to have "few rooms of good size & the rest are closets & passageways, going in & out & up & down in labyrinthine confusion."[20] When architect Karl Fredrich Schinkel visited the home in the summer of 1826, his diary also noted, as featured in this chapter's epigraph, that the house museum was full of "little deceptions."

Ellen's description perfectly narrates Soane's picturesque composition and reflected her understanding of the concept of volume in architectural space: her description was not simply based on an analysis of the plan but rather comprehension of the interlocking volumes in section. Although Ellen's architectural descriptions of Soane's Museum were brief, they are some of the most spatially expressive passages from her entire London diary.[21] For example, she visited Soane's Dulwich Picture Gallery on December 18, 1838, but made no mention of the inventive top-lit design, and her entries on other grand galleries, such as the British Museum, avoided any architectural descriptions. Something at Soane's Museum, however, inspired Ellen to pen an architectural narrative.

Even though Monticello was not directly named in her entry about Soane's Museum, Jefferson and his mountaintop creation were not far from her mind during the visit. Like her grandfather, each of her diary entries began with a meticulous record of the day's weather, noting that March 5 was "cold, dark, gloomy, thermometer down at 34°." She also called attention to one particular object in the collection, a Roman *askos,* which reminded her of the "duck." This silver pouring vase, based upon a model from Nîmes, was frequently used in the Dining Room of Monticello. Jefferson commissioned the piece from a Philadelphia silversmith and originally intended that it would be a gift for his architectural collaborator Charles-Louis Clérisseau, but it was never sent across the Atlantic.[22]

ELLEN'S PERSPECTIVES ON MONTICELLO

As Soane's Museum was tidied and formally opened to the public, Monticello slipped into further disrepair. By the time of Ellen's visit to Soane's Museum, Monticello was already under the care of its second owner since Jefferson's passing, but the home had been in a precarious state since the 1820s. In the spring of 1826, family letters reveal that a sale of Monticello was imminent due to Jefferson's rising debts and the Virginia General Assembly's general disinterest in relieving the founding father's financial troubles with a lottery.[23] Jefferson, nonetheless, made provisions that ensured certain items within the collection would be put on the proper markets: in November 1825, he asked Ellen and her husband to serve as agents for selling the art collection in Boston. He hoped that the elevated character of aesthetics in New England would bring higher revenues, but substantial revenue from a lifetime of collecting never manifested. Although many of the objects of the Indian Hall remained in place for some years before moving to the University of Virginia, the final vestige of Jefferson's collections, his retirement library, was sent to a bookseller in Washington, D.C.[24]

In terms of the attempted preservation of the home, collections, and Jefferson's financial reputation, the efforts of Jefferson's female family members, particularly Ellen, have been untold. In an effort to revive the potential lottery, or at least engender public support, Ellen drafted an essay in the fall of 1826 on the financial affairs of her grandfather, citing the causes known to her: his losses from the Revolutionary War, the depreciation of paper money, the debts he assumed from his father-in-law John Wayles (1715–1773), how his public service impacted the financial oversight of operations at Monticello, and, finally, how his continued, informal service in his retirement years burdened Monticello with visitors and ongoing requests for patronage. Neither public nor private funds from Virginia came to the aid of Monticello, and despite an offer from the South Carolina legislature and the prospects of Ellen's mother opening a school at the home, a dispersal sale was held at Monticello in January 1827. It liquidated much of the collections and the property of the plantation: on the West Front of the home, the enslaved were sold alongside furniture.

Upon Ellen's last visit to the home in 1826, she wrote: "the whole house at Monticello, with it's large apartments and lofty ceilings, appeared to me one vast monument."[25] With Jefferson's outstanding debts totaling more than $107,000, the family mourned not only Jefferson in the summer of 1826 but also the impending and unavoidable loss of Monticello. Realizing that it was practically impossible for Monticello to remain a family residence, one last effort was made to secure the property in the winter of 1828: a plan was presented to the state to transform the home into an "Asylum for deaf & dumb"; however, complications related to transportation and access to water made the mountaintop an unreasonable site.

By the summer of 1828, only two years after Jefferson's passing, there were drastic changes at Monticello. Paintings had been removed from the home, and the small arch in Jefferson's southern side of the home, once part of the richly interconnected configuration of the Library and Cabinet, had been filled to create a separate room.[26] Amid the reprogramming of the destitute house, eldest grandson Thomas Jefferson Randolph and his sister Cornelia were frantically trying to organize Jefferson's papers for publication. They hoped this endeavor would reap significant financial benefit for the family and ensure the continued ownership of Monticello; the project never met these expectations. When Washington socialite Margaret Bayard Smith, wife of the founder of the *National Intelligencer,* visited Monticello during Jefferson's lifetime, she harshly criticized the former president for his odd tastes and experimental architecture. However, her letter from August 12,

1828, displayed a different tone, and she lamented the loss of Monticello's radiance: "We entered the Hall once filled with busts & statues & natural curiosities—filled to crowding—now empty!—bare walls & defaced floor—from thence into the drawing-room—once so gay & splendid—whose walls were literally covered with pictures—like the Hall—bare & comfortless."[27] If Bayard Smith visited just a few years later, she would have found the home in an even more distressing condition. After a few tenuous years of occupation, the remainder of the family left the home in the summer of 1831 when the once 5,000-acre plantation, now parceled into a mere 552 acres, was sold to Charlottesville druggist James Turner Barclay for $7,000. Barclay spent the next three years trying, unsuccessfully, to cultivate a silkworm farm, and he let the house fall into severe disrepair. During these years, farm animals were given full command of Monticello's interior: the pigs used the mahogany and beech parquet floor of the Parlor as their new home.

Conclusion

In the early twentieth century, several scholars made significant efforts to both rediscover and reattribute the work of Jefferson and Soane, architects who were deemed passé. Following the seminal work of Fiske Kimball (1888–1955) that reinstated Jefferson's role in American architectural development and Arthur T. Bolton's (1864–1945) efforts as curator at Soane's Museum that reasserted the site as a subject of serious scholarly investigation, the architecture of Jefferson and Soane was, once again, relevant. Like Jefferson and Soane, Kimball and Bolton existed in parallel. They were both historians and practicing architects, their interests in scholarship and design were mutually informative, and they both had extensive on-site experience and knowledge of their respective case studies. Kimball spearheaded restoration efforts at Monticello following the Thomas Jefferson Memorial Foundation's acquisition of the property in 1923. At Soane's Museum, Bolton played a significant role in the organization, re-presentation of collections, and public advocacy for the preservation of Soane's architecture work as curator from 1917 until 1945. Taking cues from Kimball's and Bolton's insights, several authors pursued the importance of the work of Jefferson and Soane in national contexts through new scholarship in the latter half of the twentieth century that restored their work to the canon of architectural history.[1]

With such voluminous scholarship on the architecture of Jefferson and Soane, it seems arduous to imagine how any new research could bolster readings of Monticello or Soane's Museum. Yet, there are still uncovered histories. Presented a century after the work of Kimball and Bolton, this book identifies and traces a previously unexplored group of influential people, objects, and buildings that influenced, and connected, the work of Jefferson and Soane through a Transatlantic Design Network.

Beyond shared interests in marrying the study of precedents with new technology and geographical exploration, the members of the network displayed enduring dedication to epistolary exchange. Despite personal hardships and the perils of sending letters long distances, often without the assurance of delivery, the members of the Transatlantic Design Network were dedicated to maintaining their correspondence and, in the words of Cosway, providing their friends with the "gift of a long letter." They also circulated visual depictions and narrative descriptions of landscapes and architectural works, and through the transmission of published texts, letters of introduction, and artifacts of interest, whether ancient or innovative, the network was filled with actors who shaped design sensibilities.

Although the architectural pilgrimage sites of Monticello and Soane's Museum were at the heart of this JefferSoanean investigation, this study attempts to contextualize the house museums beyond their nationalistic lenses. Innately tied to their specific sites, the house museums were also responsive to broader, transatlantic conversations with other museums, organizations, and individuals. As illustrated, many of the key places that helped form the built and theoretical work of Jefferson and Soane have entirely disappeared, such as Stratford Place and Peale's Museum. Furthermore, many of the figures who contributed to the creative atmosphere of the Transatlantic Design Network, such as Hadfield and Godefroy, have faded into architectural obscurity despite their significant architectural contributions to the early America. Others, such as Cosway, have been overshadowed by presumed romances and the recirculation of unverified histories. By uncovering forgotten places, designers, and attributions, this study shows that Jefferson and Soane were not entirely autonomous innovators but, instead, were gifted at synthesizing ideas. Additionally, their house museums are more than autobiographical constructions: they are remarkable lenses on the interests and evolution of architectural exchange prior to the advent of modern methods of communication.

Despite such rich connections and woven unions of shared interests and aspirations, the immediate bonds of the network only lasted a generation. By the middle of the nineteenth century, letters no longer acted as the primary means of conveying ideas and information due to the increased numbers of printers and publishers, especially in America, who were circulating newspapers and books. To share information remotely, the first transatlantic cable was laid, and photography was rapidly developing. Physical travel was changing as well with the implementation of broad railroad networks and oceangoing steamships. Changes in technology and transportation were not, however, entirely responsible for the end of the network. In fact, the primary actors of the network transformed the ways designers and architectural ideas traversed the "Western Ocean." Selected members of the network spent their lifetimes collecting and were able to craft repositories of knowledge that were separate from monarchical or aristocratic assemblies. These collections then prompted intellectual investigation and new forms of scholarly tourism. The foreign designers who crossed the ocean, physically and conceptually, to explore new design ideas, such as Clérisseau, Hadfield, and Godefroy, helped introduce revivalist sensibilities to the nation as well as professional standards to architectural practice that would facilitate the development of codified, professional networks. And, finally, many of the members of the network shared a melancholier trait: they had no children to directly carry on their visions or maintain their rich tradition of personal correspondence with figures from various countries, backgrounds, and disciplines. Therefore, many members of the network shaped public institutions to act as their successors. Through the establishment of broader educational initiatives, they introduced unprecedented scholastic opportunities to the next generation. These institutions took on many of the extensive goals of members of the network, pioneering ambitious educational legislation and institutional management that had, remarkably, been shouldered by individual members of the network, such as Cosway, Jefferson, and Soane.

TODAY'S MONTICELLO AND SOANE'S MUSEUM

Jefferson and Soane spent approximately twenty years envisioning their sites as private residences, but after reassessing their family lives and professional trajectories, the homes were steadily transformed into sites for shared exploration and instruction. By the early 1800s, visitors, ranging from invited guests to clients and students, were ever-present. Today the educational programs of the sites are active and evolving with the introduction of new spaces for research and on-site investigation. At both sites, students of art and architecture still draw during class trips, groups get a glimpse into life in the early nineteenth century, and, through continuing education seminars and research facilities, scholars still have access to original objects in the collections and volumes held within the libraries.

Today Monticello and Soane's Museum are icons of intellectual curiously and architectural exploration in their respective nations, annually drawing a stream of international visitors. On a busy summer day at Monticello, when the day's timed slots for guided tours are sold out by midmorning, or on one of the candlelit Tuesday evening openings of Soane's Museum, when the queue of visitors wraps around the entire northern side of Lincoln's Inn Fields, it is difficult to imagine a time in the history of these two house museums when visitor numbers were anything but sizeable. In the late 1830s, as Jefferson's Monticello was slipping further into decay, Soane's Museum was enjoying a few years of prosperity and a constant stream of visitors carefully managed by the curator and inspectress appointed after the architect's death. Nonetheless, Soane's Museum suffered diminished visitation in the later nineteenth century, due to both the contemporary changes in taste and a lack of open days.[2] During this era, numerous proposals for additions and renovations in and around the museum were auspiciously avoided, such as a railway line underneath the home and the addition of a fourth story to no. 13. Nonetheless, modern interventions still crept into the home.[3] Across the Atlantic, Monticello continued its decline and experienced the ravages of the American Civil War. Although no major battles occurred in Charlottesville, Monticello was flooded with curious Confederate soldiers who confiscated the property, then owned by United States Naval officer Uriah Phillips Levy, and left etchings on tin shingles of the roof and graphite notes on the interior walls. Years of neglect surrounding the Civil War did nothing to improve the already-fragmented condition of railings, crumbling bricks, decaying plaster, and shattered glass. The first known photographs of Monticello, from the 1870s, depict a ruin.

Soane's Museum, too, was impacted by warfare, somehow escaping the devastation that swept through London in the first half of the twentieth century. A portion of the collections was moved during the air raids of World War I, and due to heavy bombings and the proximity of the museum to major railway targets, most of the museum's collections were evacuated during World War II, save the sarcophagus of Seti I that could only be protected by sandbags and supplications due to its size and placement. The museum was closed for seven years during World War II, and although it escaped the catastrophic destruction that crippled the Hunterian Museum on the southern side of Lincoln's Inn Fields, a bomb that landed in the northeastern corner of the fields in 1940 damaged the northern facade, marring the Portland Stone and destroying much of the original glass.[4]

Although continuously investigated by visitors and, later, trespassers during its state of dilapidation, it took nearly a century to revive Monticello. Purchased by the Thomas Jefferson Foundation in 1923 for $500,000 with the specific mission to (re)open the property as a museum, Monticello has undergone substantial restorations and renovations to depict the site as it would have been in Jefferson's retirement years. One of the most substantial acts undertaken by the foundation has been the acquisition of approximately two-thirds of the original acreage of Jefferson's plantation to ensure the preservation of an unobstructed viewshed.

A study of the recent activities of the house museums and their plans for continued development position these institutions, once again, in transatlantic conversation. During the first decades of the twenty-first century, Monticello and Soane's Museum have undergone, and continue to undergo, significant changes. For example, areas that were inaccessible to the public in the nineteenth and twentieth centuries are now the subjects of significant restoration projects so that they may be opened to visitors. With portions of the upper floors and utilitarian areas of the house museums open to visitors, there is spectacular potential for additional curatorial interpretation at the sites: the experience of the house museums will no longer be relegated to the solitary, looming figures of Jefferson and Soane but given over, in part, to the other occupants of the site: family, friends, and students as well as those who operated in service.

New educational endeavors underway at the house museums speak to the strong, enduring charge for the dissemination of knowledge left by their respective architects. The Thomas Jefferson Visitor Center and Smith

Education Center, located at the base of the mountain and designed by Baltimore-based architectural firm Ayers Saint Gross, includes classrooms, a two-story interactive gallery, museum shop, theater, and café. This project was designed to allow visitors to explore the site longer and in more depth. As a significant investment in the visitor experience, costing approximately $1 million per square foot, the project was also intended to reflect Jefferson's technical and architectural sensibilities: in 2010, it was awarded LEED Gold standing by the U.S. Green Building Council. Despite initial concerns that rising visitor numbers would be detrimental to the architectural fabric and collections, the pioneering project for Opening Up the Soane (OUTS) was facilitated by the purchase of no. 14. After this property was purchased, a restoration and construction project created an unprecedented series of spaces dedicated to the educational mission of the museum. The project moved the research library into no. 14 and created a new Robert Adam Study Centre in no. 12. The cabinets and furniture of the latter, in a wonderful twist of transatlantic construction, were crafted from American Black Walnut harvested from land that was once belonged to Jefferson's farms.

NOTES

SOURCES AND TRANSCRIPTIONS

This exploration into the nature and composition of the Transatlantic Design Network is firmly grounded in documentary evidence: diary entries, marginal notes in books, drawing annotations, as well as gossip-filled letters between friends and terse exchanges with actuaries and adversaries. The preserved voices of the members of the Transatlantic Design Network feature their original spellings, abbreviations, grammar, and capitalization. The use of *sic* would have been both redundant and interruptive; a heavy editorial hand has not been used in the transcriptions, many of which have never been published. Some punctuation has been edited: many of the letters used dashes at the end of sentences, and these have been replaced with periods. Cosway, Jefferson, Soane, and their peers often inserted words from other languages into their letters, sometimes transitioning from English to Italian to French in a single sentence. Phrases from other languages have been left in the transcriptions, noted with italicized text, and translations are included in square brackets.

Located in diverse archival collections, in several countries, the sources illuminating the Transatlantic Design Network include the following abbreviations in the endnotes:

APS   American Philosophical Society
LoC   Library of Congress
MHS   Massachusetts Historical Society

PRA   President of the Royal Academy
RA   Royal Academy
RAA   Royal Academy Archives
SJSM   Sir John Soane's Museum
SIA   Smithsonian Institute Archives
TJF   Thomas Jefferson Foundation
UVaSC University of Virginia Special Collections

Introduction

1. Sterne, *Life and Opinions of Tristram Shandy,* 11:36.
2. The Shandy note is preserved at the James Monroe Museum and Memorial Library in Fredericksburg, Virginia.
3. For a transcription of the letter delivered with Soane's copies of the book see Bolton, *Portrait of Sir John Soane,* 25.
4. Jefferson and Soane both owned other works by Sterne. Jefferson acquired *Sentimental Journey* and *The Sermons of Mr. Yorick* in the later 1760s. Soane annotated his copies of Sterne's work and used quotes from *Tristram Shandy* and *A Sentimental Journey* in his Royal Academy lectures.
5. See Latour, *Reassembling the Social.* For a modern architectural perspective see Fraser, *Architecture and the Special Relationship.*
6. See Yaneva, *Making of a Building;* Yaneva, *Made by the Office;* Yaneva, *Five Ways to Make Architecture Political;* Yaneva and Zaera, *What Is Cosmopolitical Design?*
7. For additional information on the Republic of Letters see "Mapping the Republic of Letters"; Cook, *Epistolary Bodies;* Hindley, "Mapping the Republic of Letters"; Shuffelton, Baridon, and Chevignard, "Travelling in the Republic of Letters"; Winterer, "Where Is America?"
8. Locke discusses this concept at length throughout the essay; for a brief summary see Locke, *Works of John Locke,* 1:68.
9. Jefferson, letter to Maria Cosway, December 27, 1820, in Jefferson, *Papers of Thomas Jefferson,* 16:497–99.
10. Flavell, *When London Was Capital,* 189.
11. See Hyde, "Some Evidence of Libel."
12. Soane, *Memoirs of the Professional Life.*
13. In the middle of the 1990s, a surge of new, romanticized literature emerged, alongside the depiction of the Jefferson-Cosway relationship in the Merchant and Ivory film *Jefferson in Paris* (1995).
14. Letter to Sir John Soane, December 22, 1831, manuscript, III.C.4, no. 37, Soane, "Private Correspondence."
15. Letter to Thomas Jefferson, June 16, 1823, manuscript, Jefferson, "Thomas Jefferson Papers," LoC.

16. Letter to Cosway, December 27, 1820, manuscript, Jefferson, "Thomas Jefferson Papers," LoC.
17. See "The Transatlantic Design Network, 1768–1838," http://www.archdsw.com /tdn.html.

Chapter 1: Meetings

1. Jefferson, letter to Benjamin Rush, August 17, 1811, Jefferson, *Papers of Thomas Jefferson,* ed. Boyd et al., 4:87–88.
2. According to notes in his traveling pocket book, Soane visited on September 10, 1819; he did not make any special notes about the Halle's architecture.
3. Letter, March 8, 1777, manuscript, HU/2/55, "Ozias Humphry Papers, 1753–1810," RAA, London.
4. Burnell, *Divided Affections,* 4.
5. Lloyd is particularly convinced that the story of the Hafields' murdered infants was fabricated because it appears only in Cosway's autobiography letter of 1830 and not in any other contemporary accounts. The first biography of the family transcribed Cosway's account and presented it as a dramatized fact; see Williamson, *Richard Cosway.*
6. See "Roma to Ancona" in *A Brief Account of the Roads of Italy,* 13–14. For a description of the Via Santo Spirito see Burnell, *Divided Affections,* 4.
7. See 'The Roads from Legorn to Florence by Way of Pisa' in *A Brief Account of the Roads of Italy,* 25. The unnamed author rarely cites the names of inn patrons, and commentary is typically limited to brief comments on location, inn size, and cleanliness.
8. See "The Road from Milan to Venice Through Bergamo, Brescia, Verona, and Vicenza," in *A Brief Account of the Roads of Italy,* 42.
9. See 'Viaggio da Laivorno a Firenze' in *The Roads of Italy,* 20.
10. Manuscript, HU/2/38, "Ozias Humphry Papers."
11. Letter, December 2, 1775, manuscript, HU/2/36, "Ozias Humphry Papers."
12. Lloyd, *Richard & Maria Cosway,* 42.
13. See Darley, *John Soane,* 19. At the end of his life, he hung the Hunneman portrait from 1776 in his bedroom as a reminder of his younger years.
14. "The Grand Tour," in Stevens and Richardson, *John Soane, Architect,* 96.
15. "The Grand Tour," 101. Jefferson later met Perronet.
16. See Darley, *John Soane,* 24.
17. Letter, August 5, 1774, in Bolton, *Portrait of Sir John Soane* 11–13. Stevens, A.R.A., unfortunately died in Rome in 1775.
18. Letter to Mr. Wood, May 2, 1778, in Bolton, *Portrait of Sir John Soane,* 19.
19. Soane eventually collected fifteen of Piranesi's engravings of Paestum for his museum's gallery.

20. Tait, *Adam Brothers in Rome,* 45.
21. Darley, *John Soane,* 41.
22. Maria Hadfield, letter to Ozias Humphrey, February 24, 1776, transcribed in Barnett, *Richard and Maria Cosway,* 45.
23. Burnell asserts that Cosway traveled to Rome in the summer of 1776 until early 1777 with the Gore family of London, who were traveling with their three young children; however, a review of documentary evidence does not support this claim. Additionally, the work of Darley and Lloyd, the preeminent scholar on the Cosways and curator of the unprecedented 1995 National Gallery exhibit on the couple, assert that Cosway's first visit to Rome and Naples was in 1778–1779. See Lloyd, *Richard & Maria Cosway,* 42. Additional investigation into Cosway's unpublished diary, currently being transcribed, and account books, held at the closed archive of the Foundazione Cosway in Lodi, may illuminate the date discrepancies.
24. All but Banks stayed at the inn in the summer of 1775.
25. Banks had a traveling fellowship from the Royal Academy and spent 1772–1779 in Rome.
26. Soane made arrangement prior to his departure for Italy to have his first work on architecture published, entitled *Designs in Architecture,* in 1778 with thirty-seven copper plate engravings, under the name of John Soan.
27. Northcote, *Memoirs of Sir Joshua Reynolds,* 149. For further notes on Northcote's harsh criticism of Cosway, see Burnell, *Divided Affections,* 34–36. Burnell postulates that Northcote was one of Cosway's admirers, and his advances were not accepted; hence, his embittered attitude toward her in his writings.
28. These may have come into Soane's collection in the early 1780s when William was living in London and struggling as an artist. Soane probably purchased the works, but there is no documentation that they were ever on display in the museum.
29. Darley, *John Soane,* 36.
30. It is unclear exactly when William arrived in London; he later moved to Clarges Street, where he had a studio.
31. See I.30.4, "Soane Notebooks," Archives of SJSM, London.
32. Northcote, *Memoirs of Sir Joshua Reynolds,* 149.
33. Lloyd's work represents a significant departure from this view of the Cosways' relationship and offers the explanation that following the death of their only child in 1796, Richard Cosway's interests in the mystical alienated Maria's Catholic practices and may explain her prolonged departure from London between the late 1790s and the few years preceding Richard's death in 1821. See Lloyd, *Richard Cosway.*
34. Burnell, *Divided Affections,* 65. The Townley papers at the British Museum highlight the extremely candid and verbally vulgar relationship between Richard Cosway and Townley. The graphic sexual descriptions written by Cosway about intimate relations with an Italian woman may refer to Maria Cosway and certainly

shed a different light on the miniature painter who is otherwise portrayed as a very flamboyant "macaroni."

35. Maria Cosway, letter to Sir William Cosway, May 24, 1830. Manuscript, L.961–1953, National Art Reference Library, Victoria and Albert Museum, London, https://nal-vam.on.worldcat.org/oclc/1008421436.

36. Maria Cosway showed thirty works at the Royal Academy during 1781–1789, one painting in 1796, seven in 1800, and three paintings in her last exhibit in 1801.

37. Lloyd, *Richard & Maria Cosway,* 48.

38. Letterpress copy in Adams Family, "Adams Family Papers," Massachusetts Historical Society, Boston. For the letter to John Quincy see Adams Family, *Adams Papers,* ed. Taylor et al., 12–29.

39. Brandt, *Thomas Jefferson Travels,* 2.

40. Jefferson inherited James, with 120 other slaves, when he married Martha Wayles Skelton in 1772. Jefferson paid to have James apprentice under a French chef from 1784 to 1787 in Paris, and James eventually became the head cook at Jefferson's residence at the Hôtel de Langeac. Slavery was illegal in the country, and regardless of the slave's national origin, a slave could claim freedom according to French law. With the knowledge of this provision, James negotiated his freedom with Jefferson with the condition that, upon his return to Monticello, he would teach another slave the "art of cookery." James was freed on February 5, 1796, and his manumission paper is preserved at the UVaSC.

41. Spurlin, "World of the Founding Fathers," 910.

42. Rice, *Thomas Jefferson's Paris,* 27.

43. Jefferson, letter to Charles Bellini, September 30, 1785, Jefferson, in *Papers of Thomas Jefferson,* ed. Boyd et al., 8:569.

44. Flavell, *When London Was Capital,* 189.

45. Watkin, *Architect King,* 27.

46. For a longer discussion of West's tutelage and specifics on the three generations of West's American students in London, see Evans, *Benjamin West.* Joseph Wright (1756–1793) was the Royal Academy's first American student and attended from 1775 to 1781.

47. The Mather Brown portrait is now in the National Portrait Gallery of the Smithsonian Institution (NPG.99.66) at the bequest of Charles Francis Adams. Jefferson and John Adams both sat for Brown and, in an act of friendly admiration, exchanged portraits. The Brown portraits of Jefferson and Adams in Monticello's Parlor are modern copies.

48. Trumbull resigned his military commission in May 1777, and the odd recounting of his hasty exit from the army can be found in the first chapter of Trumbull, *Autobiography.*

49. Trumbull, *Autobiography,* 92.

50. The building was demolished in 1842.

51. It is important to note that the version of the Declaration that Trumbull executed in Paris was the small, panel painting that now resides at the Yale Museum of Art and not the large canvas that hangs in the United States Capitol: this latter painting was executed 1816–1837.

52. Trumbull, *Autobiography,* 96.

53. See Trumbull, *Autobiography,* 118. The gap in his journal is from August 19 to September 10, 1786.

54. Wiebenson, "Two Domes of the Halle au Blé," 266.

55. Jefferson parted with the treatise in 1815 as part of the Library of Congress sale. See Harnsberger, "'In Delorme's Manner,'" 4. Jefferson diverged from Delorme's construction specifications and used nails, manufactured on the plantation, instead of wooden pegs, to connect the wooden ribs together. This fastening discrepancy caused the dome to slightly warp due to the expansion and contraction of dissimilar materials in the dome's composition: this problem would have been avoided if Jefferson used an all-wooden construction method as instructed.

56. Transcribed in Rice, *Thomas Jefferson's Paris,* 21.

57. The Halle au Blé's dome was redesigned by a contractor named Bélanger, and the iron structure was constructed 1808–1813. Again, structural integrity plagued the dome, probably due to the large size of the span and insufficient structural system in the bearing walls to resist compressive forces from the dome. Additionally, the structure was largely devoid of natural light, illuminated only by the lantern, and the building itself was now insufficient for the increased traffic of the market. It burned in 1854 and sat ruined for over thirty years before it was demolished in 1885 to make way for the Borse de Commerce. For additional details see Wiebenson, "Two Domes of the Halle au Blé"; J. M. Pérouse de Montclos, *Histoire de l'Architecture française.*

58. Burnell, *Divided Affections,* 166.

59. Darley, *John Soane,* 24.

60. Jefferson's payment of 6f for "seeing Desert" is noted in Bear and Stanton, *Jefferson's Memorandum Books,* 1:639.

61. Butterfield and Rice, "Jefferson's Earliest Note to Maria Cosway." Speculations cite Jefferson's injury sometime between September 13 and 22. William Franklin dated the injury to September 18 in a letter to L. G. Le Veillard; see Bear and Stanton, *Jefferson's Memorandum Books,* 1:639.

62. Jefferson, *Papers of Thomas Jefferson,* ed. Boyd et al., 10:478.

63. Jefferson, letter to Maria Cosway, December 27, 1820, manuscript, Jefferson, "Thomas Jefferson Papers," LoC.

64. Letter to Maria Cosway, October 12, 1786, in Jefferson, *Papers of Thomas Jefferson,* ed. Boyd et al., 10:443–55.

65. Letter to Cosway, October 12, 1786.

66. Letter to Cosway, October 12, 1786.

67. Letter to John Wayles Eppes, September 18, 1812, in Jefferson, *Papers of Thomas Jefferson,* ed. Looney, 5:347–50.
68. Polly was nine years old when she crossed the Atlantic and was accompanied by the enslaved domestic servant Sally Hemings with whom Jefferson would eventually have five children. See Lewis and Onuf, *Sally Hemings and Thomas Jefferson;* Gordon-Reed, *Hemingses of Monticello;* Turner, *Jefferson-Hemings Controversy;* Stanton, *Those Who Labor for My Happiness.*
69. Maria's great niece, Sarah Nicholas Randolph, cited this in Wister and Irwin, *Worthy Women of Our First Century.* The name change was also noted in Jefferson's Memorandum Book, from their debarkation at the port of Norfolk, Virginia.

Chapter 2: Ambassadors

1. Abigail Adams, letter to John Adams, April 23, 1776, in Adams Family, *Adams Papers,* ed. Butterfield, 1:369–71.
2. Eames, Eames, and the Metropolitan Museum of Art, *World of Franklin and Jefferson.*
3. The "Friends and Acquaintances" section of the catalog featured thirty-four figures and included one additional female: public writer Mercy Otis Warren (1728–1814).
4. Kennedy, *Orders from France.*
5. Recent contributions include Cook, *Epistolary Bodies;* Maudlin and Herman, *Building the British Atlantic World;* Styles and Vickery, *Gender, Taste, and Material Culture;* Wells, *Material Witness.*
6. *Encyclopedia of Diderot & d'Alembert.*
7. Madame de Tessé, née Adrienne Catherine de Noailles; Madame de Corny, née Marguérite Victorire de Palerne.
8. Franklin's time abroad was divided between three diplomatic journeys: colonial agent representing the Pennsylvania Assembly, Massachusetts, Georgia, and New Jersey (1757–1762; 1764–1775) and commissioner of Congress to the French Court, Treaty of Paris negotiator, and United States minister to France and Sweden (1776–1785).
9. Gladwell, *Tipping Point.*
10. The following political and artistic figures were born in the colonies before the American Revolution and were educated abroad, thereby illustrating that Franklin's studies, exclusively in North America, was an anomaly for some of America's first leaders: Henry Laurens (1724–1792), Richard Henry Lee (1732–1794), John Hancock (1737–1793), Silas Dean (1737–1789), Benjamin West (1738–1820), Charles Willson Peale (1741–1827), John Jay (1745–1829), Benjamin Rush (1746–1813), John Trumbull (1756–1843), Robert Fulton (1765–1815), and John Drayton (1766–1822).

11. Franklin was a member of the American Philosophical Society, Lunar Society, the Royal Society, the Society of for the Encouragement of Arts, Manufactures, & Commerce, an associate of the Académie des sciences, and the Russian Academy of Science.

12. *Catalogue of the Books.*

13. The Library Company of Philadelphia received Soane's *Description of the House and Museum* (1835) directly from the architect, and sometime before the publication of the 1835 catalog the Library Company acquired copies of Soane's *Plans, elevations, and sections of buildings* (1788), *Designs in architecture* (1790), and *Sketches in Architecture* (1798). Sometime after Soane's death, the Library Company acquired Soane's *Designs for Public and Private Buildings* (1828) and Britton's *Union of Architecture* (1827). The library also held a substantial number of dramatic titles by Soane's ne'er-do-well son George.

14. See lecture 8, Soane, *Sir John Soane: The Royal Academy Lectures,* 181.

15. Coincidentally, William Franklin (ca. 1731–1813) is buried in the same cemetery as Sir John Soane at Old St. Pancras Churchyard. Born in London, Franklin served as the colonial governor of New Jersey but returned to England after his imprisonment during the Revolutionary War.

16. S. C. K. Smith, *Bartolozzi, Zoffany, and Kauffman.*

17. Lloyd, "Maria Hadfield Cosway Exhibit."

18. One of these Academicians, pictured in the right foreground with his cane balefully braced on the abdomen of a toppled female torso from antiquity, was Richard Cosway before his marriage to Maria. Richard began his affiliation with the RA as a student on August 9, 1769. He was elected to associate of the RA in 1770 and to full Academician less than a year later.

19. The series was moved to Burlington House, ca. 1899.

20. She exhibited every year between 1769 and 1782 and then made sporadic contributions in 1786, 1788, 1791, 1796, and 1797.

21. For more on the gender imbalance in the Royal Academy during Kauffman's era see Rosenthal, *Angelica Kauffman.*

22. HU/2/33, "Ozias Humphry Papers."

23. Trumbull, *Autobiography,* 59.

24. Evans, *Benjamin West,* 74–85.

25. Trumbull, *Autobiography,* 6.

26. Trumbull, *Autobiography,* 96.

27. The friendship of Jefferson, Cosway, and Church is explored by Roberts, but like many other texts regarding Jefferson and Cosway, it is an overdramatized account that tries to weave a love story. See Roberts, *Place in History.*

28. The project was substantially altered in the 1840s and, after serving as a monastery for several decades, was demolished in the early twentieth century.

29. Letter, March 20, 1787, in Jefferson, *Papers of Thomas Jefferson,* ed. Boyd et al.,

11:226–28. At that time, the superintendant was Charles Claude Flahaut de le Billarderie.

30. For the letters, in French, detailing the gift see Jefferson, *Papers of Thomas Jefferson,* ed. Boyd et al., 15:363–64, 71. The pedestal once held the Cerrachi bust of Jefferson in Monticello's Entrance Hall but was moved to the Capitol in the 1830s and was lost in the 1851 fire.
31. Letter to Church, July 27, 1788, manuscript, Jefferson, "Thomas Jefferson Papers," LoC.
32. Randall, *Life of Thomas Jefferson,* 3:336.
33. Trumbull, *Autobiography,* 97–98.
34. The home is now a Grade II listed property, with a later addition of Toad Hall, but the Churches are not listed on any documents registering ownership; it is likely that they rented the property from John Stephenson from 1768 to 1797.
35. See Parissien, "Monkey Business"; Roscoe, "Mimic without Mind."
36. September 5, 1789, in Davenport, *Diary of the French Revolution,* I:205–6. See also G. Morris, *Diary and Letters of Gouverneur Morris.*
37. Letter translated from French, August 4, 1787, manuscript, Jefferson, "Thomas Jefferson Papers," LoC.
38. For example, see her letter to Jefferson, November 24, 1794, in Jefferson, *Papers of Thomas Jefferson,* ed. Boyd et al., 28:209–11.
39. For additional information see Silverman, "Belvidere."
40. Letter to Madame de Corny, April 23, 1802, in Jefferson, *Papers of Thomas Jefferson,* ed. Boyd et al., 37:308–10.
41. Madame de Corny, letter to Thomas Jefferson, August 15, 1803, in Jefferson, *Papers of Thomas Jefferson,* ed. Boyd et al., 41:203–5.

Chapter 3: Associates

1. Jefferson, letter to James Madison, September 20, 1785, in Jefferson, *Papers of Thomas Jefferson,* ed. Boyd et al., 8:535.
2. With seventy-nine pieces, the Fitzwilliam Museum in Cambridge, England, now holds the second largest collection of Clérisseau's works; however, Catherine the Great and Soane were the leading collectors during the artist's lifetime.
3. Soane did not own a copy of Jefferson's *Notes.* But Soane's ownership would have been quite extraordinary, considering that only approximately two hundred copies were printed, and nearly half of the lot were sent by Jefferson to his native Virginia: thirty-seven copies to his alma mater, the College of William and Mary, and fifty-seven copies to Alexander Donald, a bookseller in Richmond, Virginia. See McCormick, *Charles-Louis Clérisseau,* 193.
4. Clérisseau was elected a member of the Académie Royale de Peinture et de Sculpture in 1769.

5. For a concise summary of the Clérisseau and Adam partnership see Tait, *Adam Brothers in Rome,* 49–51.
6. Several texts assert that Clérisseau exhibited at the RA in 1775, 1776, and 1790; however, the exhaustive Graves catalog, 2:80, lists only the four 1772 entries that contained three imaginative classical architectural compositions and a view of the Forum of Nerva in Rome. Soane exhibited one entry in 1772: the front elevation for a nobleman's townhouse. Clérisseau was nominated for RA membership in 1777; however, it appears that he never became an Academician.
7. See Howard, *Thomas Jefferson, Architect,* 66–79; McLaughlin, *Jefferson and Monticello,* 25.
8. See Clérisseau's Account of Expenditures for Architectural Plans, &c., June 2, 1786, in Jefferson, *Papers of Thomas Jefferson,* ed. Boyd et al., 9:603–4.
9. James Buchanan and William Hay, letter to Jefferson, March 20, 1785, in Jefferson, *Papers of Thomas Jefferson,* ed. Boyd et al., 8:48–50. Jefferson originally envisioned a capitol building that split the three branches of the government into three separate structures, figuratively and physically. However, the Virginia Assembly passed an act in October 1784 that required the new capitol be housed in one structure for "advantage" and with "less expense."
10. Jefferson to Madison, September 20, 1785, in Jefferson, *Papers of Thomas Jefferson,* ed. Boyd et al., 8:535.
11. Buchanan and Hay to Jefferson, October 18, 1785, in Jefferson, *Papers of Thomas Jefferson,* ed. Boyd et al., 8:648.
12. Jefferson to Madame de Tessé, March 20, 1787, in Jefferson, *Papers of Thomas Jefferson,* ed. Boyd et al., 11:226.
13. Letter, November 23, 1817, manuscript, Soane, "Private Correspondence," XV.A.1.
14. See lectures 3, 4, 9, and 10 in Soane, *Royal Academy Lectures.* The perspective is preserved at Soane's Museum, 19.10.3.
15. Letter to Buchanan and Hay, January 26, 1786, in Jefferson,, *Papers of Thomas Jefferson,* ed. Boyd et al., 9:220–33.
16. Jefferson to Buchanan and Hay, January 26, 1786. The interior of the capitol was substantially remodeled in 1906.
17. The provenances of Clérisseau's works in the collection are: (1) May 20, 1797, Christie's sale, (11) November 28, 1800, Dr. Stevens sale at Christie's, (10) Dr. Monro on April 23, 1805, (2) Lord Lansdowne sale on March 25, 1806, and (4) Clark Rampling in December 1829. Soane's Museum now has twenty-five works since four additional paintings were given to Soane's Museum after Soane's death. The museum amended its policy of not adding items to Soane's collection since the painting had a Soanean provenance: the two paintings acquired in 1971 and the two acquired in 1993 had been gifted to Princess Murat by Soane in 1816. The provenance documentation is held within the Painting Inventory of the Soane's Museum Archive and was updated by Helen Dorey in 1996.

18. Lecture 5 in Soane, *Royal Academy Lectures,* 130.

19. In the 1820s, Godefroy worked on elements of Salter's Hall and designed the Roman Catholic Charities' School on Clarendon Square, Somers Town. Both were substantially damaged in World War II; the former was substantially altered, and the latter was demolished.

20. Most of the existing documentary evidence on Godefroy is held at the Maryland Historical Society and Peale Museum of Baltimore, the Library of Congress, and the Library of Virginia in Richmond.

21. Some texts have also confused the work of Maximilian Godefroy with that of fellow architect and engineer Godefroi Du Jareau (1744–1819), who actively practiced civil architecture in New Orleans before committing suicide.

22. See R. L. Alexander, "Public Memorial"; Alexander, "Maximilian Godefroy in Virginia"; Alexander, *Architecture of Maximilian Godefroy.* Reinberger delivered three new lectures on Godefroy for the Johns Hopkins University's Homewood House Museum Architectural Lecture Series on May 4, 6, and 11, 2004.

23. The discovery of this letter is due to the generous insight of the archivist of Soane's Museum, Sue Palmer, which was prompted by a discussion of Soane's connections to America during his lifetime.

24. R. L. Alexander, *Architecture of Maximilian Godefroy,* 2.

25. Cohen and Brownell, *Architectural Drawings of Benjamin Henry Latrobe,* 637–61; Latrobe, *Correspondence and Miscellaneous Papers of Benjamin Henry Latrobe,* vol. 3, *1811–1820.* During 1790–1799, Cazenove lived in Philadelphia and met Madison there. An unspecified letter of introduction to Jefferson is referenced in Madison, *Papers of James Madison: Secretary of State Series,* 8:443.

26. The extant correspondence between the two dates from December 1805.

27. The population in Baltimore was 13,503 in 1790, 26,514 in 1800, 46,555 in 1810, 62,738 in 1820, and by 1830 Baltimore was the second largest city in the United States, trailing only New York City, with 80,620 residents. For detailed statistics see Chandler, *Four Thousand Years.*

28. For additional details of the building's construction and features, see Boldrick, "St. Thomas Catholic Church."

29. For additional details on the design, see Scarff, "St. Mary's Seminary Chapel." Godefroy did not visit the site but instead conveyed the design remotely, via drawings and letters.

30. Maximilian Godefroy, *Military Reflections.* Godefroy's "expertise" proved useful during the War of 1814 when he was commissioned to reinforce and redesign elements of Baltimore's Fort McHenry. Godefroy provided vivid descriptions of his war experiences in his letter to Jefferson from January 10, 1806, stating that he "had a horse shot out from under him" and received "three honorable wounds."

31. See Wexler, "'What Manner of Woman.'"

32. In 1812, he was also advertising in the *American and Commercial Daily Advertiser* of Baltimore.
33. The original coffered dome that spanned the entire sacristy, complete with a leaded oculus, was covered in the 1890s with a false, barrel-vaulted ceiling.
34. For additional details, see *American Beacon,* June 14, 1817; *City of Washington Gazette,* September 29, 1819. The monument underwent a major restoration and conservation project in 2011.
35. At the First Presbyterian Churchyard in Baltimore, now known as Westminster Cemetery, Godefroy designed several Egyptian revival tombs (1813–1815). They were some of the earliest, if not the first, Egyptian Revival structures in the United States.
36. Letter translated from French, January 10, 1806, manuscript, Jefferson, "Thomas Jefferson Papers," LoC.
37. The appointment was conferred under Washington's presidency in 1790.
38. Letters from March 1806 between Jefferson, Madison, and Pennsylvania senator George Logan were conveyed to Godefroy, detailing the lack of federal work for military or civil engineering projects.
39. Jefferson received a patent from King George III in 1774 for the tract of land containing Natural Bridge. Prior to the purchase Jefferson had the land surveyed, and he retained the land patent until his heirs sold the property in 1833.
40. Ellen Wayles Randolph, letter to Martha Jefferson Randolph, September 27, 1816, manuscript, Box 1, "Correspondence of Ellen Wayles Randolph Coolidge, 1810–1861," in MS9090, UVaSC.
41. Letter, October 12, 1816, manuscript, Jefferson, "Thomas Jefferson Papers," LoC.
42. In recent years, archivist Sue Palmer identified the letters' erroneous placement within the collections and moved the documents to the correct place within Soane's "Private Correspondence" files.
43. See Soane, "Private Correspondence," p. xvi.H.2–3.
44. For additional details, see Graves, *Royal Academy of Arts,* 3:255–56.

Chapter 4: Architects

1. Jefferson, letter to Maria Hadfield Cosway, October 24, 1822, manuscript, Jefferson, "Thomas Jefferson Papers," LoC.
2. Like most of the pre-1836 US patents, Hadfield's Patent X289, filed on May 15, 1800, as "machine for making bricks and tiles," was lost in the December 1836 Records' Office fire. According to Hadfield's calculations, it could produce over thirty thousand bricks in twelve hours using only one horse. According to Julia King, *George Hadfield,* Hadfield owned a brick- and tile–making factory in south Washington, housed in a building he designed.
3. Graves, *Royal Academy of Arts,* 3:346.

4. King, *George Hadfield,* 39–40.
5. Correspondence from George Hadfield, manuscripts, RAA/SEC/2/77, "Records of the Secretary 1769–1968," RAA, London.
6. Graves, *Royal Academy of Arts,* 3:346.
7. Wyatt was elected associate of the Royal Academy in 1770 and elevated to Royal Academician five years later. From 1805 to 1806 he served as the RA president.
8. See Hunsberger, "Architectural Career of George Hadfield," 46. King's book best details Hadfield's complicated relationship with this patron; King, *George Hadfield,* 42, 54, 175–177.
9. Jenkins, *Architect and Patron,* 113.
10. See Stroud, *Architecture of Sir John Soane,* 66.
11. Entry from January 2, 1795, in Greig, *Farington Diary,* 85.
12. Entry from January 24, 1796, in Greig, *Farington Diary,* 137.
13. The position of commissioner of the District of Columbia was established by George Washington on January 22, 1791, and seconded by Thomas Jefferson, secretary of state. In total, eight gentlemen served as commissioners, with three men on the board at a time: Thomas Johnson (appointed January 22, 1791), David Stuart (appointed January 22, 1791), Daniel Carroll (appointed January 22, 1791), Gustavus Scott (appointed August 23, 1794), William Thornton (appointed September 15, 1794), Alexander White (appointed May 18, 1795), William Cranch (appointed January 8, 1801) and Tristram Dalton (appointed March 3, 1801). Jefferson dissolved the position under an act of Congress on May 1, 1802. President Madison briefly reinstated the position from 1815 to 1816 for the reconstruction of the public buildings destroyed by the British invasion during the War of 1812. From the Index to Proceedings of the Commissioners for the District of Columbia 1791–1802, Proceedings: April 12, 1791–September 28, 1798, "Records of the District of Columbia."
14. Cosway's letter of introduction was dated August, 19, 1789, and is now held at the UVaSC.
15. Jefferson, letter to Cosway, September 11, 1789, in Jefferson,, *Papers of Thomas Jefferson,* ed. Boyd et al., 15:413–14.
16. John Trumbull, letter to the commissioners, September 23, 1794, manuscript, "Records of the District of Columbia."
17. John Trumbull, letter to the commissioners, September 13, 1794, manuscript, "Records of the District of Columbia."
18. Commissioners, letter to John Trumbull, December 18, 1794, manuscript, "Records of the District of Columbia."
19. Letter to George Hadfield, January 2, 1797, manuscript, "Records of the District of Columbia."
20. When petitioning for a raise as architect of the Capitol, Latrobe cited the housing allowance, which was also provided to Hoban, in a letter to President Madison, March 31, 1812, in Madison, *Papers of James Madison: Presidential Series,* 4:227.

21. John Trumbull, letter to the commissioners, March 9, 1795, manuscript, "Records of the District of Columbia Commissioners."
22. Although there were small, private drafting schools in the cities of Philadelphia and Charleston, the first architecture school in the United States was founded at the Massachusetts Institute of Technology in 1865.
23. Public letter to Latrobe, April 1808, in Latrobe, *Correspondence and Miscellaneous Papers of Benjamin Henry Latrobe,* 2:602.
24. Letter to commissioners, October 27, 1795, manuscript, "Records of the District of Columbia."
25. See "Letters from the Presidents to DC Commissioners" in manuscripts 42.4.29, 42.4.31, and 42.4.39, "Records of the District of Columbia."
26. Letter to the commissioners, November 9, 1795, manuscript, 42.4.51, "Records of the District of Columbia."
27. Letter to George Hadfield, June 27, 1796, manuscript, 42.4.51, "Records of the District of Columbia."
28. See letters of May 14 and 16, 1798, from Hadfield to the commissioners, manuscripts 42.3.1361 and 42.3.1364.
29. This statement is attributed to Latrobe's eldest son, John (1803–1891), who was an author and, unlike his brother, Benjamin Henry Latrobe II (1806–1878), did not follow in his father's architectural footsteps; see Hunsberger, "Architectural Career of George Hadfield," 54–55.
30. Jefferson, *Papers of Thomas Jefferson,* ed. Boyd et al., 33:462–63.
31. Jefferson, *Papers of Thomas Jefferson,* ed. Boyd et al., 33:462–63.
32. A new building by Robert Mills replaced Hadfield's design in 1838.
33. Letter, September 10, 1822, manuscript, Jefferson, "Thomas Jefferson Papers," LoC.
34. Letter, October 24, 1822, manuscript, Jefferson, "Thomas Jefferson Papers," LoC.
35. Letter, September 22, 1822, manuscript, Jefferson, "Thomas Jefferson Papers," LoC.
36. The Panic of 1819 was the first peacetime financial crisis for the United States; for a useful survey of the crisis and other sources of literature, see Blackson, "Pennsylvania Banks and the Panic."
37. Hadfield was not listed as a visitor in any of the accounts of Jefferson or his family members; however, there are several instances where visitors to Monticello were unaccounted for in records. It is possible that Jefferson and Hadfield had conversations in Washington about the creation of a university or that Hadfield even made visits to Central College during the early years of its construction; however, once again, Hadfield does not make an appearance in the records documenting key events such as the ceremonial laying of the cornerstone on October 6, 1817, or in the notes of key figures such as carpenter James Dinsmore or members of the university community such as the Board of Visitors.

38. Arlington House was designated a national monument in 1925 and first opened to the public as a museum in 1933.

39. The mausoleum was originally located in the David Burnes burial grounds, but it was moved to Oak Hill sometime in the late 1800s. See Hunsberger, "Architectural Career of George Hadfield," 58. George de la Roche established Oak Hill cemetery in 1850, and the Van Ness Mausoleum was moved to its current location within the cemetery in 1872.

40. Hunsberger presented the precedent misattribution, and since this article was the prominent source on Hadfield until 2014, it was referenced in subsequent texts such as Price, Rudy, and Schlefer.

41. According to the Royal Academy's Collections Archive, the drawing was executed sometime between 1788 and 1795; it may have also been exhibited in the annual RA exhibition of 1795 under catalog #715. That year Hadfield also submitted a design, #650, for a national mausoleum. See Graves, *Royal Academy of Arts,* 3:336, 8:72.

42. Manuscript, RU007051 Box 3, 202–204, "Columbian Institute Records 1816–1841, with Related Papers 1791–1800," SIA, Washington, DC.

43. "Obituary of George Hadfield," *National Intelligencer,* February 13, 1826. The same obituary was reprinted in Washington's *Daily National,* in Massachusetts' *Salem Gazette,* and the *Rhode-Island American.*

44. Letter, June 16, 1823, manuscript, Jefferson, "Thomas Jefferson Papers," LoC.

Chapter 5: Societies

1. Introductory address by Edward Cutbush, January 11, 1817, manuscript, " Columbian Institute Records," SIA.

2. For the most complete history of the Columbian Institute see Rathbun, *Columbian Institute.*

3. See Flavell, *When London Was Capital,* 125. Although it gives a glimpse into the coffeehouse culture of London, Flavell's research primarily traces the Laurens family abroad and focuses on the prerevolutionary period (1755–1775).

4. Pledges ranged from £3 to £87s10 and totaled 1,300. See APSimg6759, "Subscription List for the Building of Philosophical Hall, 11 July 1785," American Philosophical Society Digital Library, Philadelphia.

5. The following institutions are just a sampling of the educational institutions and societies founded in the young nation: American Academy (1780), Georgetown College (1789; later Georgetown University), University of North Carolina (1789), Blount College (1794; later East Tennessee College, then University of Tennessee), Union College (1795), American Academy of the Fine Arts (1802), United States Military Academy at West Point (1802), and the Columbian Agricultural Society (1810).

6. See Articles 4–9 in "Columbian Institute."

7. Articles 4–9 in "Columbian Institute."
8. Charter of the Metropolitan Society, June 15, 1816, manuscript, Section 2, Article 6, "Columbian Institute Records," SIA.
9. Jefferson, letter to Thomas Law, February 24, 1817, manuscript, Jefferson, "Thomas Jefferson Papers," LoC.
10. Charter of the Metropolitan Society, June 15, 1816, manuscript, Section 3, "Columbian Institute Records," SIA.
11. John Quincy Adams, letter to Ashbury Dickens, June 1, 1824, manuscript, Box 4, "Columbian Institute Records," SIA.
12. Lingelbach, "Home of the American Philosophical Society," 200–202.
13. Edward Cutbush, Minutes from the Secretary of the Metropolitan Society, June 15, 1816, manuscript, "Columbian Institute Records," SIA.
14. Francis Barnes, letter to the Columbian Institute, July 29, 1830, manuscript, Box 1A Neg.SIA2012–2293 to 2295, "Columbian Institute Records," SIA.
15. After serving as professor of chemistry at Columbian College, he spent the final decade of his life in New York as the founder of the Geneva Medical College, now part of the State University of New York. He did not entirely sever his ties with Washington's learned societies since he accepted a corresponding membership in the National Institute in 1842. See Rathbun, *Columbian Institute,* 6.
16. Watkins, "Anniversary Discourse," 23.

Part II: Sites

1. Upton, *Architecture in the United States,* 32.

Chapter 6: Foundations

1. Wills, "The Aesthete."
2. London's own records cite the city's population as the largest in the world from 1815 to 1914.
3. Many of Jefferson's possessions are now in the permanent collections of other museums, such as the Smithsonian Institution and the Boston Athenæum. The exhibit at Monticello ran from April 13 to December 31, 1993, and was furnished with objects borrowed from over seventy-five museums. For the catalog see Stein, *Worlds of Thomas Jefferson.*
4. Wills, "The Aesthete."
5. Jefferson, letter to Benjamin Henry Latrobe, October 10, 1809, in Jefferson, *Papers of Thomas Jefferson,* ed. Boyd et al., 1:595.
6. M. B. Smith, *Winter in Washington,* 2:261.
7. Unlike Monticello, Soane's Museum has a profuse amount of students' drawings.
8. See McLean, *Henry Soane.*

9. From the inventory and appraisement of the estate of Peter Jefferson, Esq. in "Papers of Isabelle Neff Burnett, 1757–1960," Accession #MSS6634, UVaSC.

10. Wells, *Material Witness,* 149–50.

11. Jefferson, *Autobiography of Thomas Jefferson,* 6.

12. McLaughlin, *Jefferson and Monticello,* 203.

13. Jefferson, letter to Martha Jefferson Randolph, May 31, 1791, in Jefferson, *Papers of Thomas Jefferson,* ed. Boyd et al., 20:464.

14. Lerner, "Historical Statistics."

15. Jefferson, *Papers of Thomas Jefferson,* ed. Boyd et al., 13:264–76.

16. Jefferson, *Papers of Thomas Jefferson,* ed. Boyd et al., 27:449–50.

17. Lecture 1 in Soane, *Royal Academy Lectures,* 629.

18. The garden square was 7.25 acres. For a detailed description and drawings of the progression of Lincoln's Inn Fields see Palmer, "From Fields."

19. Dean, *Sir John Soane and London,* 46.

20. Palmer, *Soanes at Home,* 1.

21. District surveyor William Kinnard filed the charge that the facade of no. 13 projected beyond the plane of the terrace block; Soane won the court case.

22. Jefferson, *Autobiography of Thomas Jefferson,* 7.

23. Eliza's date of birth is unknown, but a separate certificate was not attached to her marriage license to Soane in 1784, meaning that she was at least twenty-one at the time. However, if it is assumed that Eliza was just of age, that means she was an infant when George Wyatt was named her guardian in 1763 following the death of her parents. Wyatt, of no relation to the architect James Wyatt, was occupied in the building trades as the surveyor of sewers, lamps and pavements in the city and owned several properties in Clerkenwell and Surrey. He often worked with George Dance, and Soane may have met him when apprenticing in the office from 1768 to 1772; see Darley, *John Soane,* 10, 73.

24. March 7, 1801, is the exact date mentioned in the Ealing Account Book, fol. 4; see Divitiis, "New Drawings for the Interiors"; Feinberg, "Genesis of Sir John Soane's Museum" note 1, 169.

25. Darley, *John Soane,* 6.

26. Ewing, "Pitzhangor Manor," 142.

27. Ewing, "Pitzhangor Manor," 146.

28. Letter to John Soane, June 2, 1820, manuscript, SJSM III.C.4, no. 7, Soane, "Private Correspondence"; "House of Commons Sitting."

29. Kennedy, *Architecture, Men, Women and Money;* Spurlin, "World of the Founding Fathers."

30. H. Adams, *History of the United States,* 144.

31. Letter to Martha Jefferson Randolph, September 27, 1816, manuscript, Box 1, "Correspondence of Ellen Wayles Randolph Coolidge."

32. For lecture transcriptions, see Watkin, *English Architecture.*

33. Jefferson, *Notes on the State of Virginia,* 152–53.
34. Jefferson, *Notes on the State of Virginia,* 154. For additional commentary on American resources see Shammas, "America, the Atlantic."
35. Letter to John Page, February 21, 1779, in Jefferson, *Writings of Thomas Jefferson,* 1:370.
36. The eroded bedrock produced Davidson clay loam as well as Congaree and Nason silt clay loams.

Chapter 7: Landscapes

1. Jefferson, *Papers of Thomas Jefferson,* ed. Boyd et al., 9:444–46.
2. Nichols and Griswold, *Thomas Jefferson, Landscape Architect,* 81–85; W. H. Adams, *Jefferson's Monticello,* 168–69. Adams's copy is preserved; however, Jefferson's is not: his copy, sold to the Library of Congress, was lost. Jefferson purchased another copy for his retirement library and ordered one for the University of Virginia's library.
3. Julian P. Boyd et al. provide a transcription of Jefferson's travels, combining the Jefferson's draft and manuscript copies held at the MHS and Colonial Williamsburg; see Jefferson, *Papers of Thomas Jefferson,* ed. Boyd et al., 9:369–75. Anthony Brandt provides transcriptions of several letters that contextualize the political motivations behind Jefferson's trip to London; see Brandt, *Thomas Jefferson Travels,* 99–107.
4. Kimball, *Jefferson,* 141–44.
5. Although not assertive about the impact on Jefferson's design thinking, the source that gets closest to an accurate reconstruction of Jefferson's English garden tour is Roberson, "Thomas Jefferson."
6. Letter to William Short, March 28, 1786, in Jefferson, *Papers of Thomas Jefferson,* ed. Boyd et al., 9:362–64.
7. Jefferson, letter to John Page, May 4, 1786, in Jefferson, *Papers of Thomas Jefferson,* ed. Boyd et al., 9:444–46. Jefferson recalled his visit to court in Jefferson, *Autobiography of Thomas Jefferson,* 89.
8. Jefferson, *Papers of Thomas Jefferson,* ed. Boyd et al., 9:362–64.
9. The Cosways left London for Paris on July 16, so they were in the city during Jefferson's English tour.
10. Jefferson, letter to John Page, May 4, 1786.
11. Jefferson, letter to John Page, May 4, 1786.
12. Bear and Stanton, *Jefferson's Memorandum Books,* 1:369–75.
13. In his lengthy entry for December 21, 1771, Jefferson detailed plans for Monticello that included a "small Gothic temple of antique appearance." See Bear and Stanton, *Jefferson's Memorandum Books,* 1:245–50. Although Jefferson owned a copy of Walpole's *On Modern Gardening* (1780), he did not suggest it for the university.

14. Jefferson, *Papers of Thomas Jefferson,* ed. Boyd et al., 9:369–75.
15. John Adams diary 44, April entries, Adams Family, "Adams Family Papers."
16. John Adams diary 44, April entries, Adams Family, "Adams Family Papers."
17. Adams had gardens and orchards at his home in Quincy, Massachusetts, Peacefield, but they were very small and simple in comparison to those of Monticello.
18. Jefferson, *Papers of Thomas Jefferson,* ed. Boyd et al., 9:369–75.
19. Bear and Stanton, *Jefferson's Memorandum Books,* 1:621.
20. Bear and Stanton, *Jefferson's Memorandum Books,* 1:620–21. It is unclear if Adams visited Kew, but his wife recorded a visit in the summer of 1784, in Adams, *Adams Papers,* ed. Ryerson et al., 5:417–18.
21. John Adams diary 44, "London April 20 1786 Thursday" entry, "Adams Family Papers."
22. Mrs. Conduit was appointed the first inspectress of Soane's Museum and served alongside the first curator, George Bailey, until her death in 1860. Parke entered Soane's office in November 1814.
23. Twenty-six of Parke's drawings from the trip are preserved in Soane's Museum, 7.6.1–26.
24. Pocketbook entry for August 31, 1819, SNB 154, Soane, "Soane Notebooks."
25. The Garden Pavilion visitors see today is a reconstruction based on archeological evidence.
26. Bear and Stanton, *Jefferson's Memorandum Books,* 1:245–50.
27. For an annotated drawing, see N66, "Coolidge Collection of Thomas Jefferson Manuscripts, 1705–1827," Special Collections, MHS, Boston.
28. Ellis, *American Sphinx,* 225.
29. Castell, *Villas of the Ancients Illustrated,* 44. Jefferson also owned *Plinni epistolae* (1750) and Orrey's *The letters of Pliny the Younger* (1752).
30. Fitch argues that the passage was also a critical place of communication for the operations of the plantation: Fitch, *James Marston Fitch,* 112.
31. See 143v, "Italian Sketches and Memoirs, 1778–9," Archives, SJSM, vol. 164, London. The list is transcribed as Appendix B in Du Prey, *John Soane's Architectural Education.*

Chapter 8: Libraries

1. Barbara Hofland in Soane, *Description of the House and Museum* (1835), 8.
2. Outram, *Panorama of the Enlightenment,* 18.
3. See Gilreath, "Sowerby Revirescent and Revised"; O'Neal, *Jefferson's Fine Arts Library;* Sanford, *Thomas Jefferson and His Library;* Sowerby, *Catalogue of the Library;* D. L. Wilson, "Sowerby Revisited"; Wilson, "Jefferson's Library"; Wilson, "Thomas Jefferson's Library."
4. See Harris and Savage, *Hooked on Books.*

5. Castell, *Villas of the Ancients Illustrated,* 27.
6. Bolton, *Works of Sir John Soane,* 56–57.
7. The project was largely completed between 2007 and 2013, initially led by Dr. Stephanie Coane; the creation of the online library catalog is ongoing.
8. D.L. Wilson, *Jefferson's Library,* 25–26.
9. Letter, September 21, 1814, in Jefferson, *Papers of Thomas Jefferson,* ed. Boyd et al., 7:681–84.
10. Letter to James Oldham, December 24, 1804, manuscript, "Thomas Jefferson Papers," LoC.
11. Soane did not own any works by Asher Benjamin or Owen Biddle.
12. Harris and Savage, *Hooked on Books,* 6.
13. Jefferson, letter to John Trumbull, February 15, 1789, Jefferson, *Papers of Thomas Jefferson,* ed. Boyd et al., 14:561.
14. Jefferson, letter to Trumbull, February 15, 1789.
15. Soane had the second edition of the English translation by William Smellie, volumes 1–9.
16. See Jefferson's letter to John Sullivan, October 5, 1787, in Jefferson, *Papers of Thomas Jefferson,* ed. Boyd et al., 12: 208–09.
17. Stein, *Worlds of Thomas Jefferson,* 240.
18. Jefferson, letter to Edmund Randolph, February 3, 1794, in Jefferson, *Papers of Thomas Jefferson,* ed. Boyd et al., 28:16.
19. Letter to comte de Volney, 1797, in Jefferson, *Papers of Thomas Jefferson,* ed. Boyd et al., 29:352–53.
20. Jefferson met Dinsmore in 1798 and brought him to Monticello in the fall of the same year, where he worked until 1809 and then labored for Madison at Montpelier before he undertook a series of independent ventures in Richmond, Virginia. Dinsmore returned to Jefferson's service during the construction of the University of Virginia. Neilson worked at Monticello from 1804 to 1809 and later at Montpelier and the University of Virginia.
21. Jefferson, letter to James Ogilvie, January 31, 1806, manuscript, "Thomas Jefferson Papers," LoC.
22. In 1812, the library was made accessible to members of the public if they left a deposit in place of a borrowed text, but it was not widely used beyond its legislative audience until after the Civil War. See Cole, *Library of Congress,* 1–7. A large portion of Jefferson's original books sold to Congress were lost in the fire of 1851 that struck the Capitol. Today's visitors to the Library of Congress see a re-creation of Jefferson's original catalog of books from the 1815 sale comprising the original texts, books in the Library of Congress's collections that match Jefferson's editions, other books acquired through gifts, and "place marker" books that represent the remaining titles and editions yet to be acquired to complete the exhibit. An online

exhibit of Jefferson's library at the Library of Congress is available at https://www.
loc.gov/exhibits/thomas-jeffersons-library/.

23. Harris and Savage, *Hooked on Books,* 9.

24. Letter to Samuel H. Smith, September 21, 1814, in Jefferson, *Papers of Thomas Jefferson,* ed. Boyd et al., 7:681. The Library of Congress, currently the world's largest
library, acts as a copyright depository for the United States and contains texts in
more than 450 languages.

25. Madison, *Papers of James Madison: Retirement Series,* 1:159–60.

26. Harris and Savage, *Hooked on Books,* 1:159–60.

27. Chastellux, *Voyages De M. Le Marquis De Chastellux,* 2:33–46.

Chapter 9: Cabinets

1. Hofland, *Popular Description,* 13.

2. Letter, October 12, 1786, in Jefferson, *Papers of Thomas Jefferson,* ed. Boyd et al.,
10:443–55.

3. Jefferson's residences, not including stays shorter than a month and stays at the
home of a friend, include Shadwell, two residences in Williamsburg, two residences
in Richmond, eight residences in Philadelphia, three townhouses in Paris, one
townhouse in New York, and the President's House in Washington.

4. The nine residences that Jefferson recorded and remodeled in plan form were the
Governor's Palace in Williamsburg, 1779–1781 (N242-N247), Culd-de-sac Tetebout
in Paris ca. 1785 (N245), Hôtel de Langeac in Paris, 1785 (N24), his townhouse in
New York City during his tenure as secretary of state, 1790 (N244), the Schuylkill
residence, 1793 (N251), two Philadelphia townhouses, 1790 (N252–N254), Shadwell
rebuilding plan, ca. 1800 (N296), and the President's House in Washington, ca.
1803–1805 (N404–405); see Peale, *Selected Papers of Charles Willson Peale.* Jefferson's designs for the Governor's House in Richmond are not included in this count
since his scheme presented in N283 was an unexecuted design for a new construction rather than a redesign of his rented accommodation. These documents are
located in the Massachusetts Historical Society, where the majority of Jefferson's
architectural drawings are held. Thomas Jefferson Papers, MHS, https://www
.masshist.org/thomasjeffersonpapers/arch/.

5. Jefferson, *Notes on the State of Virginia,* 152–53.

6. See N56.

7. See N52, N5, N89, N90, and N296.

8. See N56.

9. Jefferson occupied the Hôtel d'Orleans, located along present-day rue Bonaparte,
from August 10 to October 17, 1784. He occupied the Hôtel Landron from October
1784 to October 1785,; it is now known as the Rue Helder in the Ninth Arrondisse-

ment. He occupied the Hôtel de Langeac from October 1784 until September 1789.

10. See Jefferson's letter to his daughter Martha Jefferson Randolph, July 7, 1793, in Betts, *Thomas Jefferson's Garden Book,* 196–97.

11. Dependencies plan, 1796, MHS N150.

12. Monticello plan, 1796, MHS N135.

13. Letter to John Adams, January 11, 1817, in Adams, Adams, and Jefferson, *Adams-Jefferson Letters,* 2:506.

14. There are no known drawings of the space, and of the more than two hundred daily record books, known now as the Soane Notebooks, the years from 1784 to 1787 as well as 1789 are missing.

15. Soane's Museum archivist Sue Palmer has provided many of the familial insights here.

16. Palmer, *Soanes at Home,* 1.

17. See 32.2A.4 through 32.2A.18, "Drawings," Archives, SJSM, London.

18. Feinberg, "Genesis of Sir John Soane's Museum," 229.

19. Mills worked in South Carolina, Pennsylvania, Maryland, and Washington, designing significant projects such as the United States Department of the Treasury, the Washington Monument in Washington, DC, and the Baltimore Cathedral. See Bryan, *Robert Mills, Architect;* Liscombe, *Altogether American.*

20. Election Day was December 3, 1800; however, the election was not decided until February 17, 1801, when the House cast its decisive thirty-sixth vote.

21. Kennedy, *Architecture, Men, Women and Money,* 181–83.

22. The Diary of Anna Maria Thornton, "Anna Maria Brodeau Thornton Papers, 1763–1861," MMC-3412, LoC.

23. Richardson's drawings were part of his "extra-illustrated" compilation of Soane's work. Since the drawings were completed in the 1830s, it is assumed that the drawings were based on Gandy's sketches and Soane's plans rather than his own views of the space.

24. See Divitiis, "New Drawings for the Interiors"; Feinberg, "Genesis of Sir John Soane's Museum."

25. Palmer, *Soanes at Home,* 10. The other five pumps were in the Monk's Yard for kitchen use, the Scullery for sink beneath, the Butler's Pantry, in Mrs. Soane's Morning Room, and in the bathroom adjoining Soane's bedroom. There were only two other water closets in the house: at the front of no. 13 and in the Monk's Yard for the servants.

26. Randolph, *Domestic Life of Thomas Jefferson,* 401.

27. Letter, August 17, 1811, in Jefferson, *Papers of Thomas Jefferson,* ed. Looney, 4:87–88.

Chapter 10: Laboratories

1. Britton and Pugin, *Illustrations of the Public Buildings,* 320.
2. Soane was elected a fellow on November 15, 1821.
3. Hill, *Weather Architecture,* 165.
4. Le Camus de Mézières, *Genius of Architecture,* 62.
5. Hill, "Weather Architecture."
6. Soane, *Royal Academy Lectures,* 19.
7. Watkin, *Sir John Soane,* 598.
8. Soane, *Description of the House and Museum* (1835), 12, 41, 42.
9. Jefferson did not itemize all his orders in the Memorandum books, so this sum is calculated from a composite of accounts and orders expressed in letters.
10. Martha Jefferson Randolph, letter to Thomas Jefferson, June 19, 1801, in Jefferson, *Papers of Thomas Jefferson,* ed. Boyd et al., 34:389–91.
11. Letter to Mary Jefferson Eppes, June 24, 1801, in Jefferson, *Papers of Thomas Jefferson,* ed. Boyd et al., 34:428–29.
12. See the perspective view by Soane's watercolorist, Gandy, SJSM 15.4.8.
13. Soane, *Royal Academy Lectures,* 88.
14. "Italian Sketches and Memoirs," 43v.
15. Hill cites eleven instruments in *Weather Architecture,* 134.
16. Letter, June 30, 1787, in Jefferson, *Papers of Thomas Jefferson,* ed. Boyd et al., 11:509.
17. Bear and Stanton, *Jefferson's Memorandum Books,* 2:623–24.
18. Thomas Jefferson, Monticello: 1st floor of 1st version (plan), 1 page, probably before March 1771, N49.
19. Jefferson had experimented with porches earlier in his designs for the Schuylkill House. See MHS N215v.
20. Palmer, *Soanes at Home,* 13–15.
21. The label is from Jefferson's 1796 fire insurance plan.
22. Beiswanger, "Some Thoughts about Necessaries."
23. Palmer, *Soanes at Home,* 10.
24. Letter, March 3, 1826, polygraph copy, "Thomas Jefferson Papers," LoC.
25. Dorey, " 'Exquisite Hues and Magical Effects' "; Dorey, *John Soane & J. M. W. Turner;* Furján, "Sir John Soane's Spectacular Theatre"; Psarra, *Architecture and Narrative,* 110–35; Willkens, "Clouds and Cataracts."
26. See Hill, "Weather in the Architecture."
27. Woodward, "Wall, Ceiling, Enclosure, and Light," 66.
28. Furján, "Specular Spectacle," 86n3.
29. Bear and Stanton, *Jefferson's Memorandum Books,* 1:616, 618, 621.
30. Jefferson, letter to Thomas Whitney, June 13, 1802, in Jefferson, *Papers of Thomas Jefferson,* ed. Boyd et al., 37:598–99.

31. Bear and Stanton, *Jefferson's Memorandum Books*, 2:1221.
32. *Old Humphrey's Walks in London*, 237.
33. An example of this error is found in Furján's descriptions of a tilted mirror in the stairway in *Glorious Visions*.
34. Dorey, *John Soane & J. M. W. Turner*, 25.

Chapter 11: Pasticci

1. Soane, "Crude Hints towards an History," 74.
2. Julian Harrap Architects, "Conservation Report."
3. Soane, *Description of the House and Museum* (1832), 6.
4. Julian Harrap Architects, "Conservation Report," 125. Slate tiles were added to act as a barrier and create a drip edge.
5. Soane, *Description of the House and Museum* (1835), 27.
6. See SM PSA 4, 13 LIF Plans and Elevations of Pasticcio for Monument Yard, July 1819.
7. Dorey, "Soane's Pasticcio," 15.
8. P. Thornton, *Miscellany of Objects*, 30. The cast originally belonged to Lord Burlington at Chiswick, and it was gifted to Soane.
9. Dorey, "Soane's Pasticcio," 15.
10. Julian Harrap Architects, "Conservation Report," 119.
11. The diary of James Wild as cited in Dorey, "Soane's Pasticcio," 14.
12. Julian Harrap Architects, "Conservation Report," 15.
13. Soane, *Description of the House and Museum* (ed. Bolton, 1930), 7.
14. Britton, *Union of Architecture, Sculpture, and Painting*, 27.
15. Details are of conversation with TJF's former director of restoration, William Beiswanger.
16. Letter to Francis Willis, July 15, 1796, in Jefferson, *Papers of Thomas Jefferson*, ed. Boyd et al., 29:153–54.
17. Jefferson, *Papers of Thomas Jefferson*, ed. Looney, 1:473–75.
18. Semmes, *John H. B. Latrobe*, 239–51.
19. Letter to William Short, March 16, 1791, in Jefferson, *Papers of Thomas Jefferson*, ed. Boyd et al., 19:578–79.
20. Translated from French. Manuscript, "Thomas Jefferson Papers," LoC.
21. Summerson, *Heavenly Mansions*, 48.

Part III: Legacies

1. Kilbride, *Being American in Europe*, 1–2.

Chapter 12: Museums

1. John Britton, letter to Soane, April 21, 1826, in Bolton, *Portrait of Sir John Soane,* 413–14.
2. John Adams diary 44, "Adams Family Papers."
3. For further information on Lever's curatorial approach see Haynes, "'Natural' Exhibitioner.'"
4. Soane occupied the Blackfriars office during 1790; this is addressed in "Cabinets."
5. *Companion to the Museum.*
6. For an extensive history see Watkin and Hewat-Jaboor, *Thomas Hope.*
7. See Davis, *John Nash;* Mansbridge, *John Nash;* Summerson, *Life and Work of John Nash;* Tyack, *John Nash.*
8. A full history of the complex evolution of the museum can be found in Dobson, "Architectural History."
9. "Hunter Album," p. 39, in Archives and Special Collections, Royal College of Surgeons, London.
10. Letter, July 10, 1822, manuscript, "Thomas Jefferson Papers," LoC.
11. Shelfmark PC41(2), "Sale Catalogs," Archives, SJSM, London.
12. See Lloyd, *Richard & Maria Cosway,* 271.
13. See SC1(33) and PC26(7), "Sale Catalogs."
14. Williamson, *Richard Cosway,* 22–23.
15. Williamson, *Richard Cosway,* 39.
16. Arnold, *Library of the Fine Arts;,* 4:188–89; Lloyd, *Richard & Maria Cosway,* 78.
17. See vol. 5, Notebook 58, p. 55, Soane, "Soane Notebooks."
18. Manuscript, Soane, "Private Correspondence."
19. America's earliest museums are explored by Edward P. Alexander in Alexander and Alexander, *Museums in Motion.* However, he does not provide a rationale for America's stunted development.
20. Peale listed his sponsors as "Beale Bordely, Daniel Dulany, Horatio Sharpe, Robert Lloyd, Benjamin Tasker, Thomas Ringold, Benm. Calvert, Thomas Sprigg, Daniel of St. Genefer, Charles Carroll." See Hart and Ward, "Waning of an Enlightenment Ideal," 57–58.
21. Kilbride, *Being American in Europe,* 1–2.
22. Letter, October 29, 1767, in Peale, *Selected Papers of Charles Willson Peale,* 70–71. Charles Carroll is not to be confused with Charles Carroll III (1737–1832), who was a signer of the Declaration of Independence.
23. Schofield, "Science Education," 21.
24. Alderson, *Mermaids, Mummies, and Mastodons;* Hart and Ward, "Waning of an Enlightenment Ideal"; Hindle, Miller, and Richardson, *Charles Willson Peale;* Schofield, "Science Education"; Sellers, *Mr. Peale's Museum;* Ward, *Charles Willson Peale.*

25. Evans, *Benjamin West.*
26. Schofield, "Science Education," 25–26.
27. Kohlstedt, "Entrepreneurs and Intellectuals," 26.
28. Barratt and Miles, *Gilbert Stuart,* 239.
29. Jefferson, *Papers of Thomas Jefferson,* ed. Boyd et al., 1:103–4.
30. Sellers, *Mr. Peale's Museum.*
31. Letter, February 15, 1824, manuscript, "The Thomas Jefferson Papers," UVaSC.
32. For the full text of the June 19, 1788, letter see Jefferson, *Papers of Thomas Jefferson,* ed. Boyd et al., 13:264–76.
33. Letter, June 19, 1788, in Jefferson, *Papers of Thomas Jefferson,* ed. Boyd et al., 13:270.
34. Watkin, *Royal Academy Lectures,* 58.
35. William Short, letter to Thomas Jefferson, July 17, 1791, in Jefferson, *Papers of Thomas Jefferson,* ed. Boyd et al., 20:641–45.
36. Benjamin, *Country Builder's Assistant;* Benjamin, *American Builder's Companion;* Biddle, *Young Carpenter's Assistant;* Morris, *Select Architecture.*
37. See SM 32/2A/6 and 32/2A/12.
38. Soane, *Royal Academy Lectures,* 21.
39. See MHS N55v and N57.
40. See Duncan and Burns, *Lewis and Clark;* Ronda, *Voyages of Discovery;* Ronda, *Jefferson's West.*
41. The original bust was lost in the 1851 Library of Congress fire; the re-created bust was made by Joe Brown.

Chapter 13: Tokens

1. Maria Cosway, letter to John Soane, February 19, 1831, manuscript, SJSM III.c.4, no. 24, Soane, "Private Correspondence."
2. Letter to Maria Cosway, December 24, 1786, in Jefferson, *Papers of Thomas Jefferson,* ed. Boyd et al., 10:627–28 (author's translation from Italian); letter to Maria Cosway, October 13, 1786 in Jefferson, *Papers of Thomas Jefferson,* ed. Boyd et al., 10:458–59.
3. Manuscript, SJSM III.c.4, no. 24, Soane, "Private Correspondence."
4. Letter translated from Italian, November 17, 1786, in Jefferson, *Papers of Thomas Jefferson,* ed. Boyd et al., 10:538–40.
5. Manuscript, SJSM III.C.4, no. 18, Soane, "Private Correspondence."
6. Much of their letters from the early 1830s revolve around financial matters. Hoare's appointment was later terminated, in part, due to her perception that he was "confined by violent derangement of his mind." See Maria Hadfield Cosway, letter to John Soane, July 1, 1830, manuscript, SJSM III.C.4, no. 32, Soane, "Private Correspondence."

7. Soane purchased no. 14 Lincoln's Inn Fields in October 1823 and already had plans in place to extend the northeastern side of his museum with a two-story addition that would frame the back of no. 14, leaving the front of the house open to serve as rented income. By March 1825 the "moveable plans" of the Picture Room were in place. For additional information see Palin, "No. 14."

8. See Chantrell, Robert to Curators, Portraits & Mourning Cards/Cosway, Maria Ceclia (1759–1838) from "Paintings Inventory," Archives, SJSM, London.

9. See the sale catalogs held at Sir John Soane's Museum, SC1(33) and PC26(7).

10. The panel's portrait orientation, made of three pieces of pine, is typical for French paintings at the time. The construction method, however, is odd: the wood grain of the central panel is vertical, whereas the grain of the top and bottom pieces of the panel is oriented horizontally, as revealed in an unpublished conservation report of November 2010 from deputy curator Helen Dorey containing the work of conservator Anna Sandén and Simon Bobak. This cross-grain construction has caused the small panel portrait to warp since the individual pieces of the panels have separated, and large cracks in the thin paint have appeared. The most apparent crack, running along the center of the portrait to Napoleon's nose, was repaired in 2005. At this time, the conservators undertook an in-depth analysis and restoration of the painting that left them baffled. The panel construction and painting method did not align with any regional traditions, and the attempt to decipher the painting's signature was foiled even by microphotography: the image was too blurry and pixelated to read.

11. Francesco Cossia, letter to Signor Borghini, March 17, 1797, manuscript, "Paintings Inventory," Archives, SJSM, London.

12. This name appears in the 1830, 1833, and 1835/6 editions of Soane's *A Description of the House and Museum* within the table of contents of "Names of Foreign Artists Whose Works Are in This Collection" and in the section dedicated to the painting.

13. See Soane, *Description of the House and Museum* (1835), 51.

14. Lloyd, *Richard & Maria Cosway,* 49.

15. Paoli (1725–1807) and Cosway would remain friends: he was even named godfather to Cosway's only daughter.

16. Francesco Ricard, letter to Maria Ceclia Hadfield Cosway, March 26, 1797, "Paintings Inventory," Archives, SJSM, London.

17. This ring was recently rediscovered. In accordance with Soane's will, the ring was left to his grandson along with a diamond ring from the Emperor of Russia and Soane's gold medal from the Royal Academy.

18. Letter, January 5, 1828, manuscript, LAW/5/204, "Sir Thomas Lawrence, PRA, Letters and Papers 1777–1831," RAA, London.

19. Letter, February 19, 1831, manuscript, SJSM III.C.4, no. 34, Soane, "Private Correspondence."

20. Letter, February 6, 1832, manuscript, SJSM III.C.4, no. 37, and letter, March 20, 1834, manuscript, SJSM III.C.4, no. 43, both in Soane, "Private Correspondence."

21. See Soane, "Crude Hints towards an History."

22. Letter, August 19, 1830, manuscript, SJSM III.C.4, no. 32, Soane, "Private Correspondence."

23. The letter arranging the copy is dated June 8, 1830.

24. Letter, February 19, 1831, manuscript, SJSM III.C.4, no. 34, Soane, "Private Correspondence."

25. Cosway wrote: "in the second line 'Non sappiamo, etc.' there wants the word lo, 'Non lo sappiamo in Verità.' Forgive me for this trifling observation." See SJSM III.C.4, no. 34, Soane, "Private Correspondence."

26. The bust is a copy, by an unknown artist, after Antoine-Denis Chaudet (1763–1810).

27. Jefferson to Meriwether Lewis, October 26, 1806, in Jackson, *Letters of the Lewis and Clark Expedition,* 51.

28. In preparation for the journey, Napoleon apparently calculated that the sandstone building material from Great Pyramid of Khufu could be used to create a stonewall around Paris that would be one meter wide and three meters tall. See Wilson-Smith, *Napoleon and His Artists,* 73.

29. Jefferson later changed his entry for the statue in his inventory to "Ariadne reclined on the rocks of Naxos" after he acquired a copy of *Legrand's Galeries des Antiques* (1803), which featured an illustration of the original statue, housed in the Vatican.

30. Primary resources on the original placement of these objects establish critical precedent for the current placement of the Egyptian reproductions and re-creations within the museum.

31. Jane Blair Cary Smith, 1823, 69–78, from D. L. Wilson, *Jefferson's Library.*

32. Jefferson, letter to the Marquis de Chastellux, June 7, 1785, manuscript, "Thomas Jefferson Papers," LoC.

33. See Britton, *Union of Architecture,* 49–50.

34. The alabaster of the sarcophagus is now opaquer, possibility due to an unfortunate cleaning incident in the late 1900s, and it is now ensconced in a protective glass case.

35. See Soane, *Description of the House and Museum* (1835), 33.

36. Letter, February 15, 1878, manuscript, "Thomas Jefferson Papers," LoC.

37. Letter, September 26, 1788, in Jefferson, *Papers of Thomas Jefferson,* ed. Boyd et al., 13:638–39.

38. Letter, 7 December 1787, in Jefferson, *Papers of Thomas Jefferson,* ed. Boyd et al., 12:403.

39. For additional notes, see G. S. Wilson, *Jefferson on Display,* 62–66.

40. Jefferson, *Papers of Thomas Jefferson,* ed. Boyd et al., 12:647.

41. Letter, July 21, 1788, in Jefferson, *Papers of Thomas Jefferson,* ed. Boyd et al., 13:391.

42. Letter, August 17, 1788, Microfilm, Items 91–92, "Papers of Angelica Church."

43. Letter to Angelica Schuyler Church, September 21, 1788, in Jefferson, *Papers of Thomas Jefferson,* ed. Boyd et al., 13:623–24.

44. Letter, May 21, 1789, in Jefferson, *Papers of Thomas Jefferson,* ed. Boyd et al., 15:142–43.

45. Letter, September 26, 1788, in Jefferson, *Papers of Thomas Jefferson,* ed. Boyd et al., 13:638–39.

46. Letter, June 23, 1790, in Jefferson, *Papers of Thomas Jefferson,* ed. Boyd et al., 16:550–51.

47. Letter, December 4, 1795, in Jefferson, *Papers of Thomas Jefferson,* ed. Boyd et al., 34:599–600.

48. Manuscript, SJSM III.C.4, no. 43, Soane, "Private Correspondence."

Chapter 14: Academies

1. Soane, Royal Academy lecture 1 in Soane, *Royal Academy Lectures,* 41.

2. The manuscript is preserved at the Library of Congress and is transcribed in W. Thornton, *Papers of William Thornton,* 346–66.

3. W. Thornton, *Papers of William Thornton,* 352.

4. W. Thornton, *Papers of William Thornton,* 355.

5. W. Thornton, *Papers of William Thornton,* 366.

6. "Anna Maria Brodeau Thornton Papers."

7. See Ellen's letter to her mother, July 18, 1819, manuscript, Box 1, "Correspondence of Ellen Wayles Randolph Coolidge."

8. Manuscript, SJSM III.C.4, no. 37, Soane, "Private Correspondence."

9. For the full text of Jefferson's 1778 Bill see Peterson, *Thomas Jefferson Writings,* 365–73. The purview of Jefferson's educational endeavors are examined in Addis, *Jefferson's Vision for Education.* For Jefferson's hopes for a school, see Jefferson, letter to Peter Carr, September 7, 1814, in Jefferson, *Papers of Thomas Jefferson,* ed. Boyd et al., 7:636–42.

10. Letter, May 6, 1810, in Jefferson, *Papers of Thomas Jefferson,* ed. Looney, 2:365–66.

11. Letter to Antoine Louis Claude Destutt de Tracy, December 26, 1820, Jefferson, *Autobiography of Thomas Jefferson,* 174.

12. Nelson, "Architecture of Democracy," 98–101.

13. Letter, October 24, 1822, manuscript, "Thomas Jefferson Papers," LoC.

14. Nichols, *Thomas Jefferson's Architectural Drawings,* no.146.

15. The points were expressed in the "Rockfish Gap Report" to the Virginia General Assembly, August 4, 1810, in Jefferson, *Papers of Thomas Jefferson,* ed. Looney, 13:209–24.

16. Letter to Maria Cosway, October 24, 1822, manuscript, "Thomas Jefferson Papers," LoC.
17. Letter to Maria Cosway, October 24, 1822.
18. Letter, September 24, 1824, microfilm, reel 12, "Coolidge Collection of Thomas Jefferson Manuscripts."
19. Letter to Spencer Roane, March 9, 1821, in Jefferson, *Writings of Thomas Jefferson.*
20. Letter, February 6, 1832, manuscript, SJSM III.C.4, no. 37, Soane, "Private Correspondence."
21. Letter, July 10, 1822, manuscript, "Thomas Jefferson Papers," LoC.
22. Gipponi, "Il Collegio Cosway," 151.
23. Manuscript, SJSM III.C.4, no. 37, Soane, "Private Correspondence."
24. Manuscript, SJSM III.C.4, no. 24, Soane, "Private Correspondence."
25. "House of Commons Sitting"; "Act for Settling and Preserving Sir John Soane's Museum."
26. American governmental involvement in architectural preservation was not enacted until The Antiquities Act of 1906, 16 USC 431, which called for the presidential designation of national monuments, historic landmarks, historic or prehistoric structures, and other objects of historic or scientific interest; however, these sites had to be located on public property. The National Park Service, established in 1916 under the administration of President Theodore Roosevelt, was originally charged exclusively with the preservation of natural resources and added the built environment to their purview in 1966 with the National Historic Preservation Act. The Historic Sites Act of 1935 was passed in Congress as part of the Civil Works Administration and authorized the Department of the Interior to begin surveys of important historic resources.
27. Architectural preservation in Jefferson's lifetime was a private endeavor. For example, in 1816 a group of private citizens purchased the Philadelphia State House, the site where the Declaration of Independence was signed and now commonly known as Independence Hall, from the City of Philadelphia when the structure was slated for destruction. This pattern of privately driven preservation in America continued through the nineteenth and early twentieth centuries as evidenced by the 1827 efforts to save the Touro Synagogue in Newport, Rhode Island, and the foundation of the Mount Vernon's Ladies Association in 1853 to rescue George Washington's residence.
28. Letter to Henry Clay, April 2, 1833, manuscript, Henry Clay Papers, Library of Congress, Washington, DC.
29. Soane, "Crude Hints towards an History."
30. Letter to the editor of the *Richmond Enquirer,* August 1817, in Jefferson, *Papers of Thomas Jefferson,* ed. Looney, 11:664–66.
31. Letter to Jefferson, July 10, 1822, manuscript, "Thomas Jefferson Papers," LoC.
32. Gipponi, "Il Collegio Cosway," 158–62.

33. Kelsall, *Phantasm of an University.*
34. Letter, February 15, 1817, in Madison, *Papers of James Madison: Presidential Series,* 11:669–70. Jefferson ordered a copy of the book for the university in 1825. Soane had other works by Kelsall, but it does not appear that he owned *Phantasm.*
35. Madison, *Papers of James Madison: Retirement Series,* 1:136.

Chapter 15: Visitors

1. Schinkel, *English Journey,* 116.
2. In reference to scientific objects alone, Jefferson notes in a letter of 1817 that his collections rival those of Harvard College. See Birle and Francavilla, *Thomas Jefferson's Granddaughter,* xviii.
3. Letter, July 28, 1819, manuscript, Box 1, "Correspondence of Ellen Wayles Randolph Coolidge."
4. Letter, August 18, 1817, manuscript, Box 1, "Correspondence of Ellen Wayles Randolph Coolidge."
5. Letter, July 18, 1819, manuscript, Box 1, "Correspondence of Ellen Wayles Randolph Coolidge."
6. Manuscript, Box 1, "Correspondence of Ellen Wayles Randolph Coolidge."
7. Beyond her experiences in London in 1838 and 1839, Ellen traveled to China and later spent three years living in Europe in the 1840s. Like many of her siblings, she visited sites that Jefferson was only able to read about, and aside from her youngest sibling, George Wythe Randolph (1818–1867), she traveled the most extensively. George's travels were largely linked to his time with the U.S. Navy from 1831 until 1839. In a letter to Ellen from July 26, 1831, he described visiting Pompeii and Herculaneum, where he covertly stole a souvenir piece of marble from the street. Manuscript, Box 3, "Correspondence of Ellen Wayles Randolph Coolidge." George later served as the secretary of war for the Confederacy and spent two years in Europe following his resignation in 1864.
8. Jefferson, letter to John Page, May 4, 1786, in Jefferson, *Papers of Thomas Jefferson,* ed. Boyd et al., 9:444–46.
9. Birle and Francavilla, *Thomas Jefferson's Granddaughter,* 34.
10. The volume is still in the collections.
11. The volume moved from the Fiske Kimball Fine Arts Library to Special Collections in 2007, and the only note on provenance is a stamp 'GIFT Jan 31 34.'
12. From October 4, 1838, in Birle and Francavilla, *Thomas Jefferson's Granddaughter,* 75.
13. Birle and Francavilla, *Thomas Jefferson's Granddaughter,* 125.
14. From the March 24, 1835, to May 2, 1839, section of the Wister and Irwin, *Worthy Women.*
15. Visitation counts for the opening days around Ellen's visit were 6 on Tuesday,

February 12; 1 on Tuesday, February 19; 12 on Tuesday, February 26; 12 on Tuesday, March 12; 3 on Monday, March 18; and 21 on Tuesday, March 19.

16. It is of note that the location of visitors was rarely noted before 1839 in the visitor's books.

17. Jefferson owned first and second editions of the Leoni's version of Palladio and probably a copy with Inigo Jones's notations. See O'Neal, *Jefferson's Fine Arts Library,* for the full catalog entries of Jefferson's architectural books.

18. Birle and Francavilla, *Thomas Jefferson's Granddaughter,* 277–78.

19. Britton, *Union of Architecture, Sculpture, and Painting,* vii.

20. Birle and Francavilla, *Thomas Jefferson's Granddaughter,* 278.

21. Ellen mentions cork models, but it is likely these were on a table in the Picture Gallery, and the group did not visit the Model Room.

22. Birle and Francavilla, *Thomas Jefferson's Granddaughter,* 280–81.

23. The letter from Martha to Ellen of April 5, 1826, is particularly insightful. See Box 1, "Correspondence of Ellen Wayles Randolph Coolidge." In the preparation of her draft, she requested input from the two other figures who knew the most about Jefferson's finances: his daughter Martha Randolph and son-in-law Nicolas Trist.

24. D. L. Wilson, *Jefferson's Library,* 47. In Jefferson's will, his retirement library was left to the University of Virginia and duplicates to two of his grandsons, but the majority of his collection was put through to the auction. Since the late 1800s, the location and fate of the Entrance Hall items relocated to the University of Virginia has been a mystery.

25. Ellen Wayles Randolph Coolidge, letter to Martha Jefferson Randolph and Nicolas Trist, manuscript, Box 2, "Correspondence of Ellen Wayles Randolph Coolidge."

26. Mary Randolph, letter to Ellen Wayles Randolph Coolidge, August 10, 1828, manuscript, Box 2, "Correspondence of Ellen Wayles Randolph Coolidge."

27. Letter to Anna Bayard Boyd and Jane Bayard Kirkpatrick reprinted in Gizzard, "Three Grand & Interesting Objects."

Conclusion

1. Major retrospectives on the work of Jefferson and Soane were coordinated as traveling exhibitions in the 1990s and resulted in substantial catalogs. See Stein, *Worlds of Thomas Jefferson;* Stevens and Richardson, *John Soane, Architect.*

2. In 1861 the museum was only open thirty-one days.

3. Curator James Wild (1878–1892) made substantial changes to architectural fabric and layout of the museum.

4. War damages were eventually repaired, and grants during the latter half of the twentieth century allowed the museum to restore elements such as crumbling portions of the Monk's Court and purchase the property at no. 14.

BIBLIOGRAPHY

"An Act for Settling and Preserving Sir John Soane's Museum, Library, and Works of Art, in Lincoln's Inn Fields in the County of Middlesex, for the Benefit of the Public, and for Establishing a Sufficient Endowment for the Due Maintenance of the Same." April 20, 1833.

Adams, Henry. *History of the United States during the First Administration of Thomas Jefferson.* Vol. 1. New York: Charles Scribner's Sons, 1889.

Adams, John, Abigail Adams, and Thomas Jefferson. *The Adams-Jefferson Letters: The Complete Correspondence between Thomas Jefferson and Abigail and John Adams.* Edited by Lester J. Cappon. 2 vols. Chapel Hill: Univeristy of North Carolina Press, 1959.

Adams, William Howard. *Jefferson's Monticello.* New York: Abbeville Press, 1983.

Adams Family. "Adams Family Papers." Massachusetts Historical Society, Boston. https://www.masshist.org/adams/adams-family-papers.

———. *The Adams Papers.* Edited by L. H. Butterfield. Cambridge, MA: Harvard University Press, 1961.

———. *The Adams Papers: Adams Family Correspondence.* Vols. 5–6, *1782–1785.* Edited by Richard Alan Ryerson, Joanna M. Revelas, Celeste Walker, Gregg L. Lint, and Humphrey J. Costello. Cambridge, MA: Harvard University Press, 1993.

———. *The Adams Papers: Adams Family Correspondence.* Vol. 7, *January 1786—February 1787.* Edited by C. James Taylor et al. Cambridge, MA: Harvard University Press, 2005.

Addis, Cameron. *Jefferson's Vision for Education, 1760–1845.* New York: Peter Lang, 2003.

Alderson, William T., ed. *Mermaids, Mummies, and Mastodons: The Emergence of the American Museum.* Washington, DC: American Association of Museums for the Baltimore City Life Museums, 1992.

Alexander, Edward P., and Mary Alexander. *Museums in Motion: An Introduction to the History and Functions of Museums.* Lanham, MD: AltaMira Press, 2008.

Alexander, Robert L. *The Architecture of Maximilian Godefroy.* Baltimore: Johns Hopkins University Press, 1974.

———. "Maximilian Godefroy in Virginia: A French Interlude in Richmond's Architecture." *Virginia Magazine of History and Biography* 69, no. 4 (1961): 420–31.

———. "The Public Memorial and Godefroy's Battle Monument." *Journal of the Society of Architectural Historians* 17, no. 1 (1958): 19–24.

"Anna Maria Brodeau Thornton Papers, 1763–1861." In MMC-3412. Library of Congress, Washington, DC.

Arnold, M. *Library of the Fine Arts; or Repertory of Painting, Sculpture, Architecture, and Engraving.* Vol. 4. London: M. Arnold, 1832.

Barnett, Gerald. *Richard and Maria Cosway: A Biography.* Tiverton, UK: Westcountry Books, 1995.

Barratt, Carrie Rebora, and Ellen G. Miles. *Gilbert Stuart.* New York: Metropolitan Museum of Art, 2004.

Bear, James Adam, and Lucia C. Stanton, eds. *Jefferson's Memorandum Books: Accounts, with Legal Records and Miscellany, 1767–1826.* 2 vols. Papers of Thomas Jefferson, 2nd series. Princeton, NJ: Princeton University Press, 1997.

Beiswanger, William. "Some Thoughts about Necessaries at Monticello on the Occasion of the Restoration of the North Privy, August 2000." Unpublished. Thomas Jefferson Foundation, Charlottesville, VA.

Benjamin, Asher. *The American Builder's Companion.* Greenfield, MA: J. Denio, 1805.

———. *The Country Builder's Assistant.* Greenfield, MA: J. Denio, 1797.

Betts, Edwin Morris, ed. *Thomas Jefferson's Garden Book, 1766–1824: With Relevant Extracts from His Other Writings.* Whitefish, MT: Kessinger, 2010.

Biddle, Owen. *The Young Carpenter's Assistant; a System of Architecture, Adapted to the Style of Building in the United States.* Philadelphia: Benjamin Johnson, 1805.

Birle, Ann Lucas, and Lisa A. Francavilla, eds. *Thomas Jefferson's Granddaughter in Queen Victoria's England: The Travel Diary of Ellen Wayles Coolidge, 1838–1839.* Charlottesville: University of Virginia Press, 2011.

Blackson, Robert M. "Pennsylvania Banks and the Panic of 1819: A Reinterpretation." *Journal of the Early Republic* 9, no. 3 (1989): 335–58.

Boldrick, Charles C. "St. Thomas Catholic Church." Washington, DC: U.S. Department of the Interior, 1960.

Bolton, Arthur T., ed. *The Portrait of Sir John Soane, R.A., 1753–1837, Set Forth in Letters from His Friends.* London: Frome, 1927.

———. *The Works of Sir John Soane.* London: Sir John Soane Museum, 1924.

Boucher, Diane. "Maria Cosway's 'A Persian Going to Adore the Sun.'" *Burlington Magazine* 162, no. 1405 (2020): 300–305.

Brandt, Anthony, ed. *Thomas Jefferson Travels: Selected Writings, 1784–1789.* Washington, DC: National Geographic, 2006.

A Brief Account of the Roads of Italy, for the Use of Gentlemen Who Travel with the Post, with Twenty-Three Geographical Maps. London, 1775.

Britton, John. *The Union of Architecture, Sculpture, and Painting; Exemplified by a Series of Illustrations, with Descriptive Accounts of the House and Galleries of John Soane.* London, 1827.

Britton, John, and Augustus Pugin. *Illustrations of the Public Buildings of London. With Historical and Descriptive Accounts of Each Edifice.* London: J. Taylor, 1825.

Bryan, John M., ed. *Robert Mills, Architect.* Washington, DC: American Institute of Architects Press, 1989.

Burnell, Carol. *Divided Affections: The Extraordinary Life of Maria Cosway: Celebrity Artist and Thomas Jefferson's Impossible Love.* Lausanne, Switzerland: Column House, 2007.

Butterfield, L. H., and Howard C. Rice Jr. "Jefferson's Earliest Note to Maria Cosway with Some New Facts and Conjectures on His Broken Wrist." *William and Mary Quarterly* 5, no. 1 (1948): 26–33.

Castell, Robert. *The Villas of the Ancients Illustrated.* London: Printed by the author, 1728.

A Catalogue of the Books Belonging to the Library Company of Philadelphia; to Which Is Prefixed, a Short Account of the Institution, with the Charter, Laws, and Regulations. Philadelphia: C. Sherman & Co. Printers, 1835.

Catalogue of the Leverian Museum ... The Sale of the Collection, etc. (Price Catalogue.) Ms. Notes [of Prices and Purchasers]. London, 1806.

Chandler, Tertius. *Four Thousand Years of Urban Growth: An Historical Census.* Lewiston, NY: St. David's Univeristy Press, 1987.

Chastellux, François Jean. *Voyages De M. Le Marquis De Chastellux Dans L'améRique Septentrionale Dans Les AnnéEs 1780, 1781 & 1782.* Paris: Prault, 1786.

Cohen, Jeffrey A., and Charles E. Brownell, eds. *The Architectural Drawings of Benjamin Henry Latrobe.* New Haven, CT: Yale University Press, 1994.

Cole, John Y., ed. *The Library of Congress: A Documentary History.* Bethesda, MD: Congressional Information Service, 1987.

"Columbian Institute." In *Constitutional Ordinance for the Government of the Columbian Institute.* Washington, DC: S.A. Elliot, 1820.

"Columbian Institute Records 1816–1841, with Related Papers 1791–1800." In Smithsonian Institute Archives, Washington, DC.

A Companion to the Museum, Late Sir Ashton Lever's, Removed to Albion Street, etc. London, 1790.

Cook, Elizabeth Heckendorn. *Epistolary Bodies: Gender and Genre in the Eighteenth-Century Republic of Letters.* Stanford, CA: Stanford University Press, 1996.

"Coolidge Collection of Thomas Jefferson Manuscripts, 1705–1827." In Massachusetts Historical Society Special Collections, Boston.

"Correspondence of Ellen Wayles Randolph Coolidge, 1810–1861." In MS9090. University of Virginia Special Collections, Charlottesville.

Darley, Gillian. "The Grand Tour." In *John Soane, Architect: Master of Space and Light,* edited by Mary Anne Stevens and Richardson Margaret, 96–113. London: Royal Academy of Arts, 1999. Distributed by Yale University Press.

———. *John Soane: An Accidental Romantic.* New Haven, CT: Yale University Press, 1999.

Davenport, Beatrix C., ed. *A Diary of the French Revolution.* 2 vols. Freeport, NY: Books for Libraries Press, 1939.

Davis, Terence. *John Nash: The Prince Regent's Architect.* Newton Abbot, UK: David and Charles, 1973.

de Montclos, J. M. Pérouse. *Histoire de l'architecture française: De la Renaissance à la Révolution.* Paris: Mengès, 1989.

Dean, Ptolemy. *Sir John Soane and London.* Aldershot, UK: Ashgate, 2006.

Description of the House and Museum on the North Side of Lincoln's Inn Fields the Residence of Sir John Soane. Edited by Arthur T. Bolton. Oxford: Oxford University Press, 1920.

Divitiis, Bianca de. "New Drawings for the Interiors of the Breakfast Room and Library at Pitzhanger Manor." *Architectural History* 48 (2005): 163–72.

Dobson, Jessie. "The Architectural History of the Hunterian Museum." *Annal of the Royal College of Surgeons of England* 29, no. 2 (1961): 113–26.

Dorey, Helen. "'Exquisite Hues and Magical Effects': Sir John Soane's Use of Stained Glass at 13 Lincoln's Inn Fields." *British Art Journal* 5, no. 1 (2004): 30–40.

———. *John Soane & J. M. W. Turner: Illuminating a Friendship.* London: Sir John Soane's Museum, 2007. Exhibition Catalog.

———. "Soane's Pasticcio." *The Georgian,* special issue (2003): 14–17.

Du Prey, Pierre de la Ruffinière. *John Soane's Architectural Education, 1753–80.* New York: Garland, 1977.

Duncan, Dayton, and Ken Burns. *Lewis and Clark: The Journey of the Corps of Discovery.* New York: Alfred A. Knopf, 1997.

Eames, Charles, Ray Eames, and the Metropolitan Museum of Art in New York. *The World of Franklin and Jefferson: A Souvenir of the American Revolution Bicentennial Administration Exhibition.* Washington, DC: American Revolution Bicentennial Administration, 1975.

Ellis, Joseph J. *American Sphinx: The Character of Thomas Jefferson.* New York: Alfred A. Knopf, 1997.

Encyclopedia of Diderot & d'Alembert Collaborative Translation Project. University of Michigan Library. https://quod.lib.umich.edu/d/did/.

Evans, Dorinda. *Benjamin West and His American Students.* Washington, DC: Published for the National Portrait Gallery by the Smithsonian Institution Press, 1980.

Ewing, Heather. "Pitzhangor Manor." In *John Soane, Architect: Master of Space and Light,* edited by Mary Anne Stevens and Richardson Margaret, 142–49. London: Royal Academy of Arts, 1999. Distributed by Yale University Press.

Feinberg, Susan G. "The Genesis of Sir John Soane's Museum Idea: 1801–1810." *Journal of the Society of Architectural Historians* 43, no. 3 (1984): 225–37.

Fitch, James Marston. *James Marston Fitch: Selected Writings, 1933–1997.* Edited by Martica Sawin. New York: W. W. Norton, 2006.

Flavell, Julie. *When London Was Capital of America.* New Haven, CT: Yale University Press, 2010.

Fraser, Murray. *Architecture and the Special Relationship: The American Influence on Post-War British Architecture.* London: Routledge, 2007.

Furján, Helene. *Glorious Visions: John Soane's Spectacular Theater.* London: Routledge, 2011.

———. "Sir John Soane's Spectacular Theatre." *AA Files,* no. 47 (2002): 12–22.

———. "The Specular Spectacle of the House of the Collector." *Assemblage,* no. 34 (1997): 57–91.

Gilreath, James. "Sowerby Revirescent and Revised." *Papers of the Bibliographical Society of America* 78 (1984): 19–32.

Gipponi, Tino. "Il Collegio Cosway: Luoghi E Memorie." In *Maria E Richard Cosway,* edited by Tino Gipponi, 151–70. Torino: Umberto Allemandi, 1998.

Gizzard, Frank Edgar, Jr. "Three Grand & Interesting Objects: An 1828 Visit to Monticello, the University and Montpelier." *Magazine of Albemarle County History* 51 (1993).

Gladwell, Malcom. *The Tipping Point: How Little Things Can Make a Big Difference.* Boston: Little, Brown, 2000.

Godefroy, Maximilian. *Military Reflections, on Four Modes of Defence, for the United States with a Plan of Defence, Adapted to Their Circumstances and the Existing State of Things.* Translated by Eliza Anderson. Baltimore: Joseph Robinson, 1807.

Gordon-Reed, Annette. *The Hemingses of Monticello: An American Family.* New York: W. W. Norton, 2008.

Graves, Algernon. *The Royal Academy of Arts: A Complete Dictionary of Contributors and Their Work from Its Foundation in 1769 to 1904, etc.* 8 vols. London: George Bell & Sons, 1905.

Greig, James, ed. *The Farington Diary.* London: Hutchinson, 1922.

Harnsberger, Douglas. "'In Delorme's Manner': An X-Ray Probe of Jefferson's Dome at Monticello Reveals an Ingenious 16th-Century Timber Vault Construction Concealed within the Dome's Sheathing." *Bulletin of the Association for Preservation Technology* 13, no. 4 (1981): 3–8.

Harris, Eileen, and Nicholas Savage, eds. *Hooked on Books: The Library of Sir John Soane, Architect, 1753–1837.* London: Sir John Soane's Museum, 2004.

Hart, Sidney, and David C. Ward. "The Waning of an Enlightenment Ideal: Charles

Willson Peale's Philadelphia Museum, 1790–1820." *Journal of the Early Republic* 8, no. 4 (1988): 398–418.

Haynes, Clare. "A 'Natural' Exhibitioner: Sir Ashton Lever and His Holosphusikon." *British Journal for Eighteenth-Century Studies* 24 (2001): 1–14.

Hill, Jonathan. "Weather Architecture." Talk delivered at the Bartlett School of Architecture, University College London, October 25, 2012.

———. *Weather Architecture.* London: Routledge, 2012.

———. "The Weather in the Architecture: Soane, Turner and the 'Big Smoke.'" *Journal of Architecture* 14, no. 3 (2009): 361–76.

Hindle, Brooke, Lillian B. Miller, and Edgar Preston Richardson, eds. *Charles Willson Peale and His World.* New York: Harry N. Abrams, 1982.

Hindley, Meredith. "Mapping the Republic of Letters." *Humanities* 34, no. 6 (2013). https://www.neh.gov/humanities/2013/novemberdecember/feature/mapping-the-republic-letters.

Hofland, Barbara. *Popular Description of Sir John Soane's House, Museum, & Library.* Edited by Arthur T. Bolton. Oxford: Frederick Hall, 1919.

"House of Commons Sitting." House of Commons, April 1, 1833. *Hansard Parliamentary Debates*, 3d series (1830–91).

Howard, Hugh. *Thomas Jefferson, Architect: The Built Legacy of Our Third President.* New York: Rizzoli, 2003.

Hunsberger, George S. "The Architectural Career of George Hadfield." *Records of the Columbia Historical Society, Washington, DC* 51/52 (1951): 46–65.

"Hunter Album." In Archives and Special Collections, Royal College of Surgeons, London.

Hyde, Timothy. "Some Evidence of Libel, Criticism, and Publicity in the Architectural Career of Sir John Soane." *Perspecta* 37 (2005): 144–63.

"Italian Sketches and Memoirs, 1778–9." In Archives of Sir John Soane's Museum, SJSM vol. 164, London.

Jackson, Donald, ed. *Letters of the Lewis and Clark Expedition with Related Documents, 1783–1854.* 2nd ed. Urbana: University of Illinois Press, 1978.

Jefferson, Thomas. *The Autobiography of Thomas Jefferson, 1743–1790: Together with a Summary of the Chief Events in Jefferson's Life.* Edited by Paul Leicester Ford. New York: G. P. Putnam's Sons, 1914.

———. *Notes on the State of Virginia.* Edited by William Harwood Peden. Chapel Hill: University of North Carolina Press for the Institute of Early American History and Culture at Williamsburg, Virginia, 1955.

———. *The Papers of Thomas Jefferson.* Edited by Julian P. Boyd, Lyman B. Butterfield, Mina R. Bryan, et al.. Princeton, NJ: Princeton University Press, 1950–.

———. *The Papers of Thomas Jefferson: Retirement Series.* Edited by J. Jefferson Looney. 9 vols. Princeton, NJ: Princeton University Press, 2004–.

———. "Thomas Jefferson Papers." In *Library of Congress.* Washington, DC.

——. "The Thomas Jefferson Papers." In University of Virginia Special Collections, Charlottesville.

——. *The Writings of Thomas Jefferson.* 20 vols. Edited by Andrew A. Lipscomb and Albert E. Berghs. Washington, DC: Thomas Jefferson Memorial Association of the United States, 1903–20.

Jenkins, Frank. *Architect and Patron: A Survey of Professional Relations and Practice in England from the Sixteenth Century to the Present Day.* London: Oxford University Press, 1961.

Julian Harrap Architects. "Conservation Report in Connection with the Three Court-yards Project at the Sir John Soane's Museum." Unpublished report prepared for the Trustees of the Sir John Soane Museum, London, December 22, 1999.

Kelsall, Charles. *Phantasm of an University: With Prolegomena.* London: White, Cochrane, 1814.

Kennedy, Roger G. *Architecture, Men, Women and Money in America, 1600–1860.* New York: Random House, 1985.

——. *Orders from France: The Americans and the French in a Revolutionary World, 1780–1820.* New York: Knopf, 1989.

Kilbride, Daniel. *Being American in Europe, 1750–1860.* Baltimore: Johns Hopkins University Press, 2013.

Kimball, Marie Goebel. *Jefferson: The Scene of Europe, 1784 to 1789.* New York: Coward-McCann, 1950.

King, Julia. *George Hadfield: Architect of the Federal City.* London: Ashgate, 2014.

Kohlstedt, Sally Gregory. "Entrepreneurs and Intellectuals: Natural History in Early American Museums." In *Mermaids, Mummies, and Mastodons: The Emergence of the American Museum,* edited by William T. Alderson, 22–39. Washington, DC: American Association of Museums for the Baltimore City Life Museums, 1992.

Latour, Bruno. *Reassembling the Social: An Introduction to Actor-Network-Theory.* Oxford: Oxford University Press, 2005.

Latrobe, Benjamin Henry. *The Correspondence and Miscellaneous Papers of Benjamin Henry Latrobe.* Vol. 2, *1805–1810.* Edited by John C. Van Horne, Lee W. Formwalt, and Darwin H. Stapleton. New Haven, CT: Yale University Press, 1986.

——. *The Correspondence and Miscellaneous Papers of Benjamin Henry Latrobe.* Vol. 3, *1811–1820.* Edited by John C. Van Horne, Jeffrey A. Cohen, and Darwin H. Stapleton. New Haven, CT: Yale University Press for the Maryland Historical Society, 1988.

Le Camus de Mézières, Nicolas. *The Genius of Architecture; or, The Analogy of That Art with Our Sensations.* Translated by David Britt. Edited by the Getty Center for the History of Art and the Humanities. Chicago: University of Chicago Press, 1992.

Lerner, William. "Historical Statistics of the United States Colonial Times to 1970, Bicentennial Edition." Washington, DC: U.S. Government Printing Office, 1975.

Lewis, Jan Ellis, and Peter S. Onuf, eds. *Sally Hemings and Thomas Jefferson: History, Memory, and Civic Culture.* Charlottesville: University Press of Virginia, 1999.

Lingelbach, William E. "The Home of the American Philosophical Society." *Transactions of the American Philosophical Society* 43, no. 1 (1953): 43–69.

Liscombe, R. W. *Altogether American: Robert Mills, Architect and Engineer, 1781–1855.* Oxford: Oxford University Press, 1994.

Lloyd, Stephen. "The Maria Hadfield Cosway Exhibit at the Fondazione Maria Cosway, Lodi." In *International Center for Jefferson Studies,* edited by Thomas Jefferson Memorial Foundation. Charlottesville, VA, October 25, 2022. https://www.monticello.org/research-education/for-scholars/international-center-for-jefferson-studies/talks-lectures-symposia-conferences/the-maria-hadfield-cosway-exhibit/.

———. *Richard & Maria Cosway: Regency Artists of Taste and Fashion.* Edinburgh: Scottish National Portrait Gallery, 1995.

———. *Richard Cosway.* London: Unicorn Press, 2005.

Locke, John. *The Works of John Locke.* 9th ed. 9 vols. London, 1794.

Madison, James. *The Papers of James Madison: Presidential Series.* Edited by Robert A. Rutland et al. 11 vols. Charlottesville: University Press of Virginia, 1984–2020.

———. *The Papers of James Madison: Retirement Series.* Edited by David B. Mattern. 3 vols. Charlottesville, VA: University of Virginia Press, 2009–.

———. *The Papers of James Madison: Secretary of State Series.* Edited by Robert J. Brugger et al. 12 vols. Charlottesville: University of Virginia Press, 1986–.

Mallgrave, Harry Francis, and Christina Contandriopoulos, eds. *Architectural Theory: An Anthology from 1871–2005* Vol. 2. Oxford: Blackwell, 1993.

Mansbridge, Michael. *John Nash: A Complete Catalogue.* London: Phaidon Press, 1991.

"Mapping the Republic of Letters." Humanitites + Design Lab, Center for Spatial and Textual Analysis (CESTA), Stanford University, 2014. http://republicofletters.stanford.edu

Maudlin, Daniel, and Bernard L. Herman, eds. *Building the British Atlantic World: Spaces, Places, and Material Culture, 1600–1850.* Chapel Hill: University of North Carolina Press, 2016.

McCormick, Thomas J. *Charles-Louis Clérisseau and the Genesis of Neo-Classicism.* Cambridge, MA: MIT Press, 1990.

McLaughlin, Jack. *Jefferson and Monticello: The Biography of a Builder.* New York: Henry Holt, 1990.

McLean, Dabney N. *Henry Soane, Progenitor of Thomas Jefferson.* Treasure Island, FL: D. N. McLean, 1985.

Morris, Gouverneur. *The Diary and Letters of Gouverneur Morris, Minister of the United States to France.* Edited by Anne Cary Morris. New York: Charles Scribner & Sons, 1888.

Morris, Robert. *Select Architecture.* London: Robert Sayer, 1755.

National Art Reference Library. Victoria and Albert Museum, London.

Nelson, Louis P. "The Architecture of Democracy in a Landscape of Slavery: Design and Construction at Jefferson's University." In *Thomas Jefferson, Architect: Palladian Models, Democratic Principles, and the Conflict of Ideals,* edited by Lloyd DeWitt and Corey Piper, 98–118. New Haven, CT: Yale University Press in association with the Chrysler Museum of Art, 2019.

Nichols, Frederick D. *Thomas Jefferson's Architectural Drawings.* 5th ed. Charlottesville: University Press of of Virginia, 1984.

Nichols, Frederick Doveton, and Ralph E. Griswold. *Thomas Jefferson, Landscape Architect.* Charlottesville: University Press of Virginia, 1978.

Northcote, James. *Memoirs of Sir Joshua Reynolds . . . : Comprising Original Anecdotes of Many Distinguished Persons, His Contemporaries, and a Brief Analysis of His Discourses. To Which Are Added, Varieties on Art.* London: Printed for Henry Colburn, 1813–15.

"Obituary of George Hadfield." *The National Intelligencer,* February 13, 1826.

Old Humphrey's Walks in London and Its Neighbourhood. London: Religious Tract Society, 1843.

O'Neal, William B. *Jefferson's Fine Arts Library: His Selections for the University of Virginia, Together with His Own Architectural Books.* Charlottesville: University Press of Virginia, 1976.

Outram, Dorinda. *Panorama of the Enlightenment.* Los Angeles: J. Paul Getty Museum, 2006.

"Ozias Humphry Papers 1753–1810." In Royal Academy of Arts Archive, London.

"Paintings Inventory." In Archives of Sir John Soane's Museum, London.

Palin, William. "No. 14." *Georgian* 2 (Autumn/Winter 2003): 17–21.

Palmer, Susan. "From Fields to Gardens: The Management of Lincoln's Inn Fields in the Eighteenth and Nineteenth Centuries." *London Gardener* 10 (2004–5): 11–27.

———. *The Soanes at Home: Domestic Life at Lincoln's Inn Fields.* London: Sir John Soane's Museum, 1997.

"Papers of Angelica Church." In Accession #11245, University of Virginia Special Collections, Charlottesville.

"Papers of Isabelle Neff Burnett, 1757–1960." In Accession #MSS6634, University of Virginia Special Collections, Charlottesville.

Parissien, Steven. "Monkey Business." *Country Life,* November 8, 1990, 110–11.

Peale, Charles Willson. *The Selected Papers of Charles Willson Peale and His Family.* Vol. 1, *Artist in Revolutionary America, 1735–1791.* Edited by Lillian B. Miller, Sidney Hart, and Toby A. Appel. New Haven, CT: Yale University Press, 1983.

Pérouse de Montclos, J. M. *Histoire de l'Architecture française: De la Renaissance à la Révolution.* Paris: Mengès, 1989.

Peterson, Charles E. *Thomas Jefferson Writings.* New York: Literary Classics, 1894. Psarra, Sophia. *Architecture and Narrative: The Formation of Space and Cultural Meaning.* London: Routledge, 2009.

Randall, Henry S. *The Life of Thomas Jefferson*. 3 vols. New York,: Derby & Jackson, 1858.

Randolph, Sarah Nicholas. *The Domestic Life of Thomas Jefferson: Compiled from Family Letters, and Reminiscences*. New York: Harper & Brothers, Franklin Square, 1871.

Rathbun, Richard. *The Columbian Institute for the Promotion of Arts and Sciences: A Washington Society of 1816–1838, Which Established a Museum and Botanic Garden under Government Patronage*. Washington, DC: Government Printing Office, 1917.

"Records of the District of Columbia Commissioners and of the Offices Concerned with Public Buildings, 1791–1867." In Record Group 42, National Archives and Records Administration, Washington, D.C.

"Records of the Secretary 1769–1968." In Royal Academy of Arts Archive, London.

Rice, Howard C. *Thomas Jefferson's Paris*. Princeton, NJ: Princeton University Press, 1976.

The Roads of Italy, Engraved on Twenty-Six Copper Plates, from the Manuscript Drawings of a Nobleman of Distinction. 2nd ed. London: A. Dury, 1777.

Roberson, Samuel Arndt. "Thomas Jefferson and the Eighteenth-Century Landscape Garden Movement in England." PhD thesis, Yale University, 1974.

Roberts, Warren. *A Place in History: Albany in the Age of Revolution, 1775–1825*. Albany: Excelsior Editions, State University of New York Press, 2010.

Ronda, James P. *Jefferson's West: Journey with Lewis and Clark*. Charlottesville, VA: Thomas Jefferson Foundation, 2000.

———, ed. *Voyages of Discovery: Essays on the Lewis and Clark Expeditions*. Helena: Montana Historical Society Press, 1998.Roscoe, Ingrid. "Mimic without Mind: *Singerie* in Northern Europe." *Apollo* 114, no. 234 (1981): 96–103.

Rosenthal, Angela. *Angelica Kauffman: Art and Sensibility*. New Haven, CT: Yale University Press, 2006.

"Sale Catalogs." In Archives of Sir John Soane's Museum, London.

Sanford, Charles B. *Thomas Jefferson and His Library: A Study of His Literary Interests and of the Religious Attitudes Revealed by Relevant Titles in His Library*. Hamden, CT: Archon Books, 1977.

Scarff, John H. "St. Mary's Seminary Chapel." Washington, DC: U.S. Department of the Interior, ca. 1933.

Schinkel, Karl Friedrich. *The English Journey: Journal of a Visit to France and Britain in 1826*. Translated by F. Gayna Walls. Edited by David Bindman and Gottfried Riemann. New Haven, CT: Yale University Press for the Paul Mellon Centre for Studies in British Art, 1993.

Schofield, Robert E. "The Science Education of an Enlightened Entrepreneur: Charles Willson Peale and His Philadelphia Museum, 1784–1827." *American Studies* 30, no. 2 (1989): 21–40.

Sellers, Charles Coleman. *Mr. Peale's Museum: Charles Willson Peale and the First Popular Museum of Natural Science and Art.* New York,: W. W. Norton, 1980.

Semmes, John E. *John H. B. Latrobe and His Times, 1803–1891.* Baltimore: Norman, Remington, 1917.

Shammas, Carole. "America, the Atlantic, and Global Consumer Demand, 1500–1800." *OAH Magazine of History* 19, no. 1 (2005): 59–64.

Shuffelton, I., M. Baridon, and B. Chevignard. "Travelling in the Republic of Letters." *Publications Universite de Bourgogne* 66 (1988): 1–16.

Silverman, Eleni. "Belvidere." Washington, DC: U.S. Department of the Interior, National Park Service, 1984.

"Sir Thomas Lawrence, Pra, Letters and Papers 1777–1831." In Royal Academy of Arts Archive, London.

Smith, Margaret Bayard. *A Winter in Washington.* New York: E. Bliss and E. White, 1824.

Smith, S. C. Kaines, ed. *Bartolozzi, Zoffany, and Kauffman with Other Foreign Members of the Royal Academy, 1768–1792.* London: Philip Allan, 1924.

Soane, John. Archives of Sir John Soane's Museum. London.

——. "Crude Hints Towards an History of My House in L[Incoln's] I[Nn] Fields'." In *Visions of Ruin: Architectural Fantasies & Designs for Garden Follies,* 61–74. London: Sir John Soane's Museum, 1999.

——. *Description of the House and Museum, on the North Side of Lincoln's Inn-Fields, the Residence of Sir John Soane.* London: Privately printed by Levey, Robson, and Franklyn, 1832.

——. *Description of the House and Museum on the North Side of Lincoln's Inn Fields, the Residence of Sir John Soane.* Edited by Arthur T. Bolton. Oxford: Oxford University Press, 1930.

——. *Description of the House and Museum on the North Side of Lincoln's Inn Fields, the Residence of Sir J. Soane (Written by Himself). With Graphic Illustrations, etc.* London: Levey, Robson and Franklyn, St. Martin's Lane, 1835.

——. "Drawings." In Archives of Sir John Soane's Museum, London.

——. *Memoirs of the Professional Life of an Architect between the Years 1768 and 1835.* London: James Moyes Castle Street Leicster Square, Privately printed (not published), 1835.

——. "Private Correspondence." In Archives of Sir John Soane's Museum, London.

——. *The Royal Academy Lectures.* Edited by David Watkin. Cambridge: Cambridge University Press, 2000.

——. "Soane Notebooks." In Archives of Sir John Soane's Museum, London.

Sowerby, Emily Millicent. *Catalogue of the Library of Thomas Jefferson.* 5 vols. Washington, DC: Library of Congress, 1952–59.

Spurlin, Paul M. "The World of the Founding Fathers and France." *French Review* 49, no. 6 (1976): 909–25.

Stanton, Lucia C. *Those Who Labor for My Happiness: Slavery at Thomas Jefferson's Monticello.* Charlottesville: University of Virginia Press, 2012.

Stein, Susan R. *The Worlds of Thomas Jefferson at Monticello.* New York: H. N. Abrams, in association with the Thomas Jefferson Memorial Foundation, 1993.

Sterne, Laurence. *The Life and Opinions of Tristram Shandy.* 3rd ed. 9 vols. London: Printed for J. Dodsley, 1760–1767.

Stevens, Mary Anne, and Margaret Richardson, eds. *John Soane, Architect: Master of Space and Light.* London: Royal Academy of Arts, 1999. Distributed by Yale University Press.

Stroud, Dorothy. *The Architecture of Sir John Soane.* London: Studio, 1961.

Styles, John, and Vickery Amanda, eds. *Gender, Taste, and Material Culture in Britain and North America, 1700–1830.* New Haven, CT: Yale Center for British Art, 2006.

"Subscription List for the Building of Philosophical Hall, 11 July 1785." In American Philosophical Society Digital Library, Philadelphia.

Summerson, John. *Heavenly Mansions and Other Essays on Architecture.* London: W.W. Norton, 1949.

———. *Life and Work of John Nash Architect.* London: Allen and Unwin, 1980.

Tait, A. A. *The Adam Brothers in Rome: Drawings from the Grand Tour.* Edited by Sandra Pisano. London: Scala, 2008.

Thornton, Peter. *A Miscellany of Objects from Sir John Soane's Museum: Consisting of Paintings, Architectural Drawings and Other Curiosities from the Collection of Sir John Soane.* Edited by Helen Dorey. London: Lawrence King, 1992.

Thornton, William. *Papers of William Thornton.* Edited by C. M. Harris and Daniel Preston. Vol. 1, *1781–1802.* Charlottesville: University Press of Virginia, 1995.

Trumbull, John. *Autobiography, Reminiscences and Letters of John Trumbull, from 1756 to 1841.* New York: Wiley and Putnam, 1841.

Turner, Robert F., ed. *The Jefferson-Hemings Controversy: Report of the Scholars Commission.* Durham, NC: Carolina Academic Press, 2011.

Tyack, Geoffrey, ed. *John Nash: Architect of the Picturesque.* Swindon, UK: English Heritage, 2013.

Upton, Dell. *Architecture in the United States.* Oxford: Oxford University Press, 1998.

Ward, David C. *Charles Willson Peale: Art and Selfhood in the Early Republic.* Berkeley, CA: University of California Press, 2004.

Watkin, David. *The Architect King: George III and the Culture of the Enlightenment.* London: Royal Collection, 2004.

———. *English Architecture: A Concise History.* Rev. ed. London: Thames & Hudson, 2001.

———. *Sir John Soane: Enlightenment Thought and the Royal Academy Lectures.* Cambridge: Cambridge University Press, 1996.

Watkin, David, and Philip Hewat-Jaboor, eds. *Thomas Hope: Regency Designer.* New Haven, CT: Yale University Press, 2008.

Watkins, Tobias. "Anniversary Discourse. Delivered before the Columbian Institute on 7th January, 1826." Washington, DC: Davis & Force, 1826.

Wells, Camille. *Material Witness: Domestic Architecture and Plantation Landscapes in Early Virginia.* Charlottesville: University of Virginia Press, 2018.

Wexler, Natalie. "'What Manner of Woman Our Female Editor May Be': Eliza Crawford Anderson and the Baltimore Observer, 1806–1807." *Maryland Historical Magazine* 105, no. 2 (2010): 100.

Wiebenson, Dora. "The Two Domes of the Halle Au Blé in Paris." *Art Bulletin* 55, no. 2 (1973): 262–79.

Williamson, George Charles. *Richard Cosway, R.A., and His Wife and Pupils: Miniaturists of the Eighteenth Century.* London: George Bell & Sons, 1897.

Willkens, Danielle. "Clouds and Cataracts: Optical Experiments at Sir John Soane's Museum." *TAD: Technology Architecture + Design* 3 (2019): 211–20.

Wills, Garry. "The Aesthete." *New York Review of Books,* August 12, 1993.

Wilson, Douglas L. "Jefferson's Library." In *Thomas Jefferson: A Reference Biography,* edited by Merrill D. Peterson, 157–80. New York: Charles Scribners Sons, 1986.

———. *Jefferson's Library.* Charlottesville, VA: Thomas Jefferson Foundation, 1996.

———. "Jefferson's Library." In *Thomas Jefferson: A Reference Biography,* edited by Merrill D. Peterson, 157–80. New York: Charles Scribner's Sons, 1986.

———. "Sowerby Revisited: The Unfinished Catalogue of Jefferson's Library." *William and Mary Quarterly* 3rd series, 41 (1984): 615–28.

———. "Thomas Jefferson's Library and the French Connection." *Eighteenth-Century Studies* 26, no. 4 (1993): 669–85.

Wilson, G. S. *Jefferson on Display: Attire, Etiquette and the Art of Presentation.* Charlottesville: University of Virginia Press, 2018.

Wilson-Smith, Timothy. *Napoleon and His Artists.* London: Constable, 1996.

Winterer, Caroline. "Where Is America in the Republic of Letters?" *Modern Intellectual History* 9, no. 3 (2012): 597–623.

Wister, O. J., and Anges Irwin, eds. *Worthy Women of Our First Century.* Philadelphia,: Lippencott, 1877.

Woodward, Christopher. "Wall, Ceiling, Enclosure, and Light: Soane's Designs for Domes." In *John Soane, Architect: Master of Space and Light,* edited by Mary Anne Stevens and Richardson Margaret, 62–67. London: Royal Academy of Arts, 1999. Distributed by Yale University Press.

Yaneva, Albena. *Five Ways to Make Architecture Political: An Introduction to the Politics of Design Practice.* London: Bloomsbury Academic, 2017.

———. *Made by the Office for Metropolitan Architecture: An Ethnography of Design.* Rotterdam: 010 Publishers, 2009.

———. *The Making of a Building: A Pragmatist Approach to Architecture.* Oxford: Peter Lang, 2009.

Yaneva, Albena, and Alejandro Zaera-Polo, eds. *What Is Cosmopolitical Design? Design, Nature and the Built Environment.* Farnham, UK: Ashgate, 2015.

INDEX

Arrowsmith, Aaron, 104
atmosphere, atmospheric, 55–56, 115–16, 136–37, 147, 150–51, 158, 179–82, 187
Ayers Saint Gross, 241–42

Bacon, Francis, 123–24
Bailey, George, 63, 125, 144–45, 231–33, 261n22
Baltimore Exchange, 58
Bank of England, 120–21, 127, 138, 143, 194
Banks, Thomas, 21–24, 182–83
Barbary War, 61–62
Barclay, James Turner, 171, 235–36
Baroque, 22–23
Barry, Richard, 159
Bartolozzi, Francesco, 23–24
Bartram, John, 84, 134–35, 168; Bartram's Garden, 184
Baths of Diocletian, 167–68
Battle Monument, 60–61
Belvidere, 48
Belzoni, Giovanni, 210–11
Benjamin, Asher, 193–94, 262n11
Biddle, Owen, 193–94, 262n11
Biggs, James, 63
Blenheim, 110–11
Bolton, Arthur T., 159, 237
Bonomi, Joseph, 46–47
Borghini, Signor, 202–4
botany, 90, 123, 184, 222. *See also* gardens
Boullée, Étienne-Louis, 43–44, 149–50
Bowdler, Thomas, 22–23
Boyle, Caleb, 187
Bray Film Studios, 44–46. *See also* Down Place
Brettingham, Robert Furze, 20–21, 69–70
British Museum, 37–38, 144–45, 178, 185–86, 210–11, 224–25, 230–31, 233
Britton, John, 167, 232–33
Brodeau, Anna Marie, 141–43
Brown, Capability, 107–8
Brown, Mather, 26–28, 212–13, 247n47
Buchanan, William, 52–53
Buckingham Palace, 111, 179–80
Buffon, George-Louis Leclerc, comte de, 123–24, 186–87
Bulfinch, Charles, 80–81, 85–86

Bullock, William, 185–86
Buonaparte, Carlo, 204
Burdon, Rowland, 22–23
Burlington, Richard Boyle, Earl of, 107–10
Burnes, David, 78–79, 257n39

cabinets, 117–18, 130–31, 135–38, 146–48, 152–55, 159, 161, 178, 180, 186–87, 189–91, 233, 235–36. *See also* collections, collecting
Café Mécanique, 26
Canal de l'Ourcq, 112–13
Canaletto (Giovanni Antonio Canal), 56
Capitol Building, 70–76
capricci, 51–52, 162, 172–73
caricatures, 6–7
Carr, Dabny, 97–98
Carroll, Charles, 185
Carter, John, 42–43
cartoons, 6, 111
Castell, Robert, 116–17, 120
catalogs, cataloging, 9–10, 35–36, 39, 52, 94, 121–23, 125, 160, 181–82, 201–2, 211, 231–32
Cathalan, Stephen Etienne, 61–62
Catherine the Great, 51
Cavendish Square Gardens, 138
Cazenove, Theophile, 57
Ceracchi, Giuseppe, 44, 195–96
Chambers, William, 20–21, 52, 107–8, 111, 122–23
Chastellux, François-Jean de Beauvoir, Marquis de, 26, 127–29, 209–10
Château de Chaville, 43–44
Chesterfield, Lady (Elizabeth Stanhope), 69
Chiswick House, 26–27, 109–10, 230
Chovet, Abraham, 184–85
Christ Church (Philadelphia), 39–40
Church, Angelica Schuyler, 9–10, 37, 42–48, 98–99, 198–99, 212–13
Church, John Barker, 42–48, 212–13
circulation, 7, 38–39, 117–18, 137–39, 146–47, 149, 180, 209–10, 212–15, 238–39
cisterns, 155–57, 163–64, 169–70
City Hall (District of Columbia), 78
City Jail (District of Columbia), 76–77
Civil War, 89–90, 175–76, 224–25, 240
Claremont Landscape Garden, 47–48

class, 6; arts and, 15–16, 19–20, 80; education and, 216–18, 225–26; social networks and, 23–24, 63, 66

classicism, 20–21, 52–53, 66, 120, 147

classification, 125

Clavering, Robert, 39–40

Clérisseau, Charles-Louis, 9–10, 20–21, 50–56, 66, 234, 238–39, 251n2, 251n4, 252nn5–6, 252n17; *Antiquités de la France,* 52–55

Clermont, Andien de, 46

Clift, William, 180

climate, 103–4, 151–57, 184, 219–20. *See also* weather

Cobham Hall, 109–10

Cockerell, Samuel Pepys, 69–70

collaboration, 5–6, 11, 50, 52–55, 58, 67, 70, 80–81, 83, 107–8

collage, 165, 192–93

collections, collecting: access to, 38, 102–3, 141, 239–40; in America, 123, 184–90; architecture and, 7, 94–96, 119–20, 141–45, 161, 162–63, 165, 193–97, 224–25; books and, 120–27; eclecticism of, 24–25; exhibiting, 177–83, 189–90, 196–97; networks and, 10–11, 238–39; science and, 87–88, 150, 158

College of Physicians, 87

College of William & Mary, 97

Collegio delle Grazie di Lodi, 7–9, 212–14, 217, 219–20, 223–24, 226

colonialism, 4–5

Columbia College (District of Columbia), 229–30

Columbian Institute for the Promotion of the Arts and Sciences, 10–11, 13–14, 79–80, 83, 85–90, 168, 229–30

Columbus, Christopher, 83

Commandants House, 76–77

Commercial and Farmer's Bank, 60–61

community, 4–5, 7–8, 16, 70–71, 80–81, 83, 106, 219–20

Company of Surgeons, 180

Conduit, Sally, 112, 261n22

Congressional Cemetery, 81–82

conservation, 171–72, 269n10

conservatories, 44–46, 89–90

Constitutional Convention, 38–39

Cook, James, 178–79

Coolidge, Ellen Wayles Randolph, 9–10, 62–63, 102, 219, 227–36, 273n7

Coolidge, Joseph, 229–31

Coolidge, Thomas Jefferson Randolph, 230–31

Corny, Madame (Anne Mangeot) de, 9–10, 37, 43–44, 47–48, 52, 153–54

Corps of Discovery, 207–8

correspondence: friendship and, 212–15; networks of, 4–10, 37–38, 44, 50, 70, 85, 130–31, 214–15, 238–39; travel and, 15–16, 44, 68–69

Cossia, Francesco, 202–5

Cosway, Louisa Angelica Paolina, 182–83

Cosway, Maria Hadfield, 1–3, 13–14, 17, 35–37, 40–43, 46–48, 67, 70, 81–82, 101–2, 108–9, 158–59, 180–83, 245n5, 246n23, 246nn33–34; artistic pursuits, 23–25; correspondence by, 5–11, 15–16, 34, 68–69, 77, 205–7, 212–15, 268n6; as educator, 216–20, 223–24, 226; legacy of, 238–39; marriage, 23–24; *A Persian Lady Worshipping the Rising Sun,* 199–201; relationship with Jefferson, 26–34, 198–99, 207, 211–15, 222–23; relationship with Soane, 21–23, 34, 183, 198–202, 204–7, 214–15, 223–24, 268n6; romantic relationships, 16–17; youth, 16–68

Cosway, Richard, 23–25, 31, 40–41, 180–83, 199–201, 246nn33–34, 250n18

Court of St. James's, 24–25

Cranch, Mary Smith, 24–25

cryptoporticus, 116–17, 136–37

Cumming, John, 127–28

curation, 10–11, 87–88, 94–95, 177–79, 184, 186–87, 196–97, 205–6, 237, 240–41. *See also* collections, collecting; display

Custis, George Washington Park, 78

Cutbush, Edward, 89–90

Cuvier, Georges, 187–89

David, Jacques-Louis, 16–17, 202–3

deafening, 148

Deane, Hugh Primrose, 17–18

Declaration of Independence, 25–26, 38–39, 42, 127, 186, 272n27

Declaration of the Rights of Man and of the Citizen, 42–43

Delorme, Philibert, 30–31, 248n55
depression, economic, 63
Désert de Retz, Le, 31–33
Desgodetz, Antoine, 122–23, 193–94
design: ambassadors of, 37; collaboration and, 107–8; control and, 116–17; dialogue and, 15–16, 91–92, 95–96, 218; exhibition and, 177–78; iterative, 11; landscape and, 106–8, 110–12, 116–17; networks of, 13–14, 72–75, 238–39; ownership and, 80–81; practicality and, 110; process and, 91–92, 98–100; reading and, 120; science and, 149–50, 153–61; space and, 101, 114, 132–49, 151, 158–60, 233
d'Hancarville, Marquis (Pierre-François Hugues), 16–17, 31
D'Holbach's Coterie, 51
dialogue, 5; design and, 15–16, 91–92, 95–96, 218; transatlantic, 11, 41–42, 48–49
Diderot, Denis, 36–37
Dinsmore, James, 125–26, 256n37, 262n20
diplomacy, 26–27, 37–38, 41–44, 48–49, 105, 107–9, 154–55, 207–8, 249n8
display, 102–3, 124, 206–12, 246n28; architecture and, 7, 115–16, 177–89; didactic, 185–86, 190–97
Dobie, Samuel, 53
documentation, 57, 68–69, 79–80. *See also* archives
Dolland, P. and J., 158–59
domes, 30–31, 78–79, 110, 112–13, 147, 150–51, 159–61, 165–67, 193–96, 248n55, 248n57, 254n33. *See also* Monticello; Soane's Museum
domesticity, 100–103, 137–38, 208
Donath, Joseph, 151–52
Dorey, Helen, 160, 252n17
Down Place, 44–48, 212–13
drawings, 5–7, 13, 15–22, 40, 55–56, 63–65, 69, 79–80, 91–92, 96–97, 103–4, 112, 131–48, 160, 165–66, 171–72, 181, 193–95, 200–201, 214–15, 218. *See also* models; sketches
Drayton Hall, 91
Dulwich Picture Gallery, 112, 233
Dunglison, Robley, 171
Durand, Hippolyte, 59

Eames, Charles, and Ray, 35–36
East Cowes Castle, 179–80
East India Museum, 230–31
eclecticism, 24–25, 111, 113, 162–63, 172–73, 182–83
Edmond, Cyrus R., 127
education: architecture and, 11, 100–101, 105–6, 136–37, 141–48, 167, 217–26, 239–40; autodidactic, 105–6; class and, 39, 96–97, 216–18, 225–26; discourse and, 218–19; geographic location and, 216–20, 223, 226; independent, 119–20; institutions for, 216–17, 238–40; museums and, 192–95; space and, 136–37; travel and, 219–20; women's, 223–26
Edwards, Edward, 17–18
Edwards, John, 179–80
efficiency, 39–40, 43–44, 108–9, 116–17, 156–57
Egypt, Egyptomania, 58–59, 66, 88–89, 179, 206–11, 254n35, 270n28, 270n30
Egyptian Hall (London), 185–86
Elliot, William P., 79–80, 85–86
Ellis, Joseph, 116–17
Enfield Chase, 109–10
engineering, 56–60, 80–81, 106, 149–50, 153–54, 169, 254n38
English Coffee House (Piazza de Spagna), 20–21
engravings, 23–24, 54–55, 78–79, 151, 172–73, 181–82, 212, 245n19, 246n26
Enlightenment, 5, 39–40, 119–20, 150–51, 196–97
environment: built, 4, 13, 15–16, 34, 57, 105–6, 131, 147, 152–53, 272n26; education and, 226–27; monitoring, 152–57; national, 5–6, 13; natural, 15–16
epistemology, 4, 50
Esher Place, 109–11
Eton College, 46
exchange: correspondence and, 238–39; international, 36–38, 80–82, 84–85, 90–92, 94–95, 104; networks and, 238; personal interactions and, 175–76; societies and, 83–85, 90; of tokens, 198–202, 204–8
exhibitions, 35–37, 68–69, 94, 124, 160, 177–78,

186–89, 230–31, 246n23, 258n3, 262n22, 274n1. *See also* display
exterior, 114–18, 136–37, 151–52, 163–65, 222. *See also* interior, interiority

fabrication, 30–31, 109–10, 124–25, 151–52
Farington, Joseph, 69–70
Fauquier, Francis, 149–50
federal style, 48
Ferguson, James, 158–59, 168
fine arts, 85, 123–27, 186–87
fires, fireproofing, 61–62, 103–4, 120–21
First Unitarian Church, 60–61
Fitzhugh, Lee, 78
Flamsteed, John, 153–54
Fort McHenry, 60–61, 66, 253n30
fossils, 89–90, 187–89
foundations, 54–55, 74, 93, 101, 104, 166–67, 171–72
Fouquet, François, 55
Fouquet, Jean-Pierre, 55
fragments, fragmentation, 106–7, 115–16, 165, 167, 172–73, 195, 205–6
Franklin, Benjamin, 6, 9–10, 25–27, 35–42, 84, 149–50, 250n11, 250n15
Freemason's Hall, 147, 150–51
French Academy, 51–52
French Geographic Society, 87
French Revolution, 48–49, 57, 112–13
friendship, 1–2, 5–6, 11, 15–16, 27, 52–53, 77–78, 160, 198–201, 204–5, 207–8, 214–15
Fulton, Robert, 149–50

gadgetry, 124, 153–54, 158–59, 227–28
Gandy, Joseph Michael, 55–56, 163–65, 195
gardens, 15–16, 26–27, 31–33, 47–48, 122–23, 222; botanical, 87–90, 184; English, 105–12; naturalism and, 114
genealogy, 10–11
George III, King, 26–27, 40, 108–9, 184
George IV, King, 179–80
Gibbs, James, 107–8
Gladwell, Malcolm, 38
glass, 30, 147, 150–52, 157–58, 160–61, 164–65, 240–41. *See also* mirrors

Godefroy, Maximilian, 9–10, 50, 56–66, 77, 217–18, 238–39, 253nn19–21, 253n30, 254n35
Goma, Francesco, 203–4
Gothic Library at Stowe, 110–11
Gothic Revival, 58–59, 109–10
Governor's Palace, 133
Grand Tour, 1–2, 7–8, 17–23, 41, 53–54, 68–69, 112, 165–66, 172–73, 216–17, 219–20
Great Western Steamship Company, 175–76
Greek revival, 78
Green, Valentine, 23–24
Grimm, Friedreich Melchior von, 51
Gros, Antoine-Jean, 202–3

Hadfield, Charles, 17–18, 21, 245n5
Hadfield, George, 9–10, 13–14, 41–42, 67–68, 85–87, 217–18, 228, 238–39, 254n2, 256n37; as architect of U.S. Capitol, 70–76, 79–82; education, 68–70; legacy, 79–82; National Prison design, 68–69; relationship with Jefferson, 76–78; Van Ness Mausoleum, 78–79
Hadfield, William, 21–23, 68–69
Hagley Hall, 110
Halle au Blé, 15–16, 27–31, 112–13, 149–50, 248n57
Hallet, Etienne Sulpice, 71–74, 76–77
Hamels Park, 120
Hamilton, Alexander, 44, 195–96
Hampton Court, 47–48, 109–10
Hay, James, 52–53
health reform, 149
Heard, Augustine, 230–31
Hemings, James, 25, 247n40
Hemings, John, 125–26
Hemings, Sally, 249n68
hierarchy, 132–33, 139–40, 195–96
Hoare, Prince, 21–22, 199, 268n6
Hoban, James, 73–77, 85–86, 141
Hogarth, William, 122–23, 232–33
Holland, Henry, 69–70, 107–8
Holy Trinity Marylebone, 152
home: ambassadors and, 36–37, 43–44; architecture and, 34, 93, 124–25, 130–31, 149, 154–57, 159, 172; collecting and, 94–96; as museum, 7–8, 16, 34, 91–101, 108–9, 113,

Lawrence, Thomas, 205
Leasowes, 110, 114
Le Camus de Mézières, Nicolas, 30
Ledoux, Claude-Nicolas, 56–57, 60–61, 141–43, 152
Lee, Robert E., 78
legacy, 11, 16, 36–37, 56–57, 94–95, 119–20, 175–76, 217–19
Legrand, J. G., 30
L'Enfant, Pierre Charles, 73–74, 218
Leonardo da Vinci, 158–59
Lever, Ashton, 111, 177–79
Leverian Museum, 178–79, 186–87
Levy, Uriah Phillips, 240
Lewis, Henry, 22–23
Lewis, James, 180
Lewis, Meriwether, and William Clark, 187–89, 194–95, 207–8
libraries, 11, 119–29, 141–44
Library Company of Philadelphia, 38–39, 127, 184–85, 229–30, 250n13
Library of Congress, 126–27, 229–30, 262n22
light, lighting, 30, 33, 43–44, 55–56, 59, 99, 101, 115–16, 133–34, 136–37, 140, 142–43, 150–61, 165, 180, 186, 189–90, 220–22. *See also* glass; skylights; windows
Lincoln's Inn Fields, 99–101, 105, 115–16, 121–22, 131, 135, 137, 143–45, 151, 155–60, 180, 194–95, 201–2, 206, 240–41. *See also* Soane's Museum
line diagrams, 2–3
Little, Robert, 79–82
Lloyd, Stephen, 7, 245n5, 246n33
Locke, John, 2–3, 5, 123–24, 244n8
Louisiana Purchase, 61–62, 207–8
Louvre, 33–34
lumière mystèrieuse, 149–52. *See also* light, lighting
Lunar Society, 149, 250n11
Lyttelton, Lady Sarah, 199–201

Madison, James, 53–54, 57–59, 98–99, 126–27, 171, 224–26, 255n13
Maison Carrée, 53–55
Malmaison, 112–13
Malton, Thomas, 158–59

Manifest Destiny, 175, 222
Marine Barracks, 76–77
Marlborough, Duke of (John Churchill), 46
marriage, 10–11, 16–17, 23–24, 96, 100, 247n40
Maskel, Nevil, 153–54
masonry, 96–97
mass production, 149
material culture studies, 35–36
Maury, James, 97
mausoleums, 69, 78–79, 114, 189, 257n39
mechanical arts, 123
mechanization, 149, 153–57
medicine, 149, 221–22
Meigs, Henry, 88–89
memorials, 66
mentorship, 10–11, 40–41, 70–71, 97, 149–50
Metropolitan Association for the Advancement of the Sciences. *See* Columbian Institute
Metropolitan Museum of Art, Bicentennial Administration Exhibition, 35–36
Mézières, Nicolas Le Camus de, 149–50
Middleton, Ann Elbertina Van Ness, 78–79
Mignard, Pierre, 112–13
Mills, Robert, 56–57, 60–61, 80–81, 85–86, 141–43, 157, 264n19
Missouri Compromise, 224–25
Mitford, William, 122–23
models, 51, 55, 130, 150–51, 168–69, 179–80, 193–95, 198, 209–10, 274n21
modernism, 149
Molinos, Jacques, 30
Monkey Island, 46
Monroe, James, 158–59
Monticello, 7–8, 10–11, 25–26, 30–31, 33, 48, 62–63, 91–110, 130–31, 133–34; Dining Room, 43–44, 117–18, 154–55, 159, 234; display and, 177–78, 192–97; Dome Room, 151–52, 160–61, 194; education and, 141–43, 239–42; enslaved community at, 94–95, 102, 107–8, 114–17, 124, 132–33, 135, 169–70, 234–35; Entrance Hall, 44, 136–37, 161, 193, 195–96, 207–10, 251n30, 274n24; as exercise in applied science, 149–59; Garden Pavilion, 114, 116, 118, 261n25; Indian Hall, 207–8, 234; after Jefferson's death, 234–36,

Monticello (*continued*)
240; landscape and, 114–15; library, 119–20, 124–29, 141–43; Mulberry Row, 102, 114–16, 124, 156–57; Parlor, 136–37, 139–40, 159, 161, 193–95, 207–10, 229, 235–36, 247n47; pasticcio, 162–63, 167–73; redesign of, 43–44, 54–55, 74–75, 135–37, 141–43; restoration of, 237, 241; as retreat, 114; Tulip Poplar trunks, 120; visitors to, 101–2, 147–48, 192, 195–96, 234–35, 239–42, 256n37. *See also* Jefferson, Thomas

Monumental Church (Richmond), 60–61

monuments, 22–23, 52, 60–61, 66, 172–73, 272n26

Moor Park, 109–10

Morellet, André, 51

Morris, Robert, 46–47, 193–94

Moser, Mary, 40

Mount Vernon, 74–75, 78, 169–70

museums, 11; in America, 184–92; display and, 177–83, 186–89, 192–97; house, 7–8, 16, 34, 91–101, 108–9, 113, 118, 124, 130–31, 150–53, 177–83, 192, 196–97, 214–15, 224–25, 238, 241–42; narration and, 178–79, 192. *See also under* home

Napoleon, 57, 112–13, 201–9, 269n10; Armée d'Orient campaign, 208–9

narrative: museum design and, 178–79, 192; spatial, 151

Nash, John, 179–80

nation, nationalism, 83, 87; architecture and, 67–68, 70–76, 80–81, 91–92, 103–4, 167–68, 238; personal liberty and, 191–92; transatlantic influences, 5–6

National Botanic Gardens (District of Columbia), 89–90

National Gallery (London), 230–31

National Institute for the Promotion of Sciences, 89–90

National Mall (District of Columbia), 89–90

Natural Bridge, 62–63, 66, 227–28, 254n39

natural history, 123–24, 149, 178–79, 184–87

naturalism, 114, 123–24, 222

nature, 107–8, 114–16, 211, 222

Neilson, John, 125–26

neoclassicism, 51, 74–75, 114–15

networks, 80–82, 91–92; ambassadors of, 36–37, 41–44, 48–49; architecture and, 238–39; awareness of, 111; class and, 23–24, 63, 66; collaboration and, 67, 70, 80–82; correspondence and, 4–10, 37–38, 44, 50, 70, 85, 130–31, 214–15, 238–39; design and, 238–39; education and, 216–17, 219–20; international, 72–75, 79–80; professional, 69–75, 77–78, 80–82; Republic of Letters and, 4–6, 13; super-connectors, 38; tokens and, 198–99; visualizing, 5–10. *See also* Transatlantic Design Network

Newgate Prison, 76–77

Newton, Isaac, 123–24

Nicholson, Peter, 122–23

Northcote, James, 21–24

oculus, 150–52

Office of Works, 112

offices, 137–40, 143–44, 146–48

Ogilvie, James, 125–26

Oldham, James, 123

optics, 149, 157–61

Orrey, John Boyle, Earl of, 117–18

Osterley Park, 111–12

Paestum, 20–21, 53–54, 69, 245n19

Page, John, 107–8

Pain, William, 220–22

Paine, Thomas, 26

Palais-Royale, 26, 112

Palazzo Farnese, 172–73

paleontology, 187–89

Palladio, Andrea, 116–17, 122–23, 126–27, 132–33, 193–94, 220–22, 232–33

Panthéon, 112–13

Paoli, Pasquale, 16–17, 204

Paradise, John, 153–54

Parke, Henry, 22, 112–13

Parkinson, James, 178–79

parlante, 168

pasticcio (pastiche), 115–18, 162–63, 167–73

Patch, Thomas, 17

patronage, 10–11, 27, 35–37, 44–46, 48, 70–71, 211–12, 234–35